D0874031

World Aircraft
COMMERCIAL, 1935–1960

BY
ENZO ANGELUCCI
PAOLO MATRICARDI

RAND McNALLY & COMPANY
CHICAGO
NEW YORK
SAN FRANCISCO

LB

Illustrations by V. Cosentino

Posters on pages 8, 76, 154, 182, 206, 232, and 246
reproduced by kind permission
of Trans World Airlines Inc; RAF Museum,
Hendon; Aeroflot; Musée Air France;
Civico Museo Luigi Bailo (Raccolta
Salce), Treviso; Münchner Stadtmuseum;
Japan Airlines

© 1978 Europa Verlag
© 1978 Arnoldo Mondadori, Milan

Printed in Italy by Officine Grafiche
A. Mondadori Editore, Verona

Published in U.S.A., 1979
by Rand McNally & Company, Chicago, Ill.

Library of Congress Catalog Card No. 79-51520
ISBN: 0-528-88206-6

Contents

c. 1

ntroduction

n the early days of aviation the evolution of the aeroplane
progressed comparatively slowly from the first 'lighter than air' flying
machines to the more reliable aircraft which were available in 1914.

However, the advent of the First World War provided tremendous
impetus to the development of the aviation industry as a whole, and
this momentum continued after the hostilities had ceased. By 1935
commercial air transportation was becoming a more and more
common event.

Like the 1914–18 war, the Second World War increased the pace
of aircraft development and a variety of new aircraft evolved. These
included a new breed of long range transport aeroplanes, many of
which were subsequently modified for commercial use.

World Aircraft: Commercial, 1935–1960 continues the history of
commercial air transportation, and links up directly with the second
volume in the series *World Aircraft 1918–1935*.

Following the format of the previous volumes in this series, *World
Aircraft: Commercial, 1935–1960* presents a selection of 161 aircraft from eighteen countries, illustrated in 172 colour plates. For
each of the countries selected, the models chosen are presented in
chronological order, and generally listed on the basis of the year in
which the first prototype flight took place. In addition to the full-
colour illustration (in many cases more than one to an aeroplane), the
various models are shown in a variety of sectional drawings,
accompanied by tables giving their main technical specifications, and
a text. The illustration and sectional drawings often refer to different
variants of the aircraft in question to give the broadest and fullest
possible range of information. The figures given are in every case the
result of comparison between at least two sources.

The concluding sections are designed to present, in summary
form, the principal facts and figures about civil aviation in the period
in question. Lastly, a chapter devoted to the major aero-engines
shows the transition from the last piston engines to the first turbine
engines. This, in effect, is the technical phenomenon that has most
hallmarked the evolution of the aeroplane from the postwar period to
the present day.

Weather has its brighter side

AND THAT'S WHERE TWA SKYLINERS FLY

Your whole picture of winter travel will change for the better
once you've flown TWA. For all thoughts of icy roads and snowbound
delays melt away when you travel at TWA's "fair-weather" level.
Up here sunshine knows no season; the stars light your way at night.
And while your TWA Skyliner makes time, you spend it
in leisurely fashion . . . enjoying the kind of service that's made TWA
first choice of more than two million passengers each year.

*Where in the world do you want to go? For information
and reservations, call TWA or see your travel agent.*

ACROSS THE U.S. AND OVERSEAS... **FLY** *TWA*

TRANS WORLD AIRLINES
U.S.A. · EUROPE · AFRICA · ASIA

United States of America

In 1960 the 92 existing airline companies belonging to the IATA (International Air Transport Association) managed for the first time to reach and exceed the target of transporting 100,000,000 passengers. However, in 1960, more than 50% of this volume of traffic was carried by North American airlines. Of the 60 or so of these airlines in regular operation, the traditional 'big four' (United, Eastern, American and TWA) plus Pan American handled almost 40% of air traffic in the world.

The origins of this success date back to the exceptional development which air transportation underwent in the United States in the 1930s, after the relatively uneventful years of the previous decade. This commercial expansion, which had brought the United States to the top of the international ladder, had gone hand in glove with a parallel and no less significant development of the aeronautical industry; from its second-rung standing in the years immediately following the First World War it had managed not only to make up for all the disadvantages besetting it when compared with the European

industry, but it also managed to win a leading role in the international sector. Subsequently, the outbreak of hostilities in Europe and the American involvement in the war in 1941 had not had any damaging effects on the system of commercial air transportation in the United States. The distance from the theatre of war and the consequent relative normality of everyday life, in the context of a nation inhabiting a whole continent had left the by now consolidated domestic requirements virtually unaltered. What is more, these requirements were able to be all the better satisfied by the products of the immense industrial effort required by the war itself. In 1941 the domestic airline companies managed, on their own, to come very near to transporting 4,000,000 passengers. In 1942 this figure dropped dramatically to about 3,000,000, and in 1943 it remained more or less the same. Then in 1944 there was once again an abrupt rise, which brought the figure back up to the 4,000,000 level. This rate of growth continued at an even greater rate in 1945, the year in which the number of passengers carried by the domestic airlines was far in excess of 6,000,000.

It was, therefore, in this period of relative peace, many thousands of miles from the death and destruction ravaging Europe, that the American aeronautical industry laid the foundations upon which it would consolidate its own future success. In practical terms the United States had no rivals in this sector. Their fiercest competitors, Great Britain and Germany, were engaged in mortal combat in the skies over Europe. France, Holland and Italy, the other European countries traditionally in the forefront of aeronautical engineering, were little better placed either. The only other major contenders, the Soviet Union and Japan, had far more serious problems to tackle than civil or commercial aviation.

By the mid-1930s the United States had already won a most prestigious position in the field of air transportation. It was able to impose on the various international markets the revolutionary specifications and features of two exceptional aircraft which had in real terms marked the end of an era: the twin-engined Boeing and Douglas. This advantage was not only maintained during the war years, but also further consolidated by the very demands of war. The problems created by the need to be able to transport huge numbers of men and equipment nonstop, in order to refurbish and supply the arenas of war separated from the mother-country by two oceans forced the United States aeronautical industry to concentrate much of its own war effort specifically in the sector of air transport. It was during these years

that the aircraft which were to hallmark the postwar period were developed. These included the Douglas Skymaster (forbear of the future DC-6 and DC-7), the Lockheed Constellation, and the Curtiss Commando. Although the Curtiss Commando ended up enjoying only a secondary civilian career which was relatively limited, the first two, which underwent continual improvement in an effort to keep them thoroughly up-to-date, emerged as the best large-capacity, long-range transport aircraft of the 1950s.

One of the principal factors which gave the greatest momentum to the process of constant up-dating of aeronautical equipment was the fierce competition in the first years of peace between the major U.S. airlines, and especially those fighting for the biggest slice of the domestic market. The fight was particularly bitter between American, United and TWA, who were all competing directly for the most prestigious and remunerative route between the east and west coasts of the United States. It was out of this hard-fought battle that there emerged the best aircraft from the Douglas and Lockheed companies: the Super Constellation, the DC-7C and the Starliner. These aircraft represented the finest examples of passenger models powered by piston-engines. Similarly, where the increase of traffic was concerned, the results from the very outset were almost incredible: in 1951 American Airlines transported about 4,800,000 passengers; Eastern Air Lines came in second place on the domestic routes with 3,500,000 passengers; United Air Lines carried 3,000,000 passengers;

and TWA (which on May 17, 1950 had changed its name from Transcontinental and Western Air to Trans World Airlines) carried almost 2,000,000 passengers. Close behind the 'big four' domestic airlines came Capital Airlines with almost 2,200,000 passengers, while a further seven companies carried between 500,000 and 1,000,000 passengers each. These results were achieved not only thanks to the Douglas and Lockheed four-engined aircraft (which were joined, though in fewer numbers, by the Boeing Stratocruiser, another fine example of the last generation of piston-engined models) but also by the important contribution made in the short- and medium-range sector by the twin-engined Convair and Martin.

The American airlines were also very successful in the area of international routes. As far back as 1942 American Export Airlines had already interrupted the monopoly of the fifth giant of American air transport, Pan American Airways. Three years later (July 5, 1945) TWA had been authorized to open a transatlantic service flying to India via the Mediterranean and the Middle East. Subsequent to this, Northwest Airlines had set up a series of links in the north Pacific, towards Japan; Braniff International Airways in South America; and National Airlines and Chicago and Southern Air Lines in the Caribbean. However, the most sought-after route was still the North Atlantic one. This was shared by Pan American and TWA, and American Export Airlines (which had likewise changed its name on November 3, 1945 to American Overseas Airlines), but after a brief period of American monopoly, due to the temporary absence of the British BOAC company, these companies had to tackle the ever-growing competition of the major European airlines. These consisted of KLM, Air France, BOAC, SAS, Sabena, Loftleidir and Swissair which, in that order and between May 21, 1946 and July 4, 1949, all opened regular transatlantic flights to the U.S.A. In 1950 the companies operating over the North Atlantic were ten in number; by 1955 they numbered fourteen, and by 1960 eighteen.

With the beginning of the new revolution in air transport (the end of piston engine and the introduction of the turbine) the 1950s brought with them a further cause for prestige for the U.S. aeronautical industry. Even though the U.S.A. was not the first country to put a passenger aircraft driven by jet engines into service it swiftly managed to overtake both Great Britain and the Soviet Union in terms of quality and quantity. The principal merit for this went to Boeing, the time-honoured aeronautical firm which in the postwar period had opted mainly for military production, and remained comparatively outside the lively duel being enacted between Douglas and Lockheed. The Boeing 707 was not only the first commercial jet manufactured in the United States, it was also the forerunner of a whole family of aircraft which, even today, hallmarks air transport in the world. Douglas and Lockheed soon followed their old rival on the same path. As a result, once again, the North American leadership in the international sector was irreversibly consolidated.

Bellanca P-200 Airbus

In 1931 America was still reeling from the effects of the economic depression. If it had not enjoyed poor commercial success the Bellanca Airbus family, and the later Aircruiser, would have emerged as one of the most useful series of commercial transport aircraft of the day. Mario Bellanca, the Italian émigré who had managed to build up in the United States a front-line aeronautical concern, had a very specific philosophy: the commercial aircraft should be nothing more than a useful and functional means of transport, capable of carrying out its function in the best way possible. The P-200 Airbus, which took to the air for the first time in 1931, represented the best product of this concept. Its transport capacity was the equivalent of that of numerous contemporary commercial three-engined models, and its versatility and soundness were exceptional. However, only four P-200's were built for the civil market.

Aircraft: **Bellanca P-200 Airbus**
Manufacturer: **Bellanca Aircraft Corp.**
Type: **Civil transport**
Year:**1931**
Engine: **One Wright R-1820-E Cyclone, radial with 9 air-cooled cylinders, 575 hp**
Wingspan:**65 ft 0 in (19.81 m)**
Length:**42 ft 9 in (13.03 m)**
Height:**10 ft 4 in (3.15 m)**
Weight:**9,590 lb (4,344 kg) (Loaded)**
Cruising speed:**122 mph (196 km/h)**
Ceiling:**14,000 ft (4,270 m)**
Range:**720 miles (1,160 km)**
Crew:**1**
Passengers:**12**

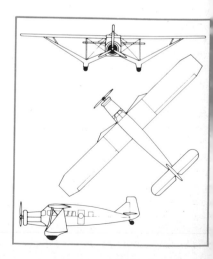

Clark G.A.43

Although virtually unknown in the annals of commercial aviation, the Clark G.A.43 was nevertheless one of the forbears of the modern aircraft. A monoplane, entirely metal-built, with a retractable undercarriage, it anticipated the features which were to be fully exploited, with greater success, by the immortal Boeing 247 and the Douglas DC-2. The reason for the commercial failure of this model for transport certainly did not lie in its technical design. The after-effects of the economic crisis in the U.S.A. were still too harsh when the General Aviation company put its aeroplane on the market. Only five examples, including the prototype, were actually completed. One was bought by Western Air Express (which put it into service between Cheyenne and Albuquerque); another by the Pan American Aviation Supply Corporation (which used it in South America); and two by Swissair, on the crowded air routes of Europe.

Aircraft: **Clark G.A.43**
Manufacturer: **General Aviation Corp.**
Type: **Civil transport**
Year: **1933**
Engine: **One Wright R-1820-F1 Cyclone, radial with 9 air-cooled cylinders, 715 hp**
Wingspan: **53 ft 0 in (16.15 m)**
Length: **43 ft 1 in (13.13 m)**
Height: **12 ft 6 in (3.81 m)**
Weight: **8,750 lb (3,964 kg) (Loaded)**
Cruising speed: **170 mph (274 km/h)**
Ceiling: **18,000 ft (5,490 m)**
Range: **425 miles (684 km)**
Crew: **1–2**
Passengers: **10–11**

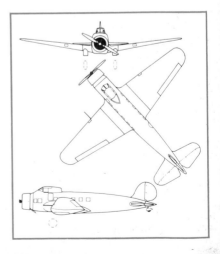

Sikorsky S.43

When it appeared the Sikorsky S.43 was described as a miniature 'clipper'. For many years this elegant, swift amphibious twin-engined type stood alongside the larger S.42, echoing its commercial success on shorter domestic routes. Designed by Igor Sikorsky, who was by now highly experienced in the manufacture of transport seaplanes, the S.43 reasserted the lines and structure of its 'bigger brother', improving on certain features, including its cargo capacity. A maximum 25 passengers could be accommodated on board and this turned out to be a useful quality on the crowded domestic routes. Four S.43's went to Air France, who used them in Africa, while others were sold to Russia, Norway, Chile and China. The first series was followed by the B version with twin rudders, which was not amphibious. The largest operator was Pan American Airways.

Aircraft: **Sikorsky S.43**
Manufacturer: **Sikorsky Aircraft**
Type: **Civil transport**
Year: **1935**
Engines: **Two Pratt & Whitney S1E(Hornet, radial, 750 hp each**
Wingspan: **86 ft 0 in (26.21 m)**
Length: **51 ft 2 in (15.60 m)**
Height: **17 ft 8 in (5.38 m)**
Weight: **19,500 lb (8,485 kg) (Loaded)**
Cruising speed: **166 mph (267 km/h)**
Ceiling: **20,000 ft (6,100 m)**
Range: **775 miles (1,250 km)**
Crew: **2–3**
Passengers: **16–25**

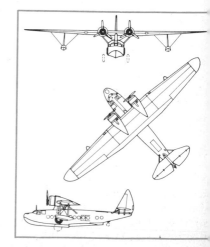

Howard DGA-6
Mr. Mulligan

Two of the most prestigious aviation competitions in America were won in 1935 by an aircraft which looked more like a 'tourer' than a 'racer'. The Howard DGA-6 raced home to victory in the annual events known as the Thompson Trophy and the Bendix Trophy. Christened *Mr. Mulligan*, this brainchild of Ben Howard (one of the world's top personalities in the various aeronautical races of the 1930s) won the first competition at an average speed of 220 mph (354.35 km/h) and the second event at an average speed of 238.7 mph (384.14 km/h). In the Thompson Trophy the aircraft was piloted by Harold Neumann, who had little trouble in winning. However, in the Bendix Trophy, Ben Howard and Gordon Israel managed to win first place by a margin of only twenty-three and a half seconds ahead of their main opponent. This was Roscoe Turner, in a single-seater Wendell Williams.

Aircraft: **Howard DGA-6** *Mr. Mulligan*
Manufacturer: **Howard**
Type: **Competition**
Year: **1935**
Engine: **One Pratt & Whitney Wasp, radial with 9 air-cooled cylinders, 830 hp**
Wingspan: **31 ft 8 in (9.65 m)**
Length: **25 ft 1 in (7.64 m)**
Height: **11 ft 0 in (3.35 m)**
Weight: **4,210 lb (1,909 kg) (Loaded)**
Maximum speed: **292 mph at 11,000 ft (470 km/h at 3,350 m)**
Ceiling: **26,000 ft (7,925 m)**
Range: **1,750 miles (2,815 km)**
Crew: **2**

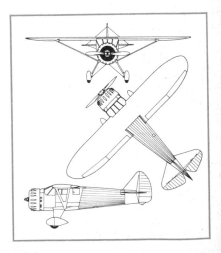

Hughes H-1

Martin Field, Santa Ana, California, September 13, 1935. A small and elegant monoplane set the world speed record at 352 mph (566.99 km/h). Some sixteen months later, on January 19, 1937, the same aircraft (fitted with longer wings) won the intercontinental speed record of the world. The journey from Los Angeles to Newark took 7 hours and 28 minutes. A total of 2,489 miles (4,006 km) was covered at the average speed of 327 mph (526.31 km/h), although the maximum speed of this aircraft was 365 mph (587 km/h). On both occasions the man at the controls of the aircraft was Howard Hughes, the 'flying millionaire'. Hughes had designed and built the H-1 merely for the pleasure of producing an exceptional model. The idea first came into being in 1935 and Hughes decided to enter his racer in the Thompson Trophy and Bendix Trophy races the following year. However, the other competitors protested and Hughes withdrew his name.

Aircraft: **Hughes H-1**
Manufacturer: **Hughes Aircraft Co.**
Type: **Competition**
Year: **1935**
Engine: **One Pratt & Whitney Twin Wasp, radial with 14 air-cooled cylinders, 1,000 hp**
Wingspan: **32 ft 0 in (9.75 m)**
Length: **28 ft 2 in (8.58 m)**
Height: **–**
Weight: **5,512 lb (2,500 kg) (Loaded)**
Maximum speed: **365 mph (587 km/h)**
Ceiling: **20,000 ft (6,000 m)**
Range: **2,490 m (4,006 km)**
Crew: **1**

Bellanca 28-90

Designed for long-distance races, the Bellanca 28-90 ended up by becoming a military aircraft, even though fairly limited in numbers. It nevertheless managed to demonstrate some very excellent features on October 29, 1936 when, piloted by James Mollison, it flew from New York to London without stopping, in the then record time of 13 hours and 17 minutes. This aircraft was fitted with a Pratt & Whitney Twin Wasp engine producing 900 hp (hence its 28-90 registration) and it was derived directly from the 28-70 model of 1934, which was identical except for the engine which could develop only 700 hp. The design had been commissioned by James Fitzmaurice who intended to pilot the aeroplane in the England–Australia race (which was to be won in fact by the de Havilland D.H.88 Comet). However, at the last minute the Bellanca 28-90, which was also christened *Irish Swoop*, was withdrawn from the race.

Aircraft: **Bellanca 28-90**
Manufacturer: **Bellanca Aircraft Corp.**
Type: **Competition**
Year: **1936**
Engine: **One Pratt & Whitney R-1830 Twin Wasp, radial with 14 air-cooled cylinders, 900 hp**
Wingspan: **46 ft 2 in (14.07 m)**
Length: **25 ft 11 in (7.90 m)**
Height: **8 ft 8 in (2.64 m)**
Weight: **7,099 lb (3,223 kg) (Loaded)**
Maximum speed: **280 mph (452 km/h)**
Ceiling: **30,500 ft (9,300 m)**
Range: **800 miles (1,280 km)**
Crew: **2**

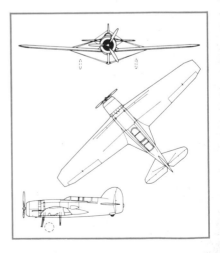

Folkerts SK-3 Jupiter

First in the 1937 Thompson Trophy event, covering the 200 mile (322 km) course at the average speed of 257 mph (413 km/h). First in the 1937 Greve Trophy event, covering 100 miles (161 km) at the average speed of 232.2 mph (373.72 km/h). In both races the Folkerts SK-3 Jupiter was piloted by Rudy Kling, an almost legendary figure in the world of American sporting aviation of the day. It was in this same aircraft that Kling was to die a year later, in Miami. Christened the *Pride of Lemont*, the small SK-3 was a racer in every detail. The designer, Clayton Folkerts, had given it an extremely short wing to improve its flying qualities. For similar reasons this aircraft also had a small undercarriage which was retractable into the fuselage by means of an ingenious mechanism. The 400 hp engine was an inverted Menasco with 6 cylinders, which could produce more than 50% over and above the original power.

Aircraft: **Folkerts SK-3 Jupiter**
Manufacturer: **Folkerts**
Type: **Competition**
Year: **1937**
Engine: **One Menasco C-6S4, air-cooled, straight 6 cylinder, 400 hp**
Wingspan: **16 ft 8 in (5.08 m)**
Length: **21 ft 0 in (6.40 m)**
Height: **4 ft 0 in (1.22 m)**
Unladen weight: **841 lb (381 kg)**
Weight: **1,385 lb (628 kg) (Loaded)**
Maximum speed: **257 mph (413 km/h)**
Ceiling: **–**
Range: **–**
Crew: **1**

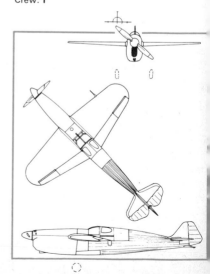

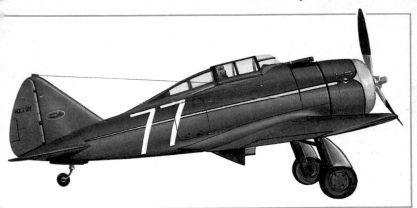

Seversky Sev-S2

Virtually identical to the military version which was at this time undergoing the Army assessment trials, the Seversky Sev-S2 was simply a racing version of the P-35, which a few enthusiasts were able to use in competitions. In fact it was during one of the most prestigious events, the Bendix Trophy, that this small, compact monoplane gave a dazzling display of its advanced qualities which were not fully acknowledged in its military use. Piloted by Frank Fuller, the Sev-S2 dominated the 1937 Bendix race, winning at the average speed of 258.2 mph (415.58 km/h), after flying for 7 hours, 54 minutes and 26 seconds. The same result recurred in the two following years: in 1938, on this occasion piloted by the woman aviator Jacqueline Cochran, at an average speed of 249.7 mph (401.91 km/h); and in 1939, once again piloted by Frank Fuller, at an average speed of 270.9 mph (435.98 km/h).

Aircraft: **Seversky Sev-S2**
Manufacturer: **Republic Aviation Corp.**
Type: **Competition**
Year: **1937**
Engine: **One Pratt & Whitney R-K30 Twin Wasp, radial with 14 air-cooled cylinders, 1,000 hp**
Wingspan: **36 ft 0 in (10.97 m)**
Length: **25 ft 6 in (7.77 m)**
Height: **9 ft 9 in (2.97 m)**
Weight: **6,390 lb (2,899 kg) (Loaded)**
Maximum speed: **305 mph (491 km/h)**
Ceiling: **29,685 ft (9,050 m)**
Range: **1,200 miles (1,930 km)**
Crew: **1**

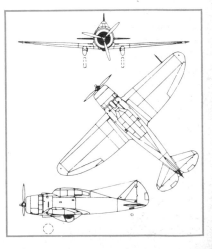

Lockheed 14 Super Electra

The Lockheed Model 14 was popular throughout the world with many major civil operators, and was successful on two levels: firstly as a commercial aircraft in the years immediately before the war, and secondly as a military aircraft throughout the war years. In both cases the Super Electra (as it was christened, in honour of the no less renowned forefather, the Lockheed 10 Electra of 1934) fully demonstrated its qualities as a tough aeroplane, which was versatile and highly reliable. In some ways its military use overshadowed its strictly civilian use: more than 2,000 examples (almost the entire production) were distributed among the allied air forces, especially to the Royal Air Force. Known as the Hudson, they played a vital role (especially in the early war years) as maritime reconnaissance aircraft.

The Lockheed 14 was derived directly from the model 10, which together with the Boeing 247 and the Douglas DC-2 had contributed handsomely to the development of modern commercial aviation. Although it retained the shape and basic structure of its forerunner, the Super Electra nevertheless included important aerodynamic improvements. In particular the adoption of the special Fowler-type wing-flaps (which among other things enabled the designer Clarence L. Johnson to earn wide recognition, in the form of the 1937 Lawrence Sperry Award) which improved the take-off performance.

The prototype flew for the first time on July 29, 1937, and on the wave of success earned by the earlier Electra, was immediately highly thought of by civil operators. These included not only domestic American companies (among which the largest orders were placed by Northwest Airlines and Continental Airlines) but also foreign companies, especially in Europe. The Dutch KLM company was the first in the old continent to use the Super Electra. It was followed by British Airways Ltd., Sabena of Belgium, LOT of Poland, and Aer Lingus of Ireland. Outside Europe there were orders from Dai Nippon Koku K.K. of Japan, Guinea

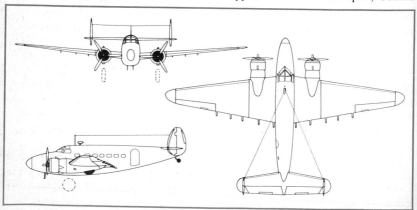

Airways, and Trans Canada Air Lines. In Japan, in particular, the Lockheed 14 enjoyed a fate not unusual to many exceptional aircraft. After 30 aircraft had been received, it was then built in more than 100 examples as a military transport aircraft. It was even used as a basis for an improved and more powerful version which the Kawasaki Kokuki Kogyo K.K. company built from 1941 onwards.

Great Britain made particularly heavy use of it. British Airways initially received eight examples of the Super Electra which, together with the pre-existing fleet of Lockheed 10s, considerably stepped up European connections, particularly those with Paris, Brussels, Frankfurt, Hamburg, Berlin, Budapest, Warsaw, Stockholm and Copenhagen. On these routes, starting from early 1939, the journey time was considerably reduced, thanks to the higher speed of the Lockheed 14 as compared with the previous models. Amongst its other distinctions it was on board a Super Electra that, in September 1938, the British Prime Minister

Aircraft: **Lockheed 14-F62 Super Electra**
Manufacturer: **Lockheed Aircraft Corp.**
Type: **Light transport**
Year: **1937**
Engines: **Two Wright GR-1820-F62 Cyclone, radial with 9 air-cooled cylinders, 760 hp each**
Wingspan: **65 ft 6 in (19.96 m)**
Length: **44 ft 2 in (13.40 m)**
Height: **11 ft 5 in (3.49 m)**
Weight: **17,500 lb (7,838 kg) (Loaded)**
Cruising speed: **225 mph at 13,000 ft (362 km/h at 3,963 m)**
Ceiling: **21,500 ft (6,558 m)**
Range: **1,590 miles (2,558 km)**
Crew: **2–3**
Passengers: **12**

Neville Chamberlain travelled to Germany for the historic Munich Conference. When hostilities broke out, however, these aircraft were taken over by the British Overseas Airways Corporation (BOAC) and used for flying to the African colonies.

In its crowded career the Super Electra also enjoyed an exceptional sporting record: in July 1938, when it flew 'around the world,' it covered the 14,792 miles (23,804 km) in three days, 19 hours and 17 minutes. The race had been organized by the American millionaire, Howard Hughes, who was on board with a four-man crew.

21

Grumman G-21

Appearing in the immediate prewar period, and designed as an amphibious commercial aircraft, the twin-engined Grumman G-21 did not have time to have a wide use, because production of it was soon monopolized by military requirements. At the end of the war, however, many examples were declared to be surplus and placed on the civil market, where they enjoyed instant success as executive and light transport aircraft, particularly in the islands of Central America and in the lakes of Canada. However, in the postwar period Grumman developed another model from the G-21 (which had been christened the 'Goose'). This was the G-73 Mallard, which was slightly larger, and went into service in 1947. These two models were accompanied by the demilitarized models of another aircraft derived from the Goose, the G-44 Widgeon. This smaller aircraft was developed in the postwar years for reconnaissance and transportation.

Aircraft: **Grumman G-21A**
Manufacturer: **Grumman Aircraft Engineering Corp.**
Type: **Light transport**
Year: **1937**
Engines: **Two Pratt & Whitney R-385-AN6 Wasp jr, radial, 450 hp each**
Wingspan: **49 ft 0 in (14.95 m)**
Length: **38 ft 4 in (11.70 m)**
Height: **12 ft 0 in (3.66 m)**
Weight: **8,000 lb (3,629 kg) (Loaded)**
Cruising speed: **190 mph (306 km/h)**
Ceiling: **22,000 ft (6,700 m)**
Range: **800 miles (1,287 km)**
Crew: **2**
Passengers: **6–7**

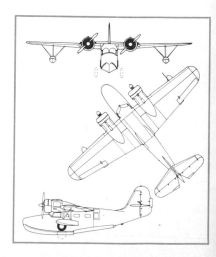

Beech 17

Even though it was the first commercial aircraft to be produced by the Beech Aircraft Corporation of Wichita, the Beech 17 showed itself to be one of the most numerous of the biplane formula with an enclosed cockpit. Even today hundreds of American enthusiasts gather annually with their 'Staggerwings' and re-live the thrill of flying in the 1930s. The 'Staggerwing' (the name by which the Beech 17 is universally known) in fact flew for the first time in 1932 and remained in production, passing through various versions, until 1948. The model F-17 was the seventh variant in the series. Although it retained the lines of its forerunners, it had a different engine and different structural details. After its success during the war years, when the Beech 17 was chosen as a military executive model and mass-produced, the last version appeared in the immediate postwar period. This was the G-17S, and it was also the best of all the variants.

Aircraft: **Beech F-17**
Manufacturer: **Beech Aircraft Corp.**
Type: **Light transport**
Year: **1938**
Engine: **One Jacobs L-6, radial with 7 air-cooled cylinders, 330 hp**
Wingspan: **32 ft 0 in (9.75 m)**
Length: **26 ft 2 in (7.98 m)**
Height: **10 ft 3 in (3.12 m)**
Weight: **3,550 lb (1,610 kg) (Loaded)**
Cruising speed: **180 mph at 10,000 ft (289 km/h at 3,050 m)**
Ceiling: **19,800 ft (6,040 m)**
Range: **700 miles (1,130 km)**
Crew: **1**
Passengers: **4**

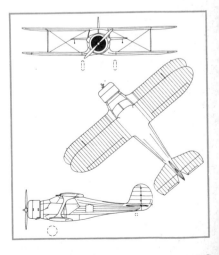

Laird-Turner L-RT Meteor

Roscoe Turner, the famous racing pilot from Latin America in the 1930s, made a triumphant return in the last two Thompson Trophy events in 1938 and 1939. The previous win for him had been back in 1934. On that occasion he was at the controls of an aircraft which was to remain one of the most celebrated in the history of aviation competitions: the Wedell Williams. The golden age of air-races nevertheless came to an end with another exceptional aircraft: the Laird-Turner L-RT Meteor. Popularly known by the nickname of 'Turner Special' this small and powerful monoplane was christened in the two last races *Pesco Special* and *Miss Champion*, respectively, and won on both occasions at an average speed of more than 280 mph (450 km/h). In fact during the 1938 Thompson Trophy he recorded a speed of 283.4 mph (456.1 km/h), and in the 1939 race he reached 282.5 mph (454.68 km/h).

Aircraft: **Laird-Turner L-RT Meteor**
Manufacturer: **Laird**
Type: **Competition**
Year: **1939**
Engine: **One Pratt & Whitney S1B3-G Twin Wasp, radial with 14 air-cooled cylinders, 1,000 hp**
Wingspan: **25 ft 0 in (7.62 m)**
Length: **23 ft 4 in (7.11 m)**
Height: **10 ft 0 in (3.05 m)**
Unladen weight: **3,310 lb (1,501 kg)**
Weight: **4,933 lb (2,238 kg) (Loaded)**
Maximum speed: **308 mph (496 km/h)**
Ceiling: **—**
Range: **—**
Crew: **1**

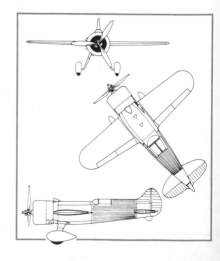

Boeing 307 Stratoliner

This was the first four-engined civil transport aircraft with a pressurized cabin. In this sense the Boeing 307 Stratoliner blazed the trail for today's commercial aeroplanes which can fly at high altitudes, even though only ten such aircraft were ever constructed. The war brought a sudden halt to all immediate ideas of developing the Stratoliner, and production of it gave way to that of the aircraft from which it had been derived. This was the bomber known as the Boeing B-17 Flying Fortress.

The design of this large four-engined transport aircraft was in fact given the go-ahead at almost the same time as that of the future B-17, towards the end of 1934. Originally known as Model 300, the aircraft was later permanently known as Model 307 when the second major variant of the bomber, the B-17C, appeared. The likenesses between the two aircraft were in fact substantial. The 307 used, virtually unmodified, the tail assembly, wing and engine installation of the military aeroplane. The fuselage was, however, completely different. It was somewhat broader and had a distinctive 'whale' form which could quite comfortably accommodate 33 passengers and a crew of five. The most marked feature, which made the Stratoliner the forbear of a whole new generation of civil transport aircraft, was nevertheless the pressurization of the cabin. This feature ensured greater passenger comfort and better operational conditions than those imposed on other commercial aircraft of the day. The latter could only fly at fairly low altitudes, and therefore could not avoid atmospheric disturbances.

For the first time the age-old dream of flying above the clouds, unaffected by storms and adverse atmospheric conditions, with greater comfort and clear-cut improvements in flying times, became a reality. TWA (at the time known as Trans Continental and Western Air) which became the major operator of the new Boeing 307s, had always been aware of this line of development. From the early 1930s this large American company had conducted and encouraged a lengthy series of experiments concerned with the possibilities of sub-stratospheric commercial flight. Wiley Post, the famous pilot who, in 1931 and in 1933 had set up spectacular distance records with the single-engined Lockheed Vega, had also been commissioned by TWA to carry out a whole series of experimental flights at high altitudes. The aim of these was to study the behaviour of both fuels and engines; the different rates of fuel consumption; and speeds. In addition, they wanted to study the possibilities of setting up a network of commercial high altitude flights.

Wiley Post carried out these test flights between 1934 and 1935 and used the same aeroplane that had enabled him to win those numerous distance records in the years before. The main modifications to the Lockheed Vega 5B, christened *Winnie Mae*, were to the engine and in the form of the addition of a supercharger. Thus equipped the monoplane showed itself to be surprisingly well suited to the purpose. In 1934 Post completed at least eight sub-stratospheric flights, in the course of which he reached altitudes of 50,000 feet (15,000 m).

Wiley protected himself from the hazards of high altitudes with a complicated pressurized flying-suit, not unlike those used by today's astronauts. In the following year, encouraged by these positive results, Wiley Post decided to give a practical demonstration of the possibilities of high altitude flight. The demonstration took the form of a flight across the American continent from the west coast to the Atlantic. To this end he once more modified his *Winnie Mae*, fitting it with an undercarriage that could be released in the air. The first attempt took place on February 22, 1935, but it was not completed because of sabotage to the engine which had been filled with abrasive powder. Three further tests also failed, but on March 15 Wiley Post achieved his aim, even though not completely. He took off from Burbank in California, and landed at Cleveland in Ohio, after a flight of 2,038 miles (3,280 km) in 7 hours and 19 minutes, at an average land-speed of 279 mph (449 km/h) — almost twice the *Winnie Mae*'s cruising speed. This incredible increase in performance was obtained simply by flying at an altitude of between 30,000 and 33,000 feet (9,000–10,000 m).

Wiley Post died a few months later on August 15, 1935, in an accident which occurred while he was taking off in a Lockheed Orion seaplane in Alaska, but this did not mean that the TWA experiments ended. Further studies were carried out by one of the company's pilots, D. W. Tomlinson, on a suitably equipped Northrop Gamma.

Boeing preferred to complete the project but await orders from the airlines before going ahead with building a prototype. Orders were not long in arriving. They came from the two major United States' companies: Pan American Airways and Trans Continental and Western Air. The former ordered four models in 1937, and TWA, at almost the same time, ordered a further six, although this figure was later reduced to five. The first aircraft for Pan American (which was also the actual prototype of the 307) took to the air on December 31, 1938, in the hands of Boeing's chief test-pilot Edmund T. Allen. This was the start of the aircraft's career. Nevertheless the prototype was destroyed three months later during a test-flight by a pilot from the Dutch KLM company. Pan American thus never received one of its ordered models and the other three

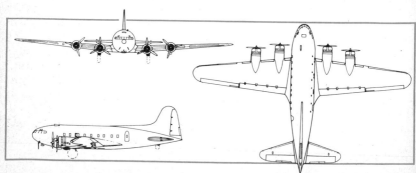

(called Model S-307s, but also known as Model PAA-307s) were delivered in 1940. They were christened *Clipper Rainbow*, *Clipper Flying Cloud* and *Clipper Comet* and were used on the South American route until 1948.

The five aircraft ordered by TWA were also delivered in 1940 (called SA-307Bs). They differed from the Pan American models in a few structural details, and also had different engines. They were christened respectively *Comanche*, *Cherokee*, *Zuni*, *Apache* and *Navajo*. They were kept particularly busy and when war broke out in the Pacific, they had together flown a total of 4,366,926 miles (7,278,210 km) without the slightest mishap. In the war years these five aircraft were requisitioned by the Armed Forces and used in Air Transport Command as C-75s. After the end of the war, they were overhauled and brought up-to-date by Boeing and returned to service on the domestic routes handled by TWA until 1951.

Aircraft: **Boeing SA-307B Stratoliner**
Manufacturer: **Boeing Aircraft Corp.**
Type: **Civil transport**
Year: **1940**
Engines: **Four Wright GR-1820 Cyclone, radial with 9 air-cooled cylinders, 900 hp each**
Wingspan: **107 ft 3 in (32.69 m)**
Length: **74 ft 4 in (22.66 m)**
Height: **20 ft 9 in (6.33 m)**
Weight: **42,000 lb (19,051 kg) (Loaded)**
Cruising speed: **222 mph (357 km/h)**
Ceiling: **26,200 ft (7,985 m)**
Range: **2,300 miles (3,700 km)**
Crew: **5**
Passengers: **33**

A very different fate lay in store for the tenth and last model produced. This was purchased by Howard Hughes, who intended to fit it out to beat his own record set up in July 1938. However, the outbreak of war prevented the new attempt to set up a distance record from ever taking place. Hughes then had the aircraft transformed into a luxurious airborne apartment, but he hardly used it and in 1949 sold it to a Texan oil magnate. In 1963 the 307 was sold again. It had flown for just 500 hours.

Lockheed 18 Lodestar

After the 1934 Electra and the 1937 Super Electra, the third member of the prolific family of twin-engined Lockheeds was the Model 18 Lodestar which in almost 30 years of service consolidated and broadened the success of the two previous aircraft. As had happened with the Lockheed 14, which had seen its excellent qualities immediately exploited for military use, so the Lodestar was widely used among the various allied air forces (the U.S. Navy alone received 1,600 examples, under the designation of PV-1 Ventura) during the war years. The war did not, however, hamper a no less exceptional civil career: towards the end of the 1940s, the Lodestars were used by half the world's airlines as short-to-medium range transport aircraft, and later they enjoyed a new phase of renown as executive and private transport aircraft.

The first Lodestar took to the air on February 2, 1940. The new Lockheed design derived closely from the Model 14. The three initial aircraft were completed by directly converting the airframes of the Super Electra. The idea which had led to the construction of the Model 18 had been basically that of considerably improving the load capacity and the general performance of the already excellent predecessor. To this end the fuselage was lengthened, the wing was structurally modified and the engines were replaced by other more powerful units. There were many engines which could be fitted to the Lodestar: from Pratt & Whitney Hornets to Wright Twin Wasps and Cyclones, with a wide range of available power. The load capacity was also considerably increased: the 12 passengers that could be carried by the Super Electra was increased to 17 (or 18 by reducing the crew by one).

Its commercial success was immediate: by 1940 Lockheed had completed 55 examples which all went

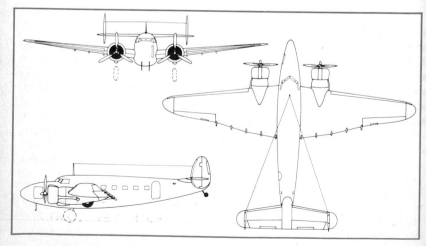

o civil operators in the United States, Latin America, France and South Africa. Initially BOAC took nine aircraft, between March and July 1941, using them in flights to and from the African colonies. Other Lodestars, released by the U.S.A.A.F., went to U.S. companies, pending the outcome of the Lend-Lease Act. Production ended in 1943 with a total of 625 aircraft built.

The end of the war gave renewed momentum to the career of this versatile twin-engined aeroplane. Many aircraft were withdrawn from the armed forces and returned to their owners or put on to the civil market. A number of companies once again used the Lockheed 18s, notably East African Airways, Linjeflyg of Sweden, and the Australian Trans-Australia Airlines. Many other Lodestars were used exclusively for freight transport but with the appearance of somewhat more modern and competitive commercial aeroplanes they became slowly less and less used.

Aircraft: **Lockheed 18-56 Lodestar**
Manufacturer: **Lockheed Aircraft Corp.**
Type: **Light transport**
Year: **1940**
Engines: **Two Wright R-1820-G205A Cyclone, radial with 9 air-cooled cylinders, 1,200 hp each**
Wingspan: **65 ft 6 in (19.96 m)**
Length: **49 ft 10 in (15.18 m)**
Height: **11 ft 1 in (3.37 m)**
Weight: **17,500 lb (7,938 kg)**
Cruising speed: **251 mph at 17,000 ft (404 km/h at 5,180 m)**
Ceiling: **27,000 ft (8,230 m)**
Range: **1,660 miles (2,671 km)**
Crew: **3**
Passengers: **17**

However, this did not mean the end of the Lockheed 18. A new wave of success opened the 1950s. The Lodestar was potentially an excellent executive model and with the greater availability caused by its withdrawal from the airlines, many specialized firms devoted themselves to converting them to VIP models. One of the best-known is the one that was christened Learstar, designed by Lear, and put on the market in 1955. With major modifications the Learstar is still flying today in many corners of the world.

29

Curtiss C-46

This was designed to replace the Douglas DC-3 on the civil market and if the demands of war had not focussed on the urgent needs of the military the Curtiss C-46 would almost certainly have done just this. Larger, more powerful and faster than the immortal twin-engined Douglas, the Commando (as the C-46 was known in every theatre of operations) offered undeniable advantages over its direct rival, especially over short-to-medium distances. The 3,200 aircraft completed nevertheless all went to the air force and this monopoly of production prevented any commercial development. Only after the end of the war were several hundred C-46s declared to be surplus and put on the market. They spread fairly slowly to the various operators, and ended up equipping many smaller companies for the transport of both freight and passengers. At the end of the 1960s there were still a couple of hundred C-46s in service with some seventy small airlines.

The Curtiss-Wright Corporation started the C-46 project in 1937 intending to develop a twin-engined transport aircraft particularly suited to a range of about 600 miles (1,000 km). The fact that these routes represented almost 90% of the domestic American lines put the new aircraft in direct competition with the already extremely popular Douglas DC-3 and the designers worked flat out to produce an aircraft with features that were fairly competitive on the civil market. The basic concept used as a springboard (which subsequently turned out to be the most valid one) was that of fitting the aeroplane with the fewest possible number of engines with the greatest potential power. The prototype, designated CW-20, appeared as a twin-engined model of considerable size and was driven by a pair of large Wright radial engines each developing 1,700 hp at take-off. Another important innovation was the pressurization of the cabin, which gave rise to the distinctive 'double bubble' shape of the fuselage. In practice this was not used because of the military requirements.

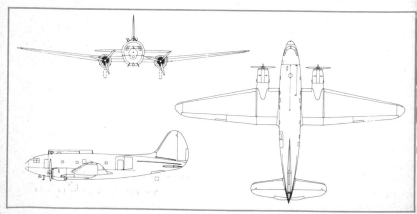

The considerable potential of the new aircraft on the civil market was demonstrated on the very day of the first prototype flight, March 26, 1940. Military observers were immediately interested by the features of the twin-engined Curtiss, particularly with regard to the load capacity and the large dimensions of the fuselage. An initial order for 25 models (considerably modified when compared with the prototype) arrived some time later and was followed by other massive orders staggered over a period of time. This led to the development of three major variants in production: the C-46A (1,491 examples); the C-46D (1,410 examples) and the C-46F (234 examples). An overall figure of 3,180 units was achieved, three other versions being built in smaller numbers. Of these aircraft the only one which was used in a civil role during the war was the prototype. This had been sent to Great Britain in 1941 and put into service by BOAC in the early months of the following year, having been christened *Spirit of St. Louis.*

Aircraft: **Curtiss C-46A**
Manufacturer: **Curtiss-Wright Corp.**
Type: **Civil transport**
Year: **1940**
Engines: **Two Pratt & Whitney R-2800-51 Double Wasp, radial with 18 air-cooled cylinders, 2,000 hp each**
Wingspan: **108 ft 1 in (32.94 m)**
Length: **76 ft 4 in (23.27 m)**
Height: **21 ft 9 in (6.63 m)**
Weight: **48,000 lb (21.772 kg) (Loaded)**
Cruising speed: **195 mph at 9,000 ft (315 km/h at 2,750 m)**
Ceiling: **24,500 ft (7,470 m)**
Range: **1,800 miles (2,896 km)**
Crew: **4**
Passengers: **40–62**

In the immediate postwar period the Curtiss company resurrected the original idea and designed a civil version, the CW-20E. This project was never completed, because of the huge availability of surplus military aircraft. Many of these were appropriately modified by specialized firms. The models CW-20T, Super 46C and C-46R were particularly successful. The modifications consisted mainly of structural improvements aimed at increasing the load capacity and the number of passengers that could be carried. In some cases this number reached 62 passengers.

Consolidated PBY Catalina

The first flight round the world (covering a distance equal to the earth's maximum circumference) made by a seaplane was completed by a PBY Catalina christened *Guba* in the hands of an American scientist called Richard Archbold. This spectacular feat was achieved between May 12 and July 6, 1939, slightly more than two years after the first flight by what was to become one of the most famous seaplanes ever made. From many points of view this episode can be considered as the start of the civil career of the 'Cat' which, after the huge and busy gap left by the war years, was revived and used in many different ways in every corner of the world. Even today various models of this versatile twin-engined aircraft are still flying, even though their number is constantly waning and the few that do remain are jealously guarded by historians and enthusiasts. The Catalina production figures have never been entirely clarified. A total of 3,290 models were

built in the United States and Canada but 'several hundred' were also built the Soviet Union, which had acquired licence in 1938. The very first one fle on March 28, 1935. It was the result a request made by the American navy to the Douglas Corporation and Co solidated on October 28, 1933, for the production of a flying-boat to replace the old Martin P3Ms and Consolidate P2Ys. The Catalina prototype (design nated XP3Y-1) borrowed the lines other aircraft in the category at the time, but also incorporated considerable technical and structural improvements. It was a flying-boat with a high wing, a central hull and a pair of radial engines. Numerous aerodynamic improvements were also made, including the use of retracting wingtip floats. The first order for 60 models was placed on June 29, 1935 and production went ahead steadily for almost five years with the initial variants PBY-1, PBY-2, PBY-3 and PBY-4. These a differed in their structural details

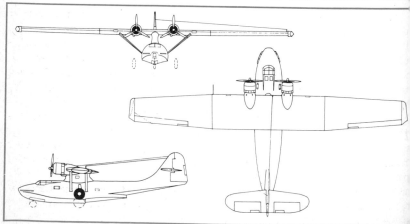

32

ttings and engines. In 1940 one of the ost popular versions appeared, the BY-5, from which, in the following ear, the first amphibious variant, the BY-5A was derived. It was from a eries modified by the Naval Aircraft actory of Philadelphia (designated BN-1 Nomad) that the last version of e Catalina, the PBY-6A, which had a ifferent hull structure, different tail ssembly and a different fuel capacity, as derived.

The end of the war, and the conse-uent demobilization of large numbers f military aeroplanes put a large umber of Catalinas on to the civil narket. These aircraft included those uilt in the United States as well as nose assembled in Canada by Canadian Vickers and Boeing Aircraft f Canada. Apart from the civil uses such as geological surveys, forest and re prevention services), for which no pecific modifications were required, nany Catalinas were used as civil ransport aircraft, especially between slands (like the Antilles and in many

Aircraft: **Consolidated PBY-5A Catalina**
Manufacturer: **Consolidated Aircraft Corp.**
Type: **Civil transport**
Year: **1941**
Engines: **Two Pratt & Whitney R-1830-92 Twin Wasp, radial with 14 air-cooled cylinders, 1,200 hp each**
Wingspan: **104 ft 0 in (31.70 m)**
Length: **63 ft 10 in (19.45 m)**
Height: **20 ft 2 in (6.14 m)**
Weight: **28,000 lb (12,701 kg)**
Cruising speed: **130 mph at 6,000 ft (209 km/h at 1,830 m)**
Ceiling: **14,700 ft (4,480 m)**
Range: **650 miles (1,046 km)**
Crew: **2–4**
Passengers: **22**

parts of south-east Asia) and for river landings (like the Amazon basin, in Brazil). One of the companies which made fullest use, with great success, of the PBYs was Panair do Brazil. They used six such aircraft up until 1965, modified for the transportation of up to 22 passengers. Finally, many Catalinas ended up being rebuilt and fitted with larger engines, so as to increase their payload. Of these modified versions a certain degree of success was earned by the one called the Super Catalina, which was to become especially popular in Canada.

Boeing 314 Yankee Clipper

The golden age of the commercial flying-boats was abruptly interrupted by the war. However, before this interruption, when the development of such aircraft was directed towards the precise needs of the military, there was one last great 'clipper' which managed to make a considerable contribution to the development of civil aviation. This was the Boeing 314 (christened Yankee Clipper), a gigantic four-engined flying-boat which represented the highest development of the formula which had started out in the form of the Sikorsky S.42 in 1935. The Boeing 314 was the first aircraft to make a regular service across the North Atlantic. This route is still the most prestigious of all today despite the immense growth of the airlines. On May 20, 1939, Pan American World Airways, at whose request the Yankee Clipper had been designed, inaugurated the first transatlantic mail service, and on June 28 inaugurated the first regular passenger service, from New York to Southampton, via Newfoundland. These developments were, however, overshadowed by the first signs of the war in Europe. Even though the outbreak of war led to the cancellation of these services, the 1? Boeing 314s built (nine went to the Pan American company and three to BOAC of Great Britain) continued to carry out vital tasks across the Atlantic and Pacific oceans until the hostilities were at an end.

The Yankee Clipper project dated back to 1935, with the start of a series of negotiations between Pan American and Boeing for the production of a flying-boat capable of guaranteeing transatlantic passenger flights with a high degree of safety, comfort and speed. On July 21 of the following year this major airline company signed a contract for six aircraft, the first of which (designation Model 314) took to the air on June 7, 1938. When it made its appearance this flying-boat was the largest civil aircraft in service. It had a central hull and adopted the wing and engine assembly of the experimental Boeing XB-15 heavy bomber. In the place of the traditional floating stabilizers at the wingtips, sponson

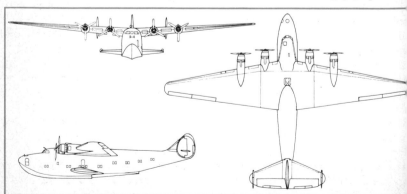

mounted on the sides of the hull were used, based on the formula developed by the German engineer Dornier. These sponsons also contained fuel-tanks, the capacity of which (together with those situated in the wings) totalled almost 3,525 gallons (16,000 litres). In the spacious fuselage there was ample room for 74 daytime passengers, or for 40 passengers in reclining seats for long night-flights.

The first six models were all delivered in the first half of 1939 and in view of their success Pan American ordered another six. These, (designation 314A), were considerably improved in their carrying capacity (77 daytime passengers), engine power, and increase in fuel capacity by about 1,000 gallons (4,500 litres). The first of these aircraft flew as a prototype on March 20, 1941, but the war was now in full swing, only half the order went to Pan American. In fact three models were bought by the British government and allotted to BOAC for use as trans-port aircraft. These aeroplanes were

Aircraft: **Boeing 314A Yankee Clipper**
Manufacturer: **Boeing Aircraft Corp.**
Type: **Civil transport**
Year: **1941**
Engines: **Four Wright GR 2600 Cyclone, radial with 14 air-cooled cylinders, 1,600 hp each**
Wingspan: **152 ft 0 in (46.33 m)**
Length: **106 ft 0 in (32.31 m)**
Height: **27 ft 7 in (8.41 m)**
Weight: **82,500 lb (37,422 kg) (Loaded)**
Cruising speed: **183 mph (294 km/h)**
Ceiling: **13,400 ft (4,085 m)**
Range: **3,500 miles (5,630 km)**
Crew: **10**
Passengers: **77**

well known for the fact that they carried Winston Churchill on his inter-continental journeys, and survived the war to be returned to the United States in 1948. The career of the Yankee Clippers, five of which were purchased by the U.S.A.A.F. and the U.S. Navy, was also a lengthy one. Apart from three which were destroyed in February 1943, November 1945 and October 1947, the others remained with Pan American until April 1946. They were then used by various small charter companies and not withdrawn from service until 1950.

Douglas DC-4

The Douglas DC-4, in a similar fashion to the Curtiss C-46, was designed for commercial use but forced to 'miss its cue' because of the needs of war. A total of 61 of these large four-engined aeroplanes (the forbear of a long and successful family) had already been ordered before the prototype had taken off, but production was immediately and completely geared to military requirements. The military had been impressed by the remarkable features of this aircraft which was ideal for the purposes of strategic transport. Under the name of C-54 Skymaster, some 1,163 models were used by Air Transport Command throughout the war years, and their contribution to victory was inestimable. In particular their intensive operational use brought to light one of the DC-4's best qualities, its safety. In the course of 79,642 flights across the various oceans, the Skymasters had just three accidents, a record which even today seems quite exceptional. With the end of the war

and the consequent flooding of the civil market with many aircraft now declared surplus, the civil career of the DC-4 got under way, although it was not as important as its makers would have liked. There were 79 completely civil models made, but these aircraft were only used to equip the airlines for a transitional period; they were replaced almost as they appeared by the new commercial aircraft of the first postwar generation.

The project which gave rise to the DC-4 initially started in the mid-1930s when the five major American airline companies started negotiations with the Douglas Corporation over making a four-engined transport aircraft designed for long-range flights. The first plan which came in the form of a prototype did not, however, satisfy the potential buyers. The four-engined type, called the DC-4E, flew for the first time on June 7, 1938 and was criticized as too large and not economical. On the basis of the new requirements, the Douglas

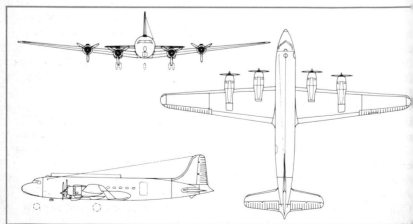

company started to work on a smaller version of this aircraft, which took to the air on February 14, 1942. It was a simpler aeroplane (omitting the cabin pressurization system that was installed in the earlier prototype) and characterized by the adoption of a single fin and rudder assembly, as compared with the triple fins and rudders of the DC-4E. The flight specifications of the new aircraft were excellent, as was the payload of 42 passengers.

The American companies were much more satisfied with the new aircraft and demonstrated their real interest by initially ordering 61 aircraft (orders placed by American Airlines, Eastern Air Lines and United Air Lines.) The similar and higher priority interest of the U.S.A.A.F. automatically settled the matter.

At the end of the war the first company to put the now veteran DC-4s into service was American Overseas Airlines which, towards the end of October 1945, inaugurated a transatlantic service between New

Aircraft: **Douglas DC-4**
Manufacturer: **Douglas Aircraft Co.**
Type: **Civil transport**
Year: **1942**
Engines: **Four Pratt & Whitney R 2000 Twin Wasp, radial with 14 air-cooled cylinders, 1,450 hp each**
Wingspan: **117 ft 6 in (35.81 m)**
Length: **93 ft 11 in (28.62 m)**
Height: **27 ft 6 in (8.38 m)**
Weight: **73,000 lb (33,112 kg) (Loaded)**
Cruising speed: **227 mph (365 km/h)**
Ceiling: **22,300 ft (6,800 m)**
Range: **2,140 miles (3,444 km)**
Crew: **5**
Passengers: **44–86**

York and London. The distance was covered in 23 hours and 48 minutes and included two stops on the way. On March 7, 1946 American Airlines was the first company to use the DC-4s on domestic American routes, starting a service between New York and Los Angeles. Subsequently the major European companies also used the reliable four-engined Douglas aircraft for regular services on all their major routes. Gradually, however, the production of modern aircraft meant that the DC-4s were converted to freight transportation, and then went to smaller airlines.

Sikorsky VS-44A

The last contributions to the development of commercial aviation made by the mighty American flying-boats are attributable to the Sikorsky VS-44A. These consisted of the transatlantic record between the United States and Europe, 3,328 miles (5,356 km) in 14 hours and 17 minutes with no stops; the fastest non-stop flight between Europe and New York, 18 hours and 5 minutes; the fastest flight between Europe and the United States with a refuelling stop in Newfoundland, 17 hours and 45 minutes; and the first nonstop flight between New York and Lisbon, 3,382 miles (5,443 km) in 20 hours and 14 minutes. Even though they referred to services run by the military during the war years (although the aircraft bore civil markings and had civilian crews), they nevertheless brought to light the exceptional performances of what can be considered to be the last aircraft of this type. If the Boeing 314 Yankee Clipper managed just in time (before donning its military uniform) to enable Pan American to run the first regular peacetime services across the North Atlantic, the Sikorsky

VS-44A had a different fate. Shortl[y] after the first prototype flight o[n] January 18, 1942, this large four[-]engined aeroplane was requisitioned b[y] the U.S. Navy. Together with the onl[y] two other models built, it was use[d] throughout the war for military trans[-]port. During this period it still kept th[e] markings of American Export Airline[s] (the company which had ordered it[)] and a civilian crew, with the sol[e] purpose of being able to have access t[o] neutral countries. Only one of the thre[e] VS-44As managed to have a real com[-]mercial career in the postwar years[.] This was the second one built (the othe[r] two were lost in 1942 and 194[?] respectively), which bore the markin[g] NC-41881.

The VS-44A derived directly from[m] the sea reconnaissance aircraft XPBS[-]1, ordered from Sikorsky by the U.S[.] Navy in 1935. When American Expor[t] Airlines decided to set up non-stop transatlantic flights, they thought o[f] using a seaplane and started t[o] negotiate with the Sikorsky firm abou[t] making an aircraft capable of flying 'a[s] far as possible, as fast as possible an[d]

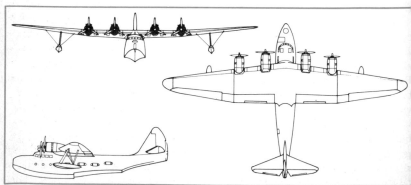

with the greatest possible cargo'. These were not easy requirements to meet, but by basing their ideas on the military project the engineers managed to build an excellent commercial aircraft which could fly (under specific load conditions) non-stop for more than 5,000 miles (8,000 km). The original transport capacity envisaged was 26 daytime passengers or 16 passengers in couchettes for long night-flights. The prototype marked NC-41880 and christened *Excalibur*, was followed not long after by the other two models, respectively marked NC-41881 *Excambian* and NC-41882 *Exeter*.

In the postwar period, after the loss of *Excalibur* and *Exeter*, the VS-44A *Excambian* had a fairly lively career. After being requisitioned by the Baltimore authorities, because it had been moored in the port for some time without paying the appropriate dues, it was bought in 1950 by a group of businessmen, for use as a freight transporter to and from Brazil. After a second long period of idleness, it was bought by Avalon Air Transport in

Aircraft: **Sikorsky VS-44A**
Manufacturer: **Sikorsky Aircraft**
Type: **Civil transport**
Year: **1942**
Engines: **Four Pratt & Whitney R-1830-S1C3G Twin Wasp, radial with 14 air-cooled cylinders, 1,200 hp each**
Wingspan: **124 ft 0 in (37.80 m)**
Length: **79 ft 3 in (24.16 m)**
Height: **27 ft 7 in (8.41 m)**
Weight: **57,500 lb (26,082 kg) (Loaded)**
Cruising speed: **160 mph at 10,000 ft (257 km/h at 3,050 m)**
Ceiling: **19,000 ft (5,790 m)**
Range: **3,600 miles (5,790 km)**
Crew: **9**
Passengers: **26–47**

1957. This company operated with seaplanes in the region of Long Beach, California. Overhauled, and converted to carry 47 passengers, it was rechristened (incorrectly) *Excalibur*. This last VS-44A remained in service for some ten years until it had to be withdrawn for want of pilots and crew specifically trained to fly multi-engined seaplanes. Nevertheless in January 1968 the aircraft was purchased once more, this time by the former Sikorsky test-pilot Charles F. Blair (who had flown the prototype in 1942), and used by the Antilles Air Boats company in the Virgin Islands.

Martin 2-0-2

Together with the large family of twin-engined Convairs, the Martin 2-0-2 marked the rebirth of commercial aviation in the United States after the end of the Second World War. It was the first civil twin-engined aircraft designed in the United States in the postwar period to become operational. The first of the two prototypes took to the air on November 22, 1946 and in all 31 aircraft were completed, 25 of them going to Northwest Orient Airlines, four to the LAN company of Chile and Two to the LAV company of Venezuela. Its regular service debut took place in Chile in October 1947. However, the career of the 2-0-2 was relatively important if compared with that of its successor, the Martin 4-0-4 of 1950. After the construction of a further twelve models with modified engines (used by TWA) the assembly lines were handed over to the construction of the Martin 4-0-4. This differed by having a pressurized cabin, more powerful engines and a larger carrying capacity.

Aircraft: **Martin 2-0-2**
Manufacturer: **Glenn L. Martin Co.**
Type: **Civil transport**
Year: **1946**
Engines: **Two Pratt & Whitney R-2800-CA18 Double Wasp, radial with 18 air-cooled cylinders, 2,100 hp each**
Wingspan: **92 ft 9 in (28.27 m)**
Length: **71 ft 11 in (21.92 m)**
Height: **25 ft 0 in (7.62 m)**
Weight: **39,300 lb (18,098 kg) (Loaded)**
Cruising speed: **286 mph at 12,000 ft (460 km/h at 3,660 m)**
Ceiling: **30,000 ft (9,150 m)**
Range: **635 miles (1,022 km)**
Crew: **3**
Passengers: **34–42**

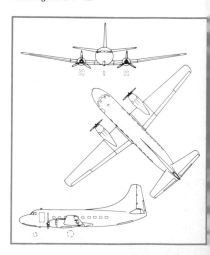

Hughes H-4 *Hercules*

Los Angeles, California, November 2, 1947. No less than 50,000 people thronging the wharves of the port witnessed an event unique in the history of aviation. The first, and only, flight of an ill-fated giant of the skies, the Hughes H-4 *Hercules*. Conceived in the agitated climate of America in its first year of the war, and built by the unpredictable millionaire Howard Hughes, this enormous seaplane with its eight engines and colossal wingspan of some 100 yards (91 m) had been completed almost out of defiance, when all and sundry had realized the absurdity of the project. And almost out of defiance it was made airborne on that morning, by Hughes himself. The flight in effect was a long hop, taking the aircraft a few feet (metres) aloft, over a distance of a mile, (1.609 km), but it was enough. For the 'flying millionaire' this demonstration not only concluded an adventure started five years earlier which had cost, at current prices, $25,000,000 but it also signed and sealed the tide of argument and criticism that had enveloped the birth and development of the *Hercules*. Having shown that it was capable of lifting itself above the water, the aircraft was then taken permanently to the immense hangar constructed on one of the wharves.

The idea had originated from a figure as unpredictable as Howard Hughes himself: the industrialist Henry J. Kaiser. Kaiser was well-known for his shipyards which built the famous Liberty Ships. These prefabricated freighters or transport ships were mass-produced in record time during the war years. Early in 1942, alarmed by the busy activity of the German submarines which were wreaking havoc among merchant shipping, Kaiser flung his proposal at the military authorities: he would build 5,000 seaplanes so large and well-designed that they would replace the convoys transporting troops and supplies.

Even though it aroused some interest in military circles, the idea to begin with seemed almost like something out of science-fiction, especially in view of Kaiser's inability to translate it into concrete technical terms. It was at this juncture that Howard Hughes appeared on the scene. Though already involved with a variety of different activities, the Texan millionaire was still under the powerful spell of flying. At that time his Hughes Aircraft Company of Culver City (Los Angeles) was busy making experimental aircraft for the Army, but it was also quite capable of tackling the demanding task of designing a huge seaplane corresponding to the specifications outlined by Kaiser. The idea fascinated Howard Hughes. In the summer of 1942, under the designation HK-1, the project started to take shape. At the same time Hughes Aircraft and the Henry Kaiser Shipping Corporation jointly formed the Kaiser–Hughes Corporation, which was to devote itself exclusively to the construction of the 5,000 flying-boats in this ambitious programme. On October 17 and 18 the military authorities were in possession of the preliminary plans with the estimated specifications regarding weights and performances. A month later Hughes and Kaiser managed to finalise the contract. This laid down the construction of three models, one for static tests and the other two for airborne tests. The prototypes were to be ready respectively not more than 15, 20 and 25 months after the date of the contract. In addition $18,000,000 was earmarked for the programme. Lastly, so as not to in any way affect the industry's war production, the aircraft were to be built of wood, with the use of metal restricted to a minimum.

The problems that Hughes and his technicians had to surmount in making the immense structure were not straightforward, and caused almost two years to be lost. However, the HK-1 gradually took shape, in the principal parts into which it was divided: hull, wings, tailplane, stabilizers, wingflaps, ailerons, rudder, elevators, lateral floating stabilizers. All these components were considerably larger in size than those of any other aircraft being built at the time. Hughes opted for eight radial Pratt & Whitney R-4360 Wasp Major engines, the most powerful units of the day. These 3,000 hp engines each drove a four-bladed propeller with a diameter of 17.1 feet

(5.23 m). The hull was more than 29 feet (9 m) high; about 26 feet (8 m) wide; and within it could carry several tanks or 700 fully-equipped troops.

The delay which held up the completion of the first prototype (which was aggravated by a series of disagreements between Hughes and his management) started to worry the military authorities at first but with the improvement in the course of the war this preoccupation turned into growing disinterest. In 1944 the initial contract was cut to one aircraft as strategically the project was no longer of any importance. As a result Henry J Kaiser abandoned the scheme dissolved the joint company and left Hughes nursing 'his baby' alone. In 1945 the programme was finally cancelled altogether by the military.

Despite these setbacks Howard Hughes was too stubborn and too proud to give up. When his partner had abandoned him, he immediately altered the designation of the aircraft to H-4 and christened it *Hercules* (the name chosen by the factory employees after a competition held among them). Then at his own expense he went ahead with the programme, determined to prove

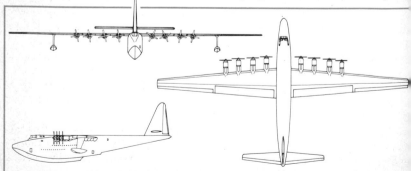

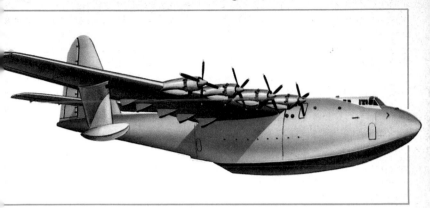

The assembly of the giant aircraft started on June 11, 1946. It was necessary to transport the various parts overland for 26 miles (45 km) to the hangar on Terminal Island. The 2,000 men involved took two days of uninterrupted work to move all the parts, and because of the very size of the convoy vehicles (especially the one carrying the hull which was transported in one piece) it was necessary to move electric pylons and cables, and cut down branches from more than 3,000 trees. By September the gigantic *Hercules* was assembled, but another year went by before it could be considered to be complete in every detail. The historic day of November 2 was organized by Howard Hughes with a keen eye. Journalists, technicians, Hollywood residents of the day, all awaited the event on board a yacht hired for the occasion by the millionaire. Then the huge crowd added the finishing touch typical of great occasions. For his part Hughes contributed a cunning ration of

Aircraft: **Hughes H-4** *Hercules*
Manufacturer: **Hughes Aircraft Co.**
Type: **Military transport**
Year: **1947**
Engines: **Eight Pratt & Whitney R-4360 Wasp Major, radial with 28 air-cooled cylinders, 3,000 hp each**
Wingspan: **320 ft 0 in (97.54 m)**
Length: **218 ft 6 in (66.60 m)**
Height: **79 ft 3 in (24.15 m)**
Weight: **400,000 lb (181,436 kg) (Loaded)***
Cruising speed: **175 mph (281 km/h)***
Range: **3,500 miles (5,633 km)***
Crew: **5**
Passengers: **500–700**
*Estimated

suspense. At 12.10, having started all eight engines, he let the mighty *Hercules* rock briefly on the water. He did the same thing half an hour later, and almost gave the impression of trying to take off. At 13.40 he made up his mind: to the excited roar of the crowd, he lifted the giant from the water and held it just a few feet above it. The official documents refer to 85 feet (26 m), but many onlookers reckon that the altitude was no more than 30–35 feet (9–10 m) for almost a mile, flying at about 95 mph (150 km/h). Then Hughes let the *Hercules* come to rest on the water again. For the first and last time.

Boeing 377 Stratocruiser

Just as the Boeing 307 Stratoliner had been developed from the B-17 bomber, so the Model 377 Stratocruiser derived nine years later from another famous military aircraft, the B-29 Super-fortress. In reality there was not a direct link, in as much as the first transport version made was military in type (C-97). However, after the huge success of this aircraft a purely commercial version of it appeared almost automatically. Thus, although only 55 models were made, the 377 Stratocruiser showed itself to be one of the best transport aircraft in the immediate postwar period. It was comfortable, safe and swift, and remained in service for more than ten years.

The request for a transport aircraft derived from the B-29 was made in 1942 by the military authorities. Boeing launched a project fairly like that of the Model 307, using the wing, tailplane, engines and undercarriage of the bomber, and modified just the fuselage. This took on the 'double bubble' form which gave the structure better possibility of standing up to the pressurization system. It also increased the space inside it, and thus the carrying capacity. The first of the three prototypes of the new aircraft (called Model 367) flew on November 15, 1944 and gave rise at once to a long cycle of evaluation tests. In the course of these, on January 9, 1945, it set up a new record for aircraft in its category, flying non-stop for 3,322 miles (5,341 km) from Seattle to Washington with a cargo of 20,000 pounds (9,070 kg) in 6 hours and 3 minutes. The high average speed, 383 mph (616 km/h), had been made possible by the high cruising altitude, more than 29,500 feet (9,000 m), permitted by the pressurization system. At the end of the trials mass production got under way and 888 models of the aircraft were completed. These were used by the military for transport and as flying tankers.

From this production model Boeing decided to derive an exclusively civil

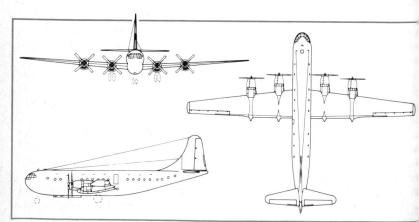

44

Aircraft: **Boeing 377-10-26 Stratocruiser**
Manufacturer: **Boeing Aircraft Co.**
Type: **Civil transport**
Year: **1947**
Engines: **Four Pratt & Whitney R-4360B-6 Wasp Major, radial with 28 air-cooled cylinders, 3,500 hp each**
Wingspan:**141 ft 3 in (43.05 m)**
Length: **110 ft 4 in (33.63 m)**
Height: **38 ft 3 in (11.66 m)**
Weight: **142,500 lb (64,434 kg) (Loaded)**
Cruising speed: **340 mph at 25,000 ft (547 km/h at 7,620 m)**
Ceiling: **33,000 ft (10,000 m)**
Range: **4,200 miles (6,760 km)**
Crew: **5**
Passengers: **55–112**

ersion, destined for the airlines. known as Model 377, this version was tted out so that it could carry a aximum of 100 passengers over long istances. Comfort on board was given pecial attention; the two deck levels ffered relatively large areas and on the ower deck there was also a bar with everal additional seats. On night ights the Stratocruiser could accommodate 55 passengers in bunks. The rototype of the Stratocruiser took to he air on July 8, 1947.

The first purchaser was Pan American, which also became the argest 377 operator with twenty aircraft. It was followed by American Airnes, with an order for eight models; Northwest with ten; United Air Lines with seven; and in Europe, BOAC and SAS of Sweden, which ordered six and our Stratocruisers respectively. The atter, however, did not go to the Scandinavian Airlines System and in he end swelled the order from the British company. Following a practice which was to become increasingly widespread, Boeing gave the aircraft in each order a special internal number, so as to distinguish them from the others on the basis of their interior preparation. The Pan American Stratocruisers were thus called 377-10-26; those of SAS 377-10-28; the eight belonging to American Airlines 377-10-29; the ten of Northwest 377-10-30; the six of BOAC 377-10-32 and the seven belonging to United 377-10-34.

The British BOAC company was perhaps the longest operator of the Stratocruisers: from December 6, 1949 to mid-1959, with a fleet which reached a total of 17 aircraft.

Lockheed Constellation
Lockheed Super Constellation

The risk of becoming withdrawn from civil use in favour of military use, which was the fate of other famous aircraft like the Curtiss C-46 and the Douglas DC-4, was brilliantly tackled and overcome by the prolific family of Lockheed Constellations. Although this family was born at the height of the war, it managed to dominate the civil market in the postwar period until the arrival of the first jets. Together with the contemporary Douglas DC-6 and DC-7, the Lockheed Constellation was the last and best expression of piston-engined civil transport.

The project had got under way in 1939, at the express request of TWA, which wanted to put forty of these new four-engined aircraft into service on its intercontinental routes. When the prototype made its first flight on January 9, 1943, the requirements of the military had nevertheless absolute priority over any civil use and under the designation C-69 the Constellation was the object of an initial order for 180 aircraft, for strategic transport. This order was subsequently reduced to 73 but of these only 22 had been delivered by the time peace was declared. It was with the 51 aircraft remaining from the military order that Lockheed went ahead with its civil production. Foreseeing the bitter fight which was to develop between the giants of the American aeronautical industry to re-supply the airlines (given new momentum by peace), the Lockheed board decided to modify the existing designs, which had already given ample proof of their validity. The decision turned out to be a good one and enabled them to gain valuable time over their most direct rivals, Douglas and Boeing. By the end of 1945, ten aircraft, designated L-049, had already been delivered. The first of these were to TWA, but the first company to put the Constellation into service was Pan American which, on February 3, 1946 inaugurated the New York–Bermuda route. Three days later TWA started its service between Washington and Paris, covering the distance in 19 hours and 46 minutes. On February 15 the Constellation was used on domestic routes

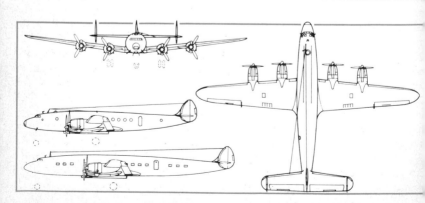

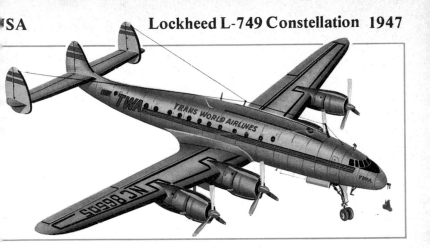

etween New York and Los Angeles. his was the start of its success story, hich was bolstered in October 1946 y the appearance of a first version hich was completely civil in design, ie L-649. This aircraft had improved ngines and carrying capacity. This as accompanied a year later by the -749 version, with appropriate iodifications to the positioning and apacity of the fuel tanks so that it ould make non-stop flights between Jew York and Paris, though not fully iden. The model L-749 together with ie version L-749A which had a tronger undercarriage and could carry n extra payload of 4,850 pounds 2,200 kg), caught the attention of the iilitary once again. They ordered a ozen, and the assembly lines for the Constellation closed with a total roduction figure of 232, giving way to he construction of the Super Con-tellation, a radically up-dated aircraft.

The first prototype of the Super Constellation, the L-1049 version, flew n October 13, 1950. Originally the

Aircraft: Lockheed L-749 Constellation
Manufacturer: **Lockheed Aircraft Corp.**
Type: **Civil transport**
Year: **1947**
Engines: **Four Wright R-3350-C18-BA3 Cyclone, radial with 18 air-cooled cylinders, 2,200 hp each**
Wingspan: **123 ft 0 in (37.49 m)**
Length: **95 ft 2 in (29.00 m)**
Height: **23 ft 8 in (7.21 m)**
Weight: **102,000 lb (46,310 kg) (Loaded)**
Cruising speed: **313 mph at 20,000 ft (504 km/h at 6,100 m)**
Ceiling: **25,000 ft (7,620 m)**
Range: **2,260 miles (3,637 km)**
Crew: **6**
Passengers: **44–81**

aircraft was one of those making up the C-69 order placed by the U.S.A.A.F., but it had been considerably revised. The most conspicuous modifications concerned the fuselage, which was lengthened by more than 18 feet (5.50 m), while other improvements were made to the structure and engines. The new Super Constellation instantly interested Eastern Air Lines, which ordered ten, followed by TWA, which ordered 14. The service was inaugurated by Eastern on December 15, 1951.

The later civil version (L-1049C) derived from the L-1049B, was in turn developed for the U.S. Navy. In these two models Lockheed overcame the problem of the under-powered engines by adopting Wright Turbo Compound engines. These were to be fitted to all the subsequently produced models. The first L-1049C flew on February 17, 1953 and production was geared initially for the Dutch KLM company and TWA, which put their new aircraft into operation respectively in August and October of that year. In all 60 aircraft were built. Some of these were converted to cargo duty and bore the designation L-1049D. There then followed 18 L-1049Es and 99 L-1049Gs. These latter, which were preceded by another military version, the L-1049F, belonged to the most popular and widely used version. The first order came from Northwest Airlines in January 1955 (just a month after the prototype flight) and was followed by orders from the world's major airline companies. The Super G

Aircraft: **Lockheed L-1049G Super Constellation**
Manufacturer: **Lockheed Aircraft Corp.**
Type: **Civil transport**
Year: **1954**
Engines: **Four Wright R-3350-DA3 Turbo Compound, radial with 18 air-cooled cylinders, 3,250 hp each**
Wingspan: **123 ft 0 in (37.49 m)**
Length: **113 ft 7 in (34.65 m)**
Height: **24 ft 9 in (7.56 m)**
Weight: **150,000 lb (68,100 kg) (Loaded)**
Cruising speed: **327 mph at 20,000 ft (526 km/h at 6,100 m)**
Ceiling: **25,000 ft (7,620 m)**
Range: **4,620 miles (7,440 km)**
Crew: **6**
Passengers: **63–99**

was accompanied by an all-cargo version, designated L-1049H.

With the end of the production of the Super Constellation (254 in all) Lockheed put another development of the project on the line. This was the model L-1649A Starliner which took to the air on October 10, 1956. However by the time it went into service it was too late in the day and had to step down when the first jets appeared. A total of 43 of these aircraft were built and were used mainly by TWA, Air France and Lufthansa.

Convair 240
Convair 540

he large family of twin-engined Con airs enjoyed a success comparable to hat of the Lockheed Constellations, lthough in a quite different sector of ir transport, medium capacity and hort-to-medium range. Just as in the nmediate postwar period the large our-engined model had made its mark n the civil market and later managed o maintain its leading position because f constant improvements, so the small nd elegant twin-engined aircraft roduced by the Convair company howed itself from the outset to be a vorthy successor to the immortal Douglas DC-3. It maintained this role or more than two decades, with continual modifications being made to the pasic model. In fact it managed to overcome the competition posed by the urbo-prop aircraft because of the extremely flexible nature of its airframe. The Convairs in the last series are still in the air today, especially with smaller companies.

The birth of the first twin-engined Convair transport aircraft dates back to the resurgence of commercial aviation after the end of the Second World War. If the long-range transport sector was already covered by numerous projects, particularly of military derivation, that of short-to-medium range transport was virtually virgin territory. The need for this type of aeroplane is demonstrated by the simultaneous appearance in numerous countries of comparable aircraft: the Ilyushin I1-12 produced in the Soviet Union, the British Vickers Viking and the Martin 2-0-2 produced in the United States. The first prototype of the Convair (called Model 110) took to the sky on July 9, 1946. It was a good-looking twin-engined aeroplane powered by a pair of Pratt & Whitney R-2,800 engines producing 2,100 hp each and capable of carrying 30 passengers. In practical terms, however, the aircraft did not appear to be competitive because of its low carrying capacity when compared with its range. As a result the Convair 110 remained in the

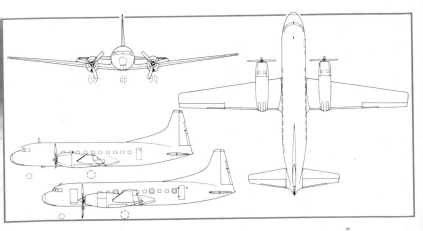

1947 – Convair 240

prototype stage, but was used as a basis for the development of the first successful model, the 240. Slightly larger with more powerful engines, this aircraft showed a clear increase in carrying capacity and range over its predecessor and met with approval from various companies shortly after the first prototype flight. This flight took place on March 16, 1947, and a year later orders reached 150 aircraft. The largest operator of the 240 was American Airlines, which ordered 75, and was followed by Pan American with 20, Western with 10 and Continental with 5. Outside the United States the aircraft was also in demand from the Dutch company KLM which ordered 12, Swissair which ordered four, Argentinian FA-MA company which ordered five and the TAA company which ordered another five. Other operators swelled the ranks bringing the overall civil production total to 176. To this figure there were added a further 395 completed for military use and put into service as transport and training aircraft (C-131

Aircraft: **Convair 240**
Manufacturer: **Convair Division of General Dynamics Corp.**
Type: **Civil transport**
Year: **1947**
Engines: **Two Pratt & Whitney R-2800 CA18 Double Wasp, radial with 18 air-cooled cylinders, 2,400 hp each**
Wingspan: **91 ft 9 in (27.98 m)**
Length: **74 ft 8 in (22.27 m)**
Height: **26 ft 11 in (8.22 m)**
Weight: **41,790 lb (18,972 kg) (Loaded)**
Cruising speed: **270 mph (432 km/h)**
Ceiling: **30,000 ft (9,150 m)**
Range: **1,800 miles (2,880 km)**
Crew: **3–4**
Passengers: **40**

and T-29 respectively). Production of the 240 ended in 1958.

In the meantime, fully aware of the potential of the project, Convair had gone ahead with producing an improved version. The first to appear was the 340, the prototype of which first took to the air on October 5, 1951. The differences consisted of the adoption of more powerful engines, an increased wingspan and a lengthened fuselage, all of which increased the carrying capacity to 44 passengers. This model enjoyed the success of its predecessor with 209 examples going on to the market, where they were

Aircraft: **Convair 540**
Manufacturer: **Convair Division of General Dynamics Corp.**
Type: **Civil transport**
Year: **1955**
Engines: **Two Napier Eland 504A turbo-props, 3,500 ehp each**
Wingspan: **105 ft 4 in (32.10 m)**
Length: **81 ft 6 in (24.84 m)**
Height: **28 ft 2 in (8.57 m)**
Weight: **53,200 lb (24,131 kg) (Loaded)**
Cruising speed: **325 mph at 20,000 ft (523 km/h at 6,100 m)**
Ceiling: **30,000 ft (9,150 m)**
Range: **1,620 miles (2,606 km)**
Crew: **3–4**
Passengers: **44**

dispersed among a host of American and European companies. A further 107 were made for military use. The Convair 340 was followed on October 5, 1955 by the further improved Model 440. This model, christened the 'Metropolitan' and capable of carrying 52 passengers was built to the tune of 186 civil and 26 military aircraft.

A new chapter in the career of this versatile twin-engined aeroplane opened with the arrival of the first turbo-prop engines. Sporadically and then in ever-growing numbers, the Convair 240-340-440 models were all converted to the new engine. The first of these successful conversions was completed late in 1954 by the English company Napier, which fitted a pair of Eland turboprops to a 340. The prototype flew for the first time on February 9, 1955 and after a series of operational trials, was hired out to the American Allegheny Airlines which used it and five others under the designation Convair 540. The second major conversion was the one which gave rise to the model 580 and which was

carried out by Pac Aaero (a division of Pacific Airmotive). The model 580 was equipped with two Allison turbo-props producing 3,750 ehp each and went into service in 1964 with Frontier Airlines. The last successful version was the one that used two Rolls-Royce Dart turbo-prop engines producing 3,025 ehp. These engines could be fitted at will to all three original series and after the prototype flight of the model that came to be known as the Convair 600 in May 20, 1965, the aircraft was adopted by numerous charter operators. The carrying capacity was increased to 56 passengers.

Douglas DC-6

The Douglas DC-6 was the natural outcome of the DC-4. Larger, with more power in the engines and a pressurized cabin, it managed to make its mark on the civil market and enjoyed the success that had eluded its predecessor. Developed in various versions (passenger, freight and military transport) more than 700 DC-6s were built and used by half the world's airlines right up to the early 1970s.

The development of a strengthened and enlarged version of the DC-4 was undertaken by Douglas in the latter years of the war, at the request of the military authorities who wanted to put into service an aircraft whose qualities would be superior to the already remarkable ones of the DC-4. The end of the war caused the U.S.A.A.F. project to be temporarily put to one side and after the construction of a military prototype, which flew on

February 15, 1946, production wa focussed on a completely civil mode Compared with the DC-4 the new four engined aircraft offered considerabl improvements in its carrying capacity range and maximum cruising speed, al features which made it an attractive proposition for the airline companies It was successful almost at once American Airlines ordered 47 and United another 35. United was the firs to put the DC-6 into service, setting up a series of domestic services throughout the United States in Apri 1947. Orders arrived from Europe, in particular from the Belgian Sabena Dutch KLM and Scandinavian SAS companies, and the total number of air craft built reached 175.

Two years later the second major production version appeared, called the DC-6A. This version was developed initially for freight transport and then

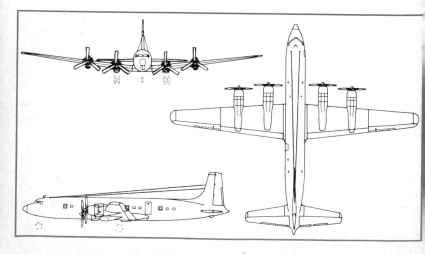

Douglas DC-6B – 1951

as a mixed aircraft (called the DC-6C) that could be converted to passenger use. It was longer than its predecessor with more powerful engines and a larger carrying capacity. The 75 civil models were followed by a further 167 for the military. The military version went into service with the U.S.A.A.F. and U.S. Navy, being designated the C-118 and the R6D Liftmaster respectively.

On January 23, 1951, the version which was to be produced in the largest numbers for the civil market made its first flight. This was the DC-6B, designed solely for passenger transport and incorporating all the improvements offered in the DC-6A and DC-6C versions. The increased range, maximum cruising speed and carrying capacity (almost double that of the original model with up to 107 passengers) made this a fairly valid aircraft capable of meeting the economic and commercial requirements of the users. Altogether 287 DC-6Bs were built and put into service on the routes run by the world's

Aircraft: **Douglas DC-6B**
Manufacturer: **Douglas Aircraft Co.**
Type: **Civil transport**
Year: **1951**
Engines: **Four Pratt & Whitney R 2800-CB16 Double Wasp, radial with 16 air-cooled cylinders, 2,400 hp each**
Wingspan: **117 ft 6 in (35.81 m)**
Length: **105 ft 7 in (32.20 m)**
Height: **28 ft 5 in (8.66 m)**
Weight: **100,000 lb (45,400 kg) (Loaded)**
Cruising speed: **307 mph (494 km/h)**
Ceiling: **25,000 ft (7,620 m)**
Range: **3,860 miles (6,270 km)**
Crew: **3**
Passengers: **54–102**

major airlines. Although the DC-6 series stopped being produced in the closing months of 1958 there were still some 200 DC-6Bs in operation towards the end of the 1960s. These were mostly in the hands of minor operating companies in the charter sector but taking all the various versions into account there were altogether about 400 aircraft still flying at this time. Its military career was even longer-lived and not only in the United States. The C-118 was also distributed as a personnel transport aircraft to many of the countries belonging to N.A.T.O.

Aero Commander

The Aero Commander series turned out to be one of the most successful and prolific in the field of executive and light transport aircraft. More than 1,200 examples and a great many versions have been produced from the early 1950s onwards. The career of this elegant twin-engined aeroplane has been considerably extended by the production of two other series derived from it: the Grand Commander of 1962 (a more powerful and larger capacity aircraft) and the Turbo Commander of 1964 which was fitted with a pair of turbo-prop engines. The founder member of the family took to the sky on April 23, 1948, but was replaced in mass-production by the first operative model, the 520 of 1951. There were 150 of the 520 built before it was replaced by the second major production version, the 560 of 1954 of which 80 were made. The success of these two versions was swollen by that enjoyed by the 12 other versions that were subsequently developed.

Aircraft: **Aero Commander 560**
Manufacturer: **Aero Design and Engineering Corp.**
Type: **Light transport**
Year: **1954**
Engines: **Two Lycoming GO-480-B with 6 horizontal air-cooled cylinders, 270 hp each**
Wingspan: **44 ft 7 in (13.59 m)**
Length: **34 ft 4 in (10.46 m)**
Height: **14 ft 9 in (4.49 m)**
Weight: **6,000 lb (2,722 kg) (Loaded)**
Cruising speed: **200 mph at 10,000 ft (320 km/h at 3,050 m)**
Ceiling: **22,000 ft (6,706 m)**
Range: **1,100 miles (1,770 km)**
Crew: **1**
Passengers: **5–7**

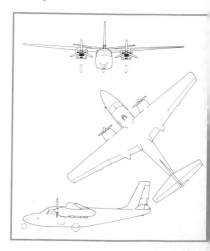

Douglas DC-7

The era of the piston-engined civil transport aircraft came to an end with two aeroplanes: the Lockheed Constellation and the Douglas DC-7. They represented the highest expression of a long line of commercial aircraft which had undergone continual development. Both came into being in the Second World War and were in direct competition for supremacy of the market in the mid-1950s. At this time the first jets manufactured by the American industry were close to coming on the international aeronautical scene and seizing that forefront role that they still play today. Similar to what had happened to the Super Constellation and the Starliner built by Lockheed, (which represented an almost exhaustive development of the original model), the Douglas DC-7 was built directly around the air-frame of the DC-6, account being taken of the need to increase its performance, carrying capacity, range and comfort on board.

The request for an improved version of the Douglas DC-6 was made in the early 1950s by American Airlines, which opened negotiations with the Californian industry to design an aircraft which would be competitive with the Super Constellations ordered by their direct rival, TWA. The Douglas technicians took as a basis the airframe of the best variant of the DC-6, the B. The DC-6B had flown for the first time on January 23, 1951 and had offered fairly impressive features for airline use. It was now subjected to an intensive series of modifications; the fuselage was lengthened to improve the capacity and the interior fittings, the entire structure was strengthened to increase considerably the amount of weight transportable, and the engines were replaced by more powerful ones. The designers adopted for the first time in the series of Douglas four-engined aircraft, the Wright Turbo Compound engines which were already fitted to the Lockheed Super Constellations. These were large radial engines with 18 cylinders in which a considerable increase of power was obtained by using the exhaust gases. These gases were channelled into three turbines installed in the rear section of the engine which then rechannelled the power received directly to the driveshaft, via a series of gears. The Wright Turbo Compound engines (once they had passed the complicated qualifying tests in October 1949 and January 1950) managed to use about 20% of the thermal energy which was normally dispersed through the exhaust gases, and were put on to the market in March 1950. The practical advantages of this system were fully demonstrated by the Wright model. In comparison to the use of conventional engines, an aircraft fitted with Turbo Compound engines could fly 20% further with the same fuel consumption. The DC-7 prototype flew for the first time on May 18, 1953 and even though it represented a clear improvement over the DC-6B in terms of payload, it did not match its predecessor in terms of running costs and the level of noise and vibration felt inside the passenger cabin. Overall, however, the aircraft was well received by the airlines and mass-production went ahead with 120 models being made. Nevertheless Douglas continued with their efforts to further improve the aircraft and make it even more competitive with a view to the most sought-after use of all, the transatlantic routes. The next version was the DC-7B. Though retaining the general lines and features (in terms of capacity and engines) of the basic model, this had been amply modified where the installation of the fuel tanks was concerned. Compared with the DC-7, the maximum weight at take-off was increased by about 4,400 pounds (2,000 kg) and the payload by about 1,545 pounds (700 kg). The prototype of the DC-7B flew for the first time on April 25, 1955 and the first company to put it into service was Pan American on its transcontinental routes. Total production of this version reached 97 aircraft.

The evolution of the DC-7 was not yet complete in view of the latest development to its constant and direct rival, the Super Constellation. At the request of TWA, Lockheed was at that very moment making the last and best version of its faithful old 'Connie', the L-1649A Starliner, which was a radical improvement over its forerunners an showed itself to be a fearsome foe o the market. The Douglas designers se to work once again to develop an eve more efficient version of the DC-7 which turned out to be undisputedly th best aircraft of the entire series.

The first prototype took to the sk on December 20, 1955. Compared with the previous version it differed principally in the wing, which was leng thened by about 10 feet (3 m), and the fuselage which was also lengthened and strengthened to increase the interio capacity. The restructuring of the wing which included enlarging the flaps and ailerons made it possible to solve the two major problems; the reduction o the noise level and the vibrations felt inside the fuselage, and the increase of the fuel capacity and consequen increase of range. In fact supple mentary fuel tanks were situated in the two additional wing sections. Modifica tions were also made to the surface area of the tailplane and the rudder. Interior fittings, such as the meteorological radar equipment and

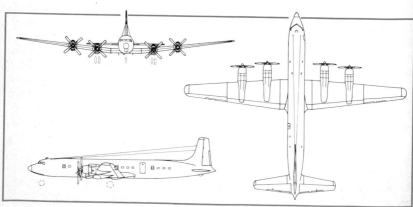

the de-icer equipment, were also improved. In addition an even more powerful version of the Turbo Compound engine was fitted.

The production-line was closed down in late 1958 with the completion of the 128th DC-7C. This brought the overall number of DC-7s produced to 338. After the introduction of the first jets many of these were converted to cargo use and called DC-7Fs. In practical terms these aircraft were used by the world's major airlines. American Airlines used the aircraft in the first series as did Aerovias Panama, Delta, Internord and United. The B version was also used by Delta, Internord, Panagra, SAA and Transair. Additionally the DC-7 was used by Airlift, Alitalia, Braniff, KLM, Martins, Northwest, Pan Am, Scanair Saturn, Sudflug and BOAC.

The British company adopted the DC-7C in March 1955 before the prototype had even taken to the air because, at that time, it was without aircraft capable of giving satisfactory

Aircraft. **Douglas DC-7C**
Manufacturer: **Douglas Aircraft Co.**
Type: **Civil transport**
Year: **1955**
Engines: **Four Wright R-3350-18EA1 Turbo Compound, radial with 18 air-cooled cylinders, 3,400 hp each**
Wingspan: **127 ft 6 in (38.80 m)**
Length: **112 ft 3 in (34.23 m)**
Height: **31 ft 10 in (9.70 m)**
Weight: **143,000 lb (64,865 kg) (Loaded)**
Cruising speed: **304 mph at 23,000 ft (486 km/h at 7,106 m)**
Ceiling: **28,000 ft (8,656 m)**
Range: **6,010 miles (9,616 km)**
Crew: **7–8**
Passengers: **69–105**

service on the North Atlantic routes. The four-engined de Havilland Comet jet was still sorting out the serious structural problems that had come to light in the initial version. The regular services across the ocean started in January 1957, when the new aircraft, nicknamed 'Seven Seas', had completed a lengthy series of tests and trials. In the course of one of these test flights on November 11, 1956 a DC-7C belonging to the British company reached New York, non-stop, in the record time for the east-west Atlantic crossing of 10 hours and 40 minutes.

Boeing 707

In the thrilling race for the first civil jet aircraft the British and Americans found themselves neck-and-neck. The British industry takes the prize for having won in terms of time, the prototype of the de Havilland Comet took to the air on July 27, 1949 and made its first regular passenger flight on May 2, 1952, while the United States industry takes the credit for having put on to the western market the first economically viable and reliable aircraft, the Boeing 707. This aircraft more than any other contributed most to transforming the world of air transport in the latter half of the 1950s, and gave it its present-day dimensions.

Boeing had started studying the possibilities of developing a jet-powered civil transport aircraft as far back as 1946 when the Model 377 Stratocruiser was undergoing its trials. The technicians at the famous Seattle firm already had considerable experience in this new field. The cessation of hostilities with Germany had given access to the top secret studies carried out by the Germans in the field of aerodynamics and jet propulsion, and they had used many aspects of that advanced technology (the swept-back wing at the fairly pronounced angle of up to 45°) in designing the first large American jet aircraft, the B-47 bomber. The revolutionary B-47 flew for the first time as a prototype on December 17, 1947 and contributed a great deal to defining the high technological level which was later fully exploited in the design of the commercial model. There were a great many studies carried out on an experimental basis. Boeing started out from the Model 367 (in production for the military as the C-97) and worked out numerous configurations, some of which were borrowed directly from the B-47 bomber. However the civil market was still fairly out of tune with the idea of an aircraft so radically different and the military authorities did not appear to be interested in a successor to the C-97. Considering the lack of orders and funds Boeing took a major risk. In April 1952 it authorized the expenditure of a sum amounting to $16,000,000 from the company funds to go ahead with what was to be the first commercial jet manufactured in the United States. The decision was made at the moment when the intensive experimental studies, carried out exclusively on the drawing-board and in the wind-tunnel, had come up with a precise definition of the project from a selection of 150 variants. Known in the inner circles of the firm as the Model 367-80 and only changed to Model 707 at a later date, the prototype was built in great secrecy starting in October 1952. It did not emerge from the vast hangars of the factory until May 15, 1954, bedecked in showy cream and brown colours, and it flew for the first time two months later on July 15.

Dash Eighty, as the mighty aeroplane was affectionately known, after the last two figures of its factory registration number, appeared to be a perfect marriage of the aircraft that had inspired its designers, Model 367 and the B-47. In fact it retained the structure and lines of the former's broad and spacious fuselage and from the latter borrowed the wing with its

distinctive 35° sweep-back angle. The aerodynamic qualities were particularly advanced: the flaps were divided into two sections for each wing to avoid interference with the flow of the exhaust gases. There were also double ailerons with one pair working at the cruising speed and another during taking-off and landing, as well as additional control surfaces including two pairs of air-brakes which could also be used as ailerons. The engines installed on the prototype were four Pratt & Whitney JT3s giving a thrust of 10,000 pounds (4,536 kg).

Dash Eighty was completed strictly as an experimental prototype to carry out all the experimental trials necessary to the final design and to the search for the best solutions for commercial use. From the day of the first flight this aircraft completed the long and intensive cycle of evaluation tests and remained the property of Boeing. It was used until the early 1970s for all its experiments on air-frames and engines, and amply repaid the initial investment of $16,000,000. The first rewards were

Aircraft: **Boeing 707-120**
Manufacturer: **Boeing Aircraft Co.**
Type: **Civil transport**
Year: **1957**
Engines: **Four Pratt & Whitney JT3C-6 turbo-jets, 13,500 lb (6,124 kg) thrust each**
Wingspan: **130 ft 10 in (39.87 m)**
Length: **144 ft 6 in (40.04 m)**
Height: **38 ft 8 in (11.79 m)**
Weight: **247,000 lb (112,039 kg) (Loaded)**
Cruising speed: **571 mph at 25,000 ft (919 km/h at 7,620 m)**
Ceiling: **31,500 ft (9,800 m)**
Range: **3,075 miles (4,950 km)**
Crew: **4**
Passengers: **121–179**

quick to arrive, on September 1, 1954, when the U.S.A.A.F. placed with Boeing an initial order for 29 models which were to be used as flying tankers (KC-135). This request, which was followed by others for several hundred aircraft altogether, did not merely provide hard cash with which to pay for production, but it once and for all released the airline companies from their state of indecision. The first to break the ice was Pan American which ordered an entire fleet of twenty Boeing 707s on October 13, 1955. Before long all the others followed suit; American

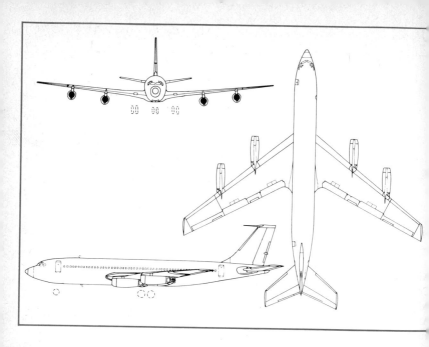

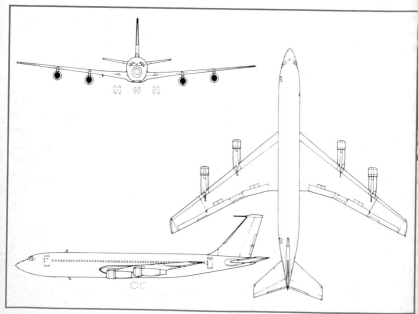

Airlines ordered thirty, then Braniff, Continental, Sabena, TWA, BOAC, Air France, Lufthansa, Quantas and Air India. Three years later the total number of 707s built reached 184, and by April 1967 some 568 Boeing 707s in the various series had been completed and delivered and a further 150 were on the waiting-list.

The first production model was the 707-120 which flew on December 20, 1957. It was delivered to Pan American in August of the following year and used on the North Atlantic route on October 26, 1958 linking New York and London. This was after a fierce race with BOAC which had managed to outdo the American company by inaugurating the same service with the de Havilland Comet 4 three weeks earlier. Compared with the prototype the 707-120 was slightly larger and heavier, had more powerful engines, and was fitted out for passenger use. Even though it had been put into service on a transatlantic route, mainly for reasons of prestige, it

Aircraft: **Boeing 707-320**
Manufacturer: **Boeing Aircraft Co.**
Type: **Civil transport**
Year: **1959**
Engines: **Four Pratt & Whitney JT4A-3 turbo-jets, 15,800 lb (7,167 kg) thrust each**
Wingspan: **142 ft 5 in (43.41m)**
Length: **152ft 11 in (46.60m)**
Height: **41 ft 7 in (12.67m)**
Weight: **312,000 lb (141,523 kg) (Loaded)**
Cruising speed: **604 mph at 25,000 ft (972 km/h at 7,620m)**
Ceiling: **37,200 ft (11,340m)**
Range: **4,630 miles (7,450 km)**
Crew: **4**
Passengers: **131–189**

was an aircraft designed for domestic use by the American companies. The 707-120 was followed by just five models belonging to the series 707-220, ordered expressly by Braniff International for its flights to and from South America. Outwardly those were similar to their predecessors. The only difference lay in the engines, the type JT4A-3 giving a thrust of 15,800 pounds (7,167 kg) and thus capable of guaranteeing better take-off performance from airports where both temperature and altitude were high.

The first 707s expressly designed for

intercontinental service belonged to series 320. The prototype took to the skies on January 11, 1959 and showed itself to be a considerably larger and heavier aircraft with a greater capacity. The engines were the same JT4A-3 type used in the five models of the 220 series. Pan American, once again, was the first to purchase these new aircraft. On August 26, 1959 Pan American put them into service on some of the longest routes across the United States. They were first put into service across the Atlantic on 10 October. The Boeing 707-320 took up most of the production line and was eventually more successful than the other series.

The last series was the 707-420 which was built at the express request of the British company, BOAC and of which 37 were produced. BOAC specified the adoption of four Rolls-Royce Conway 508 turbo-jet engines, each with a thrust of 21,470 pounds (9,738 kg), in place of the Pratt & Whitney engines. The first of these aircraft, which were substantially the same as those of the 320 series, flew on May 20, 1959. However the operational tests carried out by BOAC on the four initial models revealed the need for further aerodynamic modifications in order to improve the stability and handling of the aircraft when taking-off and landing. These modifications took the form of increasing the height of the tail fin and adding a ventral fin. Later on many 707-320s and 120s were fitted with this modification. Finally satisfied, BOAC put their 707-420s into service in May 1960.

The two principal series (120 and 320) were also produced in a more powerful version, hallmarked by the adoption of two types of turbo fan; the Pratt & Whitney JT3D-1 giving thrust of 17,000 pounds (7,711 kg) in the 707-120 and the JT3D-3 giving thrust of 18,000 pounds (8,165 kg) in the 707-320. These sub-series had the suffix B added to the model number. The first 707-120Bs were ordered by American Airlines and the prototype took to the sky on June 22, 1960. The first 707-320B flew for the first time slightly less than two years later on January 31, 1962. One of the last variants to go on the market was the 707-320C which could be used for passenger and/or freight transport and appeared in 1963. The 707-320C included provision for a large loading door on the port side of the fuselage in front of the wing. In addition its pay load was increased.

In the course of a busy operational career which is still continuing, the Boeing 707 has achieved an incredible list of prizes and records. Among the most sensational is the record set on February 23, 1960 by a Pan Am 707-320 using a very fast air stream at high altitude. At more than 140 mph (230 km/h), this aircraft managed to cover the 1,885 miles (3,033 km) between Tokyo and Hong Kong at a ground-speed of 760 mph (1,223 km/h).

A final particular feature concerns the system of designation adopted by Boeing for all the 707 series. The last two figures of the suffix which follows the factory number identify the original purchasing company: for example, 21 indicates Pan Am, 36 BOAC, 68 Saudi Arabian and so on. This code is similar to that adopted for the first time with the Boeing 377 and covers most of the world's major airlines.

Douglas DC-8

The Douglas DC-8 was the second commercial jet aircraft produced by the United States industry and was a direct rival of the Boeing 707. It went into service almost a year later on September 18, 1959 whereas the four-engined Boeing jet had gone into operation on the North Atlantic route on October 26, 1958. However the DC-8 showed itself to be just as competitive and eventually achieved a large slice of the world market which it held for many years. This success was due not least to constant improvements being made to it. In 1966 these improvements gave rise to the latest version which, with its large capacity and very long range, is still in use today with numerous companies.

Douglas embarked on their studies for a successor to the DC-7 even before the prototype of the latter had taken to the air. The choice fell inevitably on a jet-propelled aircraft, especially in view of the similar choice made by the rival

Aircraft: **Douglas DC-8 20**
Manufacturer: **Douglas Aircraft Co.**
Type: **Civil transport**
Year: **1958**
Engines: **Four Pratt & Whitney JT4A-3 turbo-jets, 15,800 lb (7,167 kg) thrust each**
Wingspan: **142 ft 5 in (43.41 m)**
Length: **150 ft 6 in (45.87 m)**
Height: **42 ft 4 in (12.91 m)**
Weight: **287,500 lb (130,410 kg) (Loaded)**
Cruising speed: **588 mph at 30,000 ft (946 km/h at 9,150 m)**
Ceiling: **30,000 ft (9,150 m)**
Range: **4,280 miles (6,888 km)**
Crew: **5**
Passengers: **116–179**

Boeing company. Contrary to the decision of Boeing's management, Douglas did not consider developing an aircraft which could also be put to military use and preferred to focus its efforts on a project destined solely for the civil market. Later on, Douglas continued to pursue this policy, preferring to avoid distractions as much as possible. While Boeing split up the 707 family into numerous series of variants the DC-8 stuck strictly to the basic design. It was not until the mid-1960s that Douglas broke this principle and produced three versions of the Super

63

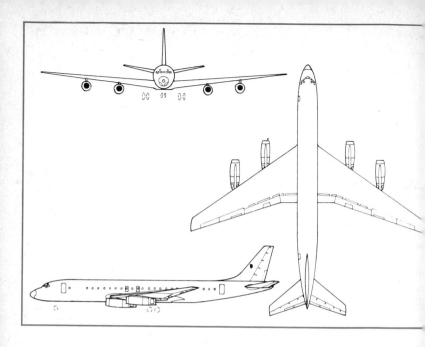

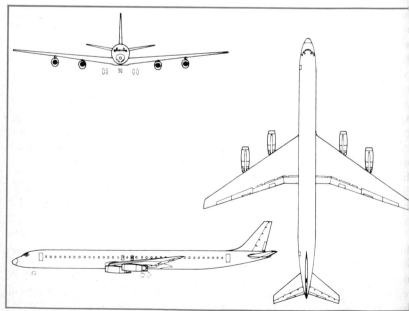

Aircraft: **Douglas DC-8-63**
Manufacturer: **Douglas Aircraft Co.**
Type: **Civil transport**
Year: **1967**
Engines: **Four Pratt & Whitney JT3D-7 turbo-jets, 19,000 lb (8,618 kg) thrust each**
Wingspan: **148 ft 5 in (45.23 m)**
Length: **187 ft 5 in (57.13 m)**
Height: **43 ft 5 in (13.23 m)**
Weight: **350,000 lb (158,760 kg) (Loaded)**
Cruising speed: **600 mph at 30,000 ft (965 km/h at 9,150 m)**
Ceiling: **30,000 ft (9,150 m)**
Range: **4,500 miles (7,240 km)**
Crew: **5**
Passengers: **259**

ixty series. These had a fuselage lengthened by more than 36 feet (11 m), aimed at increasing to the maximum the capacity and payload.

The official go-ahead to the project was given on June 7, 1955 with the intention of producing an aircraft designed essentially for domestic services. The demand for an aircraft of this category was very strong, as evidenced by the 'blind' orders received by Douglas straight after the announcement of the programme. Pan American was the first company to ask for the DC-8, ordering 25 in October 1955. There followed orders from three other American airlines as well as, at the end of the year, orders from two European companies. On the day of the first prototype flight orders were in excess of 130 units.

The DC-8-10 was the forbear of all the DC-8s, and started its trials on May 30, 1958. It was followed by the first models of four other basic production series. The DC-8-20 prototype, designed for domestic flights but fitted

with more powerful engines, made its maiden flight on November 29, 1958. The DC-8-30 was the first intercontinental series with a choice of even more powerful engines and a larger fuel capacity. The prototype of this series took off on February 21, 1959. The DC-8-40 prototype first flew on July 23, 1959. These aircraft used British Rolls-Royce Conway 509 engines producing a thrust of 17,500 pounds (7,945 kg). The DC-8-50, the prototype of which made its first flight on December 20, 1960, was fitted with turbofans producing a thrust of 18,000 pounds (8,165 kg). The aircraft in this last series were also developed as a mixed passenger-freight version, called the DC-8F Jet Trader, which was shown in October 1962. In the course of the production of these different versions Douglas made a whole series of structural and aerodynamic improvements which were standard features of the DC-8-50, and incorporated retroactively in many aircraft in the preceding series. This comprehensive task of up-dating existing aeroplanes contributed more than a little to the overall success of the aircraft. In 1967, after the appearance of the first large-capacity versions, some 280 DC-8s of the five initial series had been delivered and were in use with companies across the globe. The major users were Alitalia, Iberia, KLM, Pan American, SAS, United, Air Canada, JAL and Swissair but there were many more.

A new momentum to the production and success of the four-engined Douglas jet came in April 1965 when the company announced three new versions of the DC-8: the 61, the 62 and the 63. The difference to the five previous series was the carrying capacity which was almost doubled. This had been achieved by considerably lengthening the fuselage. This feature gave the aircraft a rather unconventional appearance. In addition the models in all three series could be fitted out for either all passenger, or all freight; or alternatively mixed passenger and freight use. The first DC-8-61 flew on March 14, 1966 and went into service with United in November of that same year. It was fundamentally an aircraft designed for domestic routes, with a maximum capacity of 251 passengers.

It was followed on August 29 by the first DC-8-62 which was even further modified. The fuselage had been lengthened by not much more than 6 feet (m) compared with the 36 feet (11 m) of the DC-8-61 and numerous variations had been made to the wing structure, the installation of the engines, and the positioning and capacity of the fuel tanks which could now ensure a very long range indeed. The last variant, the DC-8-63, incorporated the solutions adopted in the two earlier models so that the fuselage was lengthened as in the DC-8-61, giving the same high passenger capacity, and it had the new wing of the DC-8-62.

The success of the Super Sixty series was far-reaching and immediate thanks to the excellent features which made them competitive, even with the 'wide bodies' which were in the advanced design stage at that time. In 1970 when the first giant Boeing 747 went into service, the total number of DC-8s of all series ordered had risen to more than 550. A particular highly competitive feature of the Super Sixties was the ratio of payload to range. This feature was also fully exploited in the all-cargo variants (DC-8-61F, DC-8-62F and DC-8-63F) which were popular with all the specialized companies and ended up by being as successful as the passenger versions. Among the highlights of its busy career one merits special mention; it concerns the high structural soundness and the excellent aerodynamic features of the four engined Douglas jet which allowed a DC-8-40 to become the first airliner to fly at a speed in excess of Mach 1, on August 21, 1961. To be precise it achieved Mach 1.012.

Grumman G-159 Gulfstream

he Grumman G-159 Gulfstream was e first and one of the most successful f this very specific category of turbo- rop twin engined executive aircraft. nnounced in 1956, the prototype ersion took to the air on August 14, 958 and started to be delivered as om May in the following year. It was handsome twin-engined type with a w wing, capable of holding 10–12 assengers in the normal version and 9 in the tightly-packed seating ersion. It also boasted the most up-to- ate navigation and flying aids. The uccess it enjoyed with private buyers, he companies that needed aircraft for apid communications and transport, as demonstrated by the large orders eceived by Grumman in a fairly short eriod of time. In 1960, 60 examples ere delivered and more than 180 ircraft were completed in 1966.

Aircraft: **Grumman G-159 Gulfstream 1**
Manufacturer: **Grumman Aircraft Engineer- ing Corp.**
Type: **Light transport**
Year: **1958**
Engines: **Two Rolls-Royce Dart 529 turbo- props, 2,210 ehp each**
Wingspan: **78 ft 6 in (23.93 m)**
Length: **63 ft 8 in (19.40 m)**
Height: **22 ft 10 in (6.95 m)**
Weight: **36,000 lb (16,329 kg) (Loaded)**
Cruising speed: **356 mph at 25,000 ft (573 km/h at 7,620 m)**
Ceiling: **35,000 ft (10,670 m)**
Range: **2,350 miles (3,780 km)**
Crew: **2**
Passengers: **10–19**

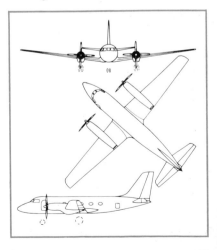

Lockheed L.188 Electra

In 1955 Lockheed tackled the short-to-medium range civil transport market and revived the name 'Electra' after a gap of 22 years. The new aircraft designated L.188 and christened like the famous twin-engined model of 1933, was the first turbo-prop commercial model designed and manufactured by the American aeronautical industry.

The design stage got under way in 1954 at the request of American Airlines. After experience acquired in making the C-130 Hercules military aeroplane, the Lockheed technicians confidently chose turbo-prop propulsion rather than the jet engine. The first result was a fairly compact aircraft with a high wing and powered by either Rolls-Royce Dart or Napier Eland engines. Known by the factory designation CL-303 the aircraft was well able to meet the specifications of American Airlines with regard to speed and range, which were 350 mph (563 km/h) and 745 miles (1,200 km) respectively. However, it was reckoned to be too small and uneconomical, as well as potentially unsafe when landing or making a forced touch-down because of the shape of the high wing. This resulted in a second design, the CL-310, being prepared. In the meantime Eastern Air Lines had joined forces with American. Eastern Air Lines wanted better specifications in terms of range, maximum cruising speed and payload and so the design of the CL-310 was not considered valid. Eventually both airlines agreed about the final specifications and Lockheed prepared the final design, which was announced in June 1955 and known officially as Model L.188 Electra. By this time American Airlines had already placed an order for 35 such aircraft and at the end of September Eastern added a further order for 40 units. This commercial success was consolidated still further even before the prototype had been completed. On December 6, 1957, the date of the first flight, the total number ordered had reached 144.

The first prototype was followed by two more, which flew respectively on February 13 and April 10, 1958. The

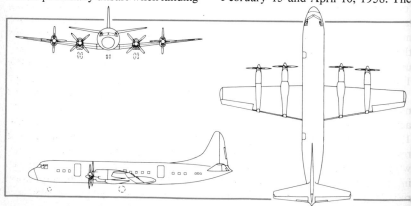

ast of the three was used as a basis for he development of the maritime reconnaissance version which was to be used by the U.S. Navy and was called the P-3 Orion. The first of the aircraft in he initial L.188A series flew in May and deliveries got under way in October for Eastern and in November for American. Eastern Air Lines was he first company to inaugurate services with the new Electra on January 12, 1959, followed by American eleven days later. On the production lines the model L.188A was followed by the C variant, which had a larger fuel capacity and could carry more passengers. This version became the standard one and remained unaltered until the completion of the 170th and last model.

The success of the Electra was nevertheless jolted by two serious accidents which occured in September 1959 and March 1960. Both accidents revealed structural weaknesses in the wing. While the results of the technical investigation were pending, strict speed restrictions were imposed on all the air-

Aircraft: **Lockheed L.188A Electra**
Manufacturer: **Lockheed Aircraft Corp.**
Type: **Civil transport**
Year: **1958**
Engines: **Four Allison 501-D13A turboprops, 3,750 ehp each**
Wingspan: **99 ft 0 in (30.18 m)**
Length: **104 ft 6 in (31.85 m)**
Height: **32 ft 11 in (10.03 m)**
Weight: **116,000 lb (52,618 kg) (Loaded)**
Cruising speed: **405 mph at 22,000 ft (652 km/h at 6,700 m)**
Ceiling: **27,000 ft (8,230 m)**
Range: **2,770 miles (4,458 km)**
Crew: **5**
Passengers: **66–99**

craft in service as from March 25, 1960. Subsequently, in January 1961, Lockheed launched a far-reaching programme aimed at strengthening the engine nacelles and certain wing sections and both the aircraft still on the production line and those being used by the airlines underwent modification. This entailed a major loss of time and money which had an adverse effect on the career of the Electra. The psychological consequences were also considerable and induced many operators to brand the modified aircraft Electra II, to give the impression that they were a different model.

Boeing 720

The Boeing 720 was the third model based on the successful 707. Its similarity to its predecessors in the 120 and 320 series was only outward and in reality it was structurally a quite different aircraft.

The announcement of the imminent appearance of a 'younger brother' of the 707 was made by Boeing in July 1957. Abiding by its policy of diversifying production as much as possible to meet the various demands of a varied market, the company was confident of the success of its new 'baby'. Those airlines operating on the domestic routes needed an aircraft which not only guaranteed a large capacity and reduced flight-times, but also low running costs. This turned out to be an accurate market assessment which was proved by numerous 'blind' orders placed with Boeing immediately after the official announcement was made. The first company was United, which placed an order for 11 aircraft in

November. By this time the new aircraft had been designated Model 720. At the outset the company designation had been 707-020, which linked the design and project directly with it forerunners. However as the programme got under way the differences turned out to be so substantial that they justified a completely different designation.

The Boeing 720 incorporated a whole series of aerodynamic improvements and structural modifications aimed at maintaining high performance and reducing weight. The most markedly modified part was the wing which was very sharply swept back in the section between the fuselage and the inboard engine mountings, and included leading-edge flaps on the outermost sections. In addition the reduced fuel capacity and the adoption of lighter engines and a lighter undercarriage contributed considerably to keeping the unladen weight within sufficiently low figures. The engines used were four Pratt &

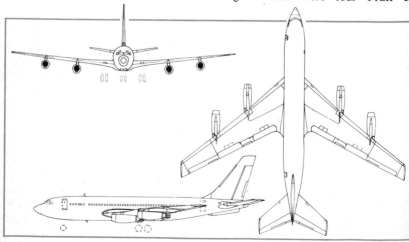

Whitney JT3C-7s with a thrust of 12,000 pounds (5,443 kg) each. The cabin could hold 108 passengers in the standard version and 165 in the all-tourist version.

The prototype took to the air for the first time on November 23, 1959 and services were started by United on July 5 of the following year. This company became the principal operator of 720s, with a fleet of 29 aircraft. Ten were bought by American Airlines, 15 by Eastern, three by Irish International, four each by Western and Braniff and two by Pacific Northern. The aircraft continued to evolve, however, with the adoption, as had been the case with the 120 and 320 series of the Boeing 707, of turbofan engines in the 720B version. This version appeared in October 1960 and revealed a clear improvement in performance. The JT3D-1 engines with a thrust of 17,000 pounds (7,711 kg) made it possible to reduce fuel consumption by 15% and as a result gave the 720 a range that was comparable with that of the 707-320.

Aircraft: **Boeing 720**
Manufacturer: **Boeing Aircraft Co.**
Type: **Civil transport**
Year: **1959**
Engines: **Four Pratt & Whitney JT3C-7 turbo-jets, 12,000 lb (5,443 kg) thrust each**
Wingspan: **130 ft 10 in (39.87 m)**
Length: **136 ft 9 in (41.68 m)**
Height: **37 ft 11 in (11.56 m)**
Weight: **229,000 lb (103,875 kg) (Loaded)**
Cruising speed: **601 mph at 25,000 ft (967 km/h at 7,620 m)**
Ceiling: **38,500 ft (11,735 m)**
Range: **5,240 miles (8,430 km)**
Crew: **4**
Passengers: **90–149**

The 720Bs turned out to be the most versatile in the entire range of four-engined Boeing jets. The increased power of the engines, together with the aerodynamic and structural improvements, enhanced the already excellent features of the model to the full.

The first company to put the Boeing 720B into service was American Airlines, on March 12, 1961. It was followed by numerous other airlines, especially outside the United States; these included Lufthansa, Ethiopian Air Lines, Pakistan International, El Al, and Saudi Arabian Airlines.

Convair 880

After Boeing and Douglas a third major American aeronautical company, Convair, focussed on the sector of jet-powered civil transport. Convair aimed directly at the domestic market and proposed to produce a valid and competitive aircraft, the 880 model, which offered very good performance. The quality of the result was excellent, but the initial success came up against fierce competition from Boeing and Douglas which effectively choked the development of the Convair 880. In fact only 65 units, including 18 aircraft belonging to the intercontinental M version, were completed before production ceased.

The go-ahead for the project was given in April 1956 when Delta Air Lines and TWA ordered 40 models from Convair of a four-engined high-performance jet for use on the domestic routes. Some time before, the company had made a detailed analysis of the market in search of an inroad into that

market. After setting aside the sector of intercontinental transport because this was monopolized by Boeing and Douglas the possibility emerged of meeting a consistent demand for an aircraft with a relatively low carrying capacity and range, together with comfort and speed.

The project took the form of a four-engined jet with a low, sharply swept-back wing, and engines mounted in separate nacelles, all of which was not unlike its two direct rivals. To start with it was called the Convair 600 Skylark, but this was changed some time later to Golden Arrow on the basis of a curious proposal whereby the outer surfaces of the aircraft could be painted gold with a special method of anodizing. The idea was scrapped and in the end the design was known as the Convair 880, with a factory designation of Model 22. The number 880 indicated the speed of the aircraft in feet per second. The first prototype flight took place on January

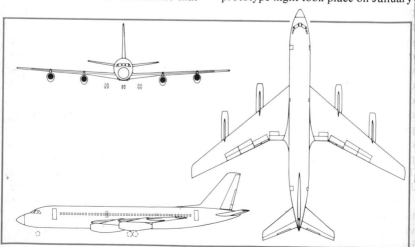

27, 1959. The operational trials and lengthy evaluation tests brought to light the excellent performance of the Convair 880, particularly where speed was concerned. The four General Electric CJ805-3 engines with a thrust of 11,200 pounds (5,080 kg) ensured a very fast cruising speed, 615 mph (990 km/h) at 25,000 feet (7,620 m), which was higher than that of its direct rivals. The prototype was followed by three production models, which completed the series of tests necessary for approval by the authorities. This was obtained on May 1, 1960 and just two weeks later Delta Air Lines put the first of its new 880s into service. Operation of them by TWA was delayed by the company's financial troubles and they preferred to hire six of the 30 models ordered by Northeast Airlines, which put them into service in December. TWA started using the Convair 880 in January of the following year.

In the meantime, on October 3, 1960 the prototype of a more ambitious version, the 880-M designed for intercontinental flights, had taken to

Aircraft: **Convair 880**
Manufacturer: **Convair Division of General Dynamics Corp.**
Type: **Civil transport**
  Year: **1959**
Engines: **Four General Electric CJ805-3 turbo-jets, 11,200 lb (5,080 kg) thrust each**
Wingspan: **120 ft 0 in (36.58 m)**
Length: **129 ft 4 in (39.42 m)**
Height: **36 ft 4 in (11.00 m)**
Weight: **189,500 lb (85,957 kg) (Loaded)**
Cruising speed: **615 mph at 25,000 ft (990 km/h at 7,620 m)**
Ceiling: **41,000 ft (12,600 m)**
Range: **3,200 miles (5,150 km)**
Crew: **5**
Passengers: **84–130**

the air. This aircraft had a larger fuel capacity, more powerful engines and aerodynamic improvements, although it retained the same passenger capacity as the domestic version. The first delivery was made in June of the following year to the Chinese CAT company, and others followed. The orders were fairly scant, however, and made by only a few companies. The market, especially in the long-range sector, was dominated by the giants Boeing and Douglas. Gradually production of the Convair 880 faded, and then dried up altogether.

Beech 18

More than 9,000 models built in 30 years. This is the main yardstick that gives an idea of the incredible career of the Beech 18. It was a small twin-engined type which was designed for civil use and was in fact more successful as a military transport aircraft. It ended up by returning to the commercial market in the immediate postwar period, and clinched a leading position in the sector of light and executive aeroplanes. Thanks to its being constantly up-dated (with specific modifications and conversions by specialized firms) the Beech 18, in its most recent versions, still enjoys great success today despite the fierce competition from more modern aircraft.

The first model 18 was developed way back in 1936, as a light transport aeroplane for six people and the prototype made its maiden flight on January 20 of the following year. There was a reasonable market response and production went ahead with the A18 and B18 versions, which differed mainly in terms of the engines used. The latter variant also aroused interest from the military authorities who saw the small, versatile twin-engined type as a useful aircraft for use in the sectors of communications and general transport. It was this interest that blessed the Beech 18. The first modest orders placed on the eve of the United States involvement in the war, were followed by huge requests from the U.S.A.A.F. and the U.S. Navy, which ended up totalling several thousand units. Known principally as the C-45 in the Air Force and as the JRB in the Navy, these aircraft undertook a wide variety of tasks during the war years, from training to transport and general communications, and they remained in service until the late 1960s.

The end of the war brought on to the market a host of aircraft declared surplus by the military authorities and gave momentum to purely commercial production. Production of a further 1,030 models of the C18 and D18 versions were completed, thus swelling the numbers of those already in service. The next variant, which was also the

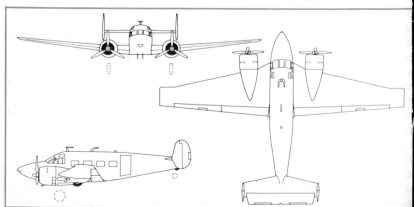

rst to be conspicuously modernized, ppeared in 1953: the maiden flight of he prototype of the model E18 Super 8 took place on 10 December 1953. In his version, in addition to structural nodifications of the wing, more power-ul engines were adopted and the nterior fittings were improved giving greater comfort to passengers. Special navigational equipment could also be nstalled at the request of the client. The adoption of a pair of auxiliary rockets was also possible, to assist at take-off.

Further improvements and moder-nization took place in the G18S version of 1959, which ended up totalling more han 500 models completed. The wing, particularly, was further modified with a slightly increased wingspan, while the structure was reinforced and the engines replaced by more powerful ones. This resulted in an increase in take-off weight of about 550 pounds 250 kg) as well as a considerable ncrease in performance. In addition special attention was paid to the nterior fittings, with particular care to soundproof the cabin.

Aircraft: **Beech G18S-Super 18**
Manufacturer: **Beech Aircraft Corp.**
Type: **Light transport**
Year: **1959**
Engines: **Two Pratt & Whitney R-985-AN14B Wasp Junior, radial with 9 air-cooled cylinders, 450 hp each**
Wingspan: **49 ft 8 in (15.14 m)**
Length: **35 ft 2 in (10.70 m)**
Height: **9 ft 8 in (2.94 m)**
Weight: **9,700 lb (4,400 kg) (Loaded)**
Cruising speed: **204 mph at 5,000 ft (328 km/h at 1,525 m)**
Ceiling: **21,000 ft (6,400 m)**
Range: **1,585 miles (2,550 km)**
Crew: **2**
Passengers: **5–9**

Most of the Beech 18s produced are still being used today by airline com-panies and large firms, as well as by private owners. There have been numerous conversions by specialized firms, some of which have made radical changes. The Dumond Corporation, for instance, has modified the Beech 18 models with a tricycle undercarriage and considerably modified the interior to the point where this small twin-engined aircraft resembles an airline model. Similarly, Volpar Inc. also added a tricycle undercarriage, and has even replaced the two radial engines with a pair of turbo-props.

75

fly **BEA**

VISCOUNT

BEA 'DISCOVERY' CLASS

world's first *TURBO-PROP* airliner

TO

SWITZERLAND

OR

MEDITERRANEAN

BRITISH EUROPEAN AIRWAYS

Great Britain

'The magnificent false start': this is how various aviation historians have defined the hapless beginning of the age of the commercial jet. The second disaster that befell the de Havilland Comet (which occurred in 1954, on April 8, near Stromboli, just three months after the similar crash near Elba) marked the beginning of a long lull, which lasted almost four and a half years. During the course of this period the major initial advantage of the British aeronautical industry in the sector of turbine engines risked being seriously endangered. The disaster was, however, in no way a death-blow, although it was a major let-down to British national pride. In fact the birth of the Comet had been greeted as something of a trump-card, after the years of intensive efforts to regain a major role in the field of international air transport.

The real blow had been dealt by time. The Second World War, which had involved Great Britain both directly and totally, had put a halt to the phase of major expansion of the British airlines in the previous decade. Even in the latter half of the 1930s Imperial Airways had started to suffer from the growing spread of modern aircraft produced by the United States and Germany. This expansion was showing itself to be something of a threat especially on those European routes which the British airline had basically overlooked, preferring to concentrate on the long and prestigious 'Empire routes'. These European routes stimulated fierce competiton among the major European airlines. To remedy this situation, while the industry strove to prepare new and more directly competitive models, a programme of radical restructuring was got under way. This had started in March 1938, when a special government commission had suggested putting into effect a major re-allocation of duties: Imperial Airways was to be in sole charge of the 'Empire routes', while the network of European routes was to be handled by British Airways, (the powerful organization that had come into being on October 1, 1935 out of the merger of Spartan Airlines, United Airways, Hillman's Airways and British Continental Airways). This suggestion had only been adhered to in part and it was eventually decided to merge the two companies into a single State airline. After two years of debate the British Overseas Airways Corporation (BOAC) was formed on April 1, 1940. Throughout the war BOAC served the Allied cause, keeping the old routes towards South Africa and even Australia virtually intact. At the end of the war, having used 160 aircraft of different types and origins, it had transported about 280,000 passengers and covered more than 56,500,000 miles (91,000,000 km). This was a remarkable achievement, but not enough to surmount the serious problems entailed by the return of peace. These were basically technical problems, as well as structural and organizational ones. Not only was there a shortage of modern aircraft, but there was also a lack of strong-currency funds (i.e. dollars) with which to buy the sound products of the American industry, which at that time were the only ones capable of being competitive. It was, therefore, necessary to start from scratch with the task of designing new transport and passenger aircraft and thus recover from the technological and production setbacks suffered.

The results, taken all in all, were fairly positive. On the strictly organizational and structural level it was decided to make a clear-cut dividing-line between the handling of the European routes and the handling of the intercontinental services. On August 1, 1946 the British European Airways company (BEA) was created; a company which, by demonstrating a high degree of flexibility and other excellent features, grew constantly in importance and status. In addition, where the South American routes were concerned, in September 1945 BOAC took over the entire fleet belonging to British Latin American Air Lines (BLAIR) and changed the name of the company to British South American

Airways (BSAA). To begin with, as far as the aircraft stock was concerned, the situation was not particularly promising. From the early days of peace BOAC operated with converted military aircraft (the various Lancastrians, Yorks, Halifaxes and so on). The BSAA also used, for a while, a certain number of the hapless Tudors, while BEA started with DC-3s supplied by the Royal Air Force. However, as time passed things got slightly better, both because it was possible to buy American aircraft, and because the British aeronautical industry, working flat out, was preparing to launch the new generation of commercial aircraft. In this field the technical personnel managed to make fullest use of the results obtained in the field of engines, which were a direct consequence of the desperate efforts made during the war years. Great Britain was the nation that had produced the first valid turbine engines, thus securing for itself a leading position among the major industrial powers. All this emerged in two fundamental stages – fundamental not only for the history of aviation, but also for that of the British airlines: the first flight of the Viscount, on July 16 1948, and the first flight of the Comet on July 27 of the following year. If the Comet had an unfortunate debut (but it was only the debut that was), the Viscount was the aircraft that quickly marked (and this time irreversibly) the beginning of the new period of success. With the enthusiastic test-flights between London and Paris and London and Edinburgh made by the new turbo-prop aircraft flying the BEA colours, the 1950s got under way in a climate of great optimism.

Airspeed A.S.5 Courier

Designed in 1932 at the request of Sir Alan Cobham, who wanted to make a non-stop flight from Great Britain to India, the A.S.5 Courier was the forbear of a successful series of Airspeed light transport aircraft. A monoplane with a low wing made entirely of wood, and a smooth aerodynamic line, it was also the first mass-produced British aeroplane to be fitted with a retractable undercarriage. After more than a year of tests to improve a system of mid-air refuelling, the prototype trials commenced on September 24, 1934. Although this flight was cut short almost at once after a forced landing, the construction of 15 aircraft finally went ahead. These aircraft were designated A.S.5A. They were used by various small companies, such as London, Scottish and Provincial Airways, North Eastern Airways, P.S. and I.O.W. Aviation, all operating on domestic routes and on flights to Paris.

Aircraft: **Airspeed A.S.5A Courier**
Manufacturer: **Airspeed Ltd.**
Type: **Light transport**
Year: **1933**
Engine: **One Armstrong Siddeley Lynx IVC, radial with 7 air-cooled cylinders, 240 hp**
Wingspan: **47 ft 0 in (14.33 m)**
Length: **28 ft 6 in (8.69 m)**
Height: **8 ft 9 in (2.67 m)**
Weight: **3,900 lb (1,769 kg) (Loaded)**
Cruising speed: **132 mph (212 km/h)**
Ceiling: **13,500 ft (4,115 m)**
Range: **600 miles (965 km)**
Crew: **1**
Passengers: **5**

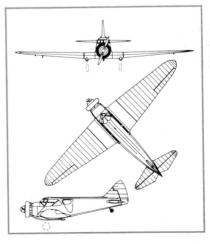

Percival P.3 Gull Six

From Great Britain to Brazil with a record time for crossing the southern Atlantic of 13 hours and 15 minutes. From Great Britain to Australia in 5 days, 21 hours and 3 minutes, and then to New Zealand in the record overall time of 11 days and 45 minutes. Of the many sporting feats achieved by the Percival P.3 Gull Six, these of 1935 and 1936 by the woman aviator Jean Batten are the most indicative of the excellent characteristics of this small single-engined monoplane. The Gull Six was made in 1934, by modifying the engine and in particular the undercarriage and fuselage of its direct predecessor the Percival P.1 Gull Four. This had been designed in 1932 and from its first appearance in the King's Cup Race of that year it had given ample proof of its speed. The Percival monoplanes proved most popular among private owners and enthusiasts, but a few were also used by small companies.

Aircraft: **Percival P.3 Gull Six**
Manufacturer: **Percival Aircraft Co. Ltd.**
Type: **Light transport**
Year: **1934**
Engine: **One de Havilland Gipsy Six, 6 straight cylinders, air-cooled, 200 hp**
Wingspan: **36 ft 2 in (11.02 m)**
Length: **24 ft 9 in (7.54 m)**
Height: **7 ft 4 in (2.24 m)**
Weight: **2,450 lb (1,111 kg) (Loaded)**
Cruising speed: **168 mph (270 km/h)**
Ceiling: **20,000 ft (6,100 m)**
Range: **640 miles (1,030 km)**
Crew: **1**
Passengers: **3**

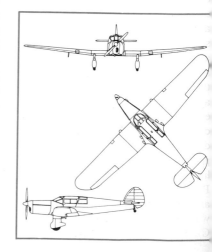

Airspeed A.S.6 Envoy

As a logical development of the A.S.5 Courier, the Airspeed company produced the larger A.S.6 Envoy in 1934. Despite the twin-engined design of the new aircraft, it had many features in common with its predecessor. These included the type of structure and covering, certain sections of the wing, and a retractable undercarriage. After the production of a few models belonging to the first series, production was concentrated on a version with more powerful engines and improved control surfaces. The third, and further improved, version appeared in 1936. The Airspeed twin-engined aircraft had a brief sporting career but was used mainly by small domestic companies. The Envoys were particularly successful with those airlines, such as North Eastern Airways, P.S. and I.O.W. Aviation, which had already used the Courier. Some models were also sold to Chinese, Indian and Czechoslovakian companies.

Aircraft: **Airspeed A.S.6 Envoy II**
Manufacturer: **Airspeed Ltd.**
Type: **Light transport**
Year: **1934**
Engines: **Two Armstrong Siddeley Lynx IVC, radial with 7 air cooled cylinders, 240 hp each**
Wingspan: **52 ft 4 in (15.95 m)**
Length: **34 ft 6 in (10.52 m)**
Height: **9 ft 6 in (2.90 m)**
Weight: **5,830 lb (2,645 kg) (Loaded)**
Cruising speed: **153 mph (246 km/h)**
Ceiling: **16,500 ft (5,030 m)**
Range: **650 miles (1,045 km)**
Crew: **1**
Passengers: **6–8**

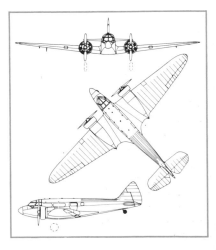

Short S.16 Scion

One of the most used pre-war British light transport aircraft, the S.16 Scion appeared as a prototype in 1933 and astounded both technicians and observers. Short Brothers Ltd, were already known for their activity in the field of water-borne and ocean-going aircraft and so the production of a landplane was a radical breakaway from their traditional tendency. The first four production aircraft were subjected to a lengthy series of tests and assessments. On the basis of the results obtained from these tests the principal version, called Scion 2, appeared in 1935. Capable of carrying six passengers, safely, quietly, and comfortably, this small twin-engined aeroplane with its high wing enjoyed an immediate success with the minor companies which specialized in short tourist flights. It was particularly in this capacity that the Short Scion became well known in Great Britain. A total of 16 aircraft were built.

Aircraft: **Short S.16 Scion 2**
Manufacturer: **Short Brothers Ltd.**
Type: **Light transport**
Year: **1935**
Engines: **Two Pobjoy Niagara III, radial with 7 air-cooled cylinders, 90 hp each**
Wingspan: **42 ft 0 in (12.80 m)**
Length: **31 ft 4 in (9.56 m)**
Height: **10 ft 4 in (3.15 m)**
Weight: **3,200 lb (1,452 kg) (Loaded)**
Cruising speed: **105 mph (169 km/h)**
Ceiling: **13,000 ft (3,960 m)**
Range: **390 miles (628 km)**
Crew: **1**
Passengers: **6**

Short S.23 C-Class Empire Boat

In the British aeronautical circles of the 1930s the name of Short Brothers was synonymous with flying-boats. It was in effect the products of this fine company that confirmed the validity of this particular means of air transport in the period immediately preceding the outbreak of the Second World War. In the years during which the British Empire was at the height of its glory, Imperial Airways managed to serve it with a complex and efficient network of regular routes. This was possible because of the existence of the long series of Short flying-boats, which were cally nothing less than airborne liners. Like the aircraft being produced in the United States at the same time they represented the highest expression of this type of machine. The forbear of the entire family was the Short S.23.

In 1935 the British government decided to order the manufacture of a fleet of new commercial aeroplanes capable of transporting freight (mainly mail) and passengers around the various territories in the Empire. In practical terms this meant virtually all over the world. Imperial Airways, which had its finger firmly on the pulse of the potential of intercontinental air transport and envisaged as a result an immense and rapid development in that sector, laid down the technical and operative specifications for the design and at the same time ordered 28 aircraft. The new aircraft was to be capable of carrying 24 passengers in great comfort and have room for at least one ton of cargo as well. Its cruising speed was to be around 155 mph (250 km/h), and its normal range 685 miles (1,100 km), with the possibility of extension to 2,000 miles (3,200 km). With a reduced load and the increased range, it could be used on the North Atlantic routes. The final specification, was that the aircraft was to be of the flying-boat type.

The production of an aeroplane of this type entailed solving numerous technical and technological problems. The first obstacle to overcome was represented by the internal capacity of the fuselage, which had been laid down in rigid specifications by Imperial Airways. It was this feature that finally gave the aircraft its general line, with the deep hull which directly supported the wing, without any superstructure. The large calculated weight of the aeroplane (in the region of 18 or 19 tons) created serious difficulties, deriving from the high wind resistance. This was so high that it made take-off hazardous, and it was thus necessary to complete a long series of experiments in tanks and modify the design of the submerged part of the hull several times before reaching a good solution. Finally the aeroplane assumed its definitive shape: a large flying-boat with a central hull and stabilizing floats at the sides, driven by four Bristol Pegasus radial engines driving three-bladed metal propellers. The hull incorporated two decks, with the passengers being accommodated in four large compartments on the lower deck, and the spacious flight-deck on the upper one. Holds for freight or mail had been provided in the rear section of both decks. The wing had been the object of specific aerodynamic research. In order to improve the take-off and landing performance, Arthur Gouge fitted it with special flaps, which he designed himself, which could increase by 30% the lift and at the same time reduce the speed by about 12 mph (20 km/h) without altering the trim. All the aerodynamic experiments and the study of the flight specifications were conducted first on a Short S.16 Scion, and then on a Scion Senior. The latter aircraft had been modified with the adoption of four engines so that it became an aerodynamic prototype, scaled-down to half the actual size.

The first S.23 Empire Boat made its maiden flight on July 4, 1936, piloted by Short's chief test-pilot, John Lankester Parker. Christened *Canopus* (all the flying-boats in this series adopted names beginning with the letter C, which led to the creation of the C-Class), it confirmed the predictions made about the project. It displayed excellent flight characteristics, and in particular a take-off time, when fully laden, of just 21 seconds. The aircraft

was delivered to Imperial Airways on September 17, 1936 and used in the Mediterranean from the October 2 onwards. The second S.23 was of the long-range type and this was delivered on December 4, 1936. The other 26 aircraft followed punctually at intervals with the last one, christened *Coorong* delivered on February 26, 1938.

The first regular service on the 'Empire' routes opened on February 8 1937. In the month of June the service was fully operational and had been extended from Australia to the African colonies. In 1938 the S.23s made in all 16 weekly flights to Egypt, India, East Africa, southern Africa, Malaya, Hong Kong and Australia. In the meantime the North Atlantic route had also been gained. *Caledonia*, the second of the S.23s, with modifications made to its fuel tanks, had reached New York on July 9, 1937, having taken off from Foynes (Ireland) on the night of the July 5/6. The experimental flight from Foynes to Botwood (in Newfoundland) took 15 hours and 3 minutes.

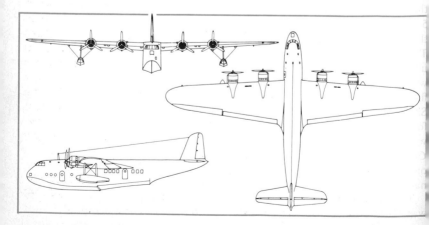

The commercial success of the S.23s was demonstrated in concrete terms at the end of 1937 when Imperial Airways ordered a further batch of 11 aircraft. The first three were completed to the standard specifications of the basic series, but the other eight were modified and called S.30s. Compared with their predecessors, they differed in the adoption of Bristol Perseus engines producing 890 hp; in numerous structural reinforcements; and in the increase of the maximum weight at take-off to 53,000 pounds (24,000 kg). In addition they could be refuelled in mid-air. These aircraft had been prepared for use on the North Atlantic route, which was inaugurated with a one-way mail flight on August 8, 1939. Another Short S.30 was ordered in 1939, and followed by the last two aircraft built, which were christened *Clifton* and *Cleopatra*; although identical to the original S.23, they were both designated S.33.

The civil career of the Empire Boats was abruptly interrupted by the war,

Aircraft: **Short S.23 C-Class Empire Boat**
Manufacturer: **Short Brothers Ltd.**
Type: **Civil transport**
Year: **1936**
Engines: **Four Bristol Pegasus XC, radial with 9 air-cooled cylinders, 920 hp each**
Wingspan: **114 ft 0 in (34.74 m)**
Length: **88 ft 0 in (26.82 m)**
Height: **31 ft 10 in (9.72 m)**
Weight: **40,500 lb (18,371 kg) (Loaded)**
Cruising speed: **165 mph (265 km/h)**
Ceiling: **20,000 ft (6,100 m)**
Range: **760 miles (1,225 km)**
Crew: **2**
Passengers: **24**

but this did not check the activity of these irreplaceable flying-boats which were used on the hazardous operational flights to the various theatres of operations, especially in the Pacific and Mediterranean. Many were destroyed, but thirteen survived and some returned to civil use. The final flight of the last S.23 (*Coriolanus*) took place on December 23, 1947, between the Fiji Islands and Sydney, flying in the colours of the Australian Qantas company. In eleven years of service the Empire Boats had covered altogether almost 38,000,000 miles (61,000,000 km) across all five continents.

Airspeed A.S.40 Oxford

Among the 8,751 examples of Airspeed Oxford used between 1937 and 1954 in the flying schools of the Royal Air Force and the Commonwealth, a fair number were also used for civilian purposes. These aircraft were the forerunners of the demilitarized models which were converted shortly after the end of the war. The first of these was delivered to British Airways Ltd in September 1938, to be used in the field of radio communications research. Six aircraft were then given to British Airways for training purposes, while other Oxfords became communications aircraft. These particular aircraft were assigned to the aeronautical industries during the war. Following the end of the Second World War they were also used for commercial transport, but with its small space available for passengers the Oxford was not very successful and eventually continued its civil career as a survey and aerial photography aeroplane.

Aircraft: **Airspeed A.S.40 Oxford**
Manufacturer: **Airspeed Ltd.**
Type: **Light transport**
Year: **1937**
Engines: **Two Armstrong Siddeley Cheetah X, radial with 7 air-cooled cylinders, 375 hp each**
Wingspan: **53 ft 4 in (16.25 m)**
Length: **34 ft 6 in (10.51 m)**
Height: **11 ft 1 in (3.38 m)**
Weight: **7,600 lb (3,447 kg) (Loaded)**
Cruising speed: **166 mph at 5,000 ft (266 km/h at 1,525 m)**
Ceiling: **19,500 ft (5,945 m)**
Range: **900 miles (1,450 km)**
Crew: **1–2**
Passengers: **4**

T.K.4

This tiny competition model had just three weeks of active life before being destroyed in an attempt to set a speed record. Despite its brief existence, however, the T.K.4 managed to display the soundness of the design. It touched on a speed of 244 mph (393 km/h) with just 137 hp at its disposal! The T.K.4 was built and designed in 1937 by students at the de Havilland Aeronautical Technical School, a hothouse for future technicians and designers founded by de Havilland in 1928. The aircraft was built around the Gipsy Major III engine and its dimensions were kept down to a minimum. With a wooden structure and 'skin', retractable undercarriage and carefully studied lines to make the aerodynamic shape as good as possible, it weighed only 1,357 pounds (615 kg). The first flight took place on July 30, 1937 and on September 10 the T.K.4 was ninth in the King's Cup Race. On October 1 the aircraft crashed.

Aircraft: **de Havilland T.K.4**
Manufacturer: **de Havilland Aeronautical Technical School**
Type: **Competition**
Year: **1937**
Engine: **One de Havilland Gipsy Major III, with 4 straight cylinders, air-cooled, 137 hp**
Wingspan: **19 ft 2 in (5.84 m)**
Length: **15 ft 10 in (4.83 m)**
Height: **–**
Weight: **1,357 lb (615 kg) (Loaded)**
Maximum speed: **244 mph at 1,500 ft (393 km/h at 457 m)**
Ceiling: **21,000 ft (6,400 m)**
Range: **450 miles (724 km)**
Crew: **1**

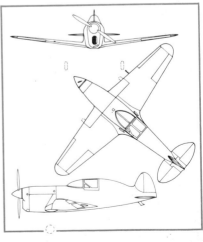

de Havilland D.H.91 Albatross

The de Havilland D.H.91 Albatross was one of the most elegant commercial aircraft of its day. Although the extremely aerodynamic lines of this aeroplane were not expressly aesthetic in purpose they made an exceptional performance possible, particularly where range was concerned. In the mail version, the Albatross could fly almost 3,100 miles (5,000 km) at a cruising speed of more than 200 mph (320 km/h). Just five aircraft were built, plus two prototypes which went into service in October 1938 on the competitive routes to France and the rest of Europe. They remained in service until July 1943.

The D.H.91 was designed in 1936, in response to a request by the government for a fast transatlantic mail aeroplane. When the first prototype made its maiden flight on May 20, 1937, at the hands of Robert Wright, it seemed to be a completely different air-craft compared with the immediately preceding designs put out by de Havilland. These had included the family of D.H.84 Dragon and D.H.86 and D.H.89 Dragon Rapide commercial biplanes. The D.H.91 was a sleek, entirely wood-built monpolane with a long, circular fuselage, twin fins and rudders and a retractable undercarriage. The engines were four de Havilland Gipsy Twelves (new V-12 air-cooled models in the 500 hp class) each of which drove a variable-pitch metal twin-bladed propeller. The aerodynamic research had produced an unusual solution for cooling the engines: the air was channelled from four intakes on the leading edge of each wing, through a tube, and then from inside to the rear section of the engines. As a result the engines were housed in four nacelles with a circular section which were perfectly tapered.

The first prototype (registered G-AEVV and christened *Faraday*) was joined on August 27, 1938 by a second, called *Franklin*. After modifications to

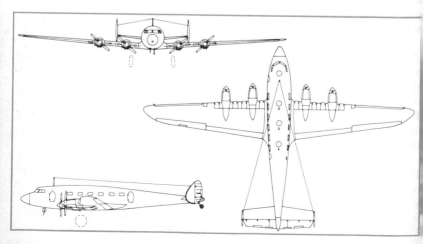

the structure of the tail surfaces and also the fuselage, the first production-line Albatross, called *Frobisher*, was delivered two months later to Imperial Airways. This gave rise to a new class of aircraft called 'F Class', from the initial letter of the names given to the aeroplanes. In all there were five production D.H.91s (*Frobisher* was followed by *Falcon*, *Fortuna*, *Fingal* and *Fiona*); they were fitted out for passenger use while the two prototypes were used for mail transport.

With their excellent features the Albatrosses showed themselves to be very competitive on the most prestigious routes. In the course of a series of experimental flights to France and Belgium, they managed to considerably reduce the flight times on the Croydon–Paris and Croydon–Brussels routes. The service to the French capital continued until June 13 of the following year, when it had to be suspended because of the approaching war. Similarly a service between London, Bordeaux and Lisbon, which

Aircraft: **de Havilland D.H.91 Albatross**
Manufacturer: **de Havilland Aircraft Co. Ltd.**
Type: **Civil transport**
Year: **1937**
Engines: **Four de Havilland Gipsy Twelve I, air-cooled V-12 type, 525 hp each**
Wingspan: **104 ft 8 in (31.90 m)**
Length: **70 ft 0 in (21.34 m)**
Height: **20 ft 2 in (6.15 m)**
Weight: **28,500 lb (12,928 kg) (Loaded)**
Cruising speed: **210 mph at 11,000 ft (338 km/h at 3,355 m)**
Ceiling: **16,800 ft (5,121 m)**
Range: **3,230 miles (5,197 km)**
Crew: **4**
Passengers: **22**

started on June 4, 1940, had to be dropped after only a few days. In the end, the Second World War put an end to all development of commercial flights. The two prototypes were used by the Royal Air Force, and the others suffered from the ravages of war: in 1940 *Frobisher* and *Fingal* were destroyed, and in July 1943 *Fortuna* suffered the same fate. This accident put a virtual end to the career of the D.H.91s. The survivors, *Fiona* and *Falcon*, were dismantled on September 29 and October 1, 1943, after an inspection revealed damage to the structure.

Armstrong Whitworth A.W.27 Ensign

After the 1926 Argosy and the 1932 Atalanta, Armstrong Whitworth decided in 1935 to continue with the development of their civil models. This third project, the A.W.27 Ensign (the initial letter of which created the 'E Class' of commercial aircraft) came into being at the express request of the British government, which wanted them to produce a large, high-performance aircraft capable of ensuring rapid mail transport across the Empire. The Armstrong Whitworth design was slow to take shape because of the company's priority commitments to design and produce the Whitley bomber. However, once defined, it gave rise to the largest transport aeroplane ever built to date for Imperial Airways. Fourteen Ensigns were completed. They went into service in 1938 and remained operational throughout the ups and downs of war, until the spring of 1945.

The prototype (christened Ensign and registered G-ADSR) flew for the first time on January 24, 1938. In its lines and general aspect it echoed its direct predecessor, the Armstrong Whitworth A.W.15 Atalanta: a monoplane with the wing set high up four-engined, with a long, sleek fuselage. The designer, John Lloyd, had also designed the two previous civil models. However, despite the outward similarities the A.W.27 was a more modern, and, in particular, larger and heavier aeroplane. At the end of the operational trials and the evaluation tests G-ADSR was delivered to Imperial Airways, which put it into service on the Paris route on October 20, 1938. The aircraft had been fitted out in the so-called 'Empire style', with a maximum capacity of 27 passengers.

The Imperial Airways order was for a total of 12 and all were delivered by the beginning of 1940. The prototype was followed by G-ADST *Elsinore*, G-ADSU *Euterpe*, G-ADSS *Egeria*, G-ADSV *Explorer*. These aircraft

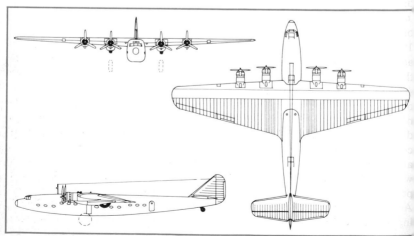

all with the same capacity as Ensign, were followed by four models (G-ADSW *Eddystone*, G-ADSX *Ettrick*, G-ADSY *Empyrean* and G-ADSZ *Elysian*) which were fitted out to accommodate 40 passengers and were called the 'European version'. There then followed G-ADTA *Euryalus*, G-ADTB *Echo* and G-ADTC *Endymione*, which went back to the original interior arrangement. The continuing hostilities in Europe caused inevitable losses. The A.W.27s, which operated on flights to France until June 1940, were the object of German attacks and three were shot down. At the same time it was decided to make substantial modifications to the engines of two further aircraft, to make up for a noticeable lack of power that had been dramatically revealed by the wartime conditions of use: G-AFZU *Everest* and G-AFZV *Enterprise* were fitted with Wright GR-1820 Cyclone engines producing 950 hp. These replaced the Armstrong Siddeley Tiger IXs producing 850 hp, and the new aircraft were consequently designated A.W.27

Aircraft: **Armstrong Whitworth A.W.27 Ensign 1**
Manufacturer: **Armstrong Whitworth Aircraft Ltd.**
Type: **Civil transport**
Year: **1938**
Engines: **Four Armstrong Siddeley Tiger IXC, radial with 14 air-cooled cylinders, 850 hp each**
Wingspan: **123 ft 0 in (37.49 m)**
Length: **111 ft 0 in (33.83 m)**
Height: **23 ft 0 in (7.01 m)**
Weight: **49,000 lb (22,226 kg) (Loaded)**
Cruising speed: **170 mph at 7,000 ft (274 km/h at 2,135 m)**
Ceiling: **22,000 ft (6,106 m)**
Range: **860 miles (1,384 km)**
Crew: **4**
Passengers: **27–40**

Ensign 2. From 1941 onwards, this modification was extended, to all the remaining eight aircraft in the first series.

In the midst of the world war the Ensigns were widely used for military type flights, even though most of them were made under the civil colours of BOAC, particularly on the routes to Africa and India. These services ended in May 1945. Seven aircraft that survived then returned to Great Britain, in the first months of the following year, where they were all broken-up.

de Havilland D.H.95 Flamingo

Designed for medium-range light transport, the de Havilland D.H.95 Flamingo served its purpose mainly in the war, during which time the flights were handled by BOAC. The project, which appeared in the form of a prototype on December 28, 1938, astounded onlookers in as much as it was the first entirely metal-built aircraft produced by de Havilland, which was renowned for its specialization in wooden construction. The D.H.95 Flamingo was a high-winged twin-engined aeroplane with a passenger capacity varying between 12 and 17. The operational tests and trials ended in May 1939 and the prototype was then loaned to Guernsey and Jersey Airways. The outbreak of hostilities prevented any commercial development. The first 16 aircraft ordered were followed by a further seven and these were used by the R.A.F and Fleet Air Arm, including two allotted to the King's Flight.

Aircraft: **de Havilland D.H.95 Flamingo**
Manufacturer: **de Havilland Aircraft Co. Ltd.**
Type: **Civil transport**
Year: **1938**
Engines: **Two Bristol Perseus XVI, radial with 9 air-cooled cylinders, 930 hp each**
Wingspan: **70 ft 0 in (21.33 m)**
Length: **51 ft 7 in (15.72 m)**
Height: **15 ft 3 in (4.65 m)**
Weight: **17,600 lb (7,983 kg) (Loaded)**
Cruising speed: **184 mph (296 km/h)**
Ceiling: **20,900 ft (6,370 m)**
Range: **1,210 miles (1,950 km)**
Crew: **3**
Passengers: **12–17**

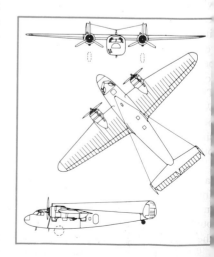

hort-Mayo S.20/S.21 Composite

non-stop flight of 6,045 miles (9,728 m) in 42 hours and 5 minutes between undee (Scotland) and Alexander Bay at the mouth of the Orange river in outh Africa). This spectacular feat arted on October 6, 1938. The rotagonists were two aeroplanes, nked together by fate in one of the ost ambitious projects in the history f commercial aviation: the Short-Mayo S.20/S.21 Composite. As well as eating the international record for ong-distance flights by seaplanes, the ight also served to prove the theory which had initiated the project in 1932: onsidering that the load and range of n aeroplane were heavily influenced by the need for power and fuel ecessary for take-off and reaching the ruising altitude, why not make an airraft free of these problems altogether? The solution appeared to be the bvious one: a large seaplane appropriately designed and built, which would carry a smaller aircraft on t; this latter aircraft, which would be itted for mail transport only, would be eleased once the right altitude had been reached, and would thus be able o reach its final long-range destination. The outbreak of the Second World War stopped the project getting beyond the experimental phase, but similar ideas were taken up again on other occasions.

The original project, which was aunched by the technical chief of Imperial Airways, R. H. Mayo, was ncluded in the series of studies carried out by the British company to improve he postal services across the long intercontinental routes, especially towards America. Mayo's idea was greeted with much interest by the technical authorities, who approved it on the operational level, thus giving the green light for executing the idea. In 1935 a special company was founded: the Mayo Composite Aircraft Co. Ltd. This company had the job of supervising the project as it progressed, while the actual execution of the programme was in the hands of the Short company.

The designers set to work on two aircraft, called the S.20 *Mercury* and the S.21 *Maia* respectively. The first aircraft was the upper half of the project: a high-winged monoplane with twin floats, and smooth aerodynamic lines powered by, originally, four Napier Rapier V engines (16 air-cooled cylinders in II-formation) each producing 340 hp. The *Mercury* alone had a take-off weight of 12,500 pounds (5,670 kg) but this figure was increased by 8,300 pounds (3,765 kg) when the aircraft was transported by the S.21. This, in its turn, was a large flying-boat with a central hull, not unlike the S.23, but considerably modified.

Maia and *Mercury* were made and tested separately, under the watchful eyes of test-pilots John Lankester Parker and Harold Piper. The *Maia* had its maiden flight on July 27, 1937, the *Mercury* on September 5, 1937. On January 20, 1938 the two aircraft were taken up into the air together, and on February 6 *Mercury* parted from *Maia* in mid-air for the first time.

The first attempt at a commercial flight across the North Atlantic was on July 21, 1938. This was the day that the take-off had been planned for, and the final destination was to be Canada.

Maia-Mercury, piloted respectively by Captains Wilcockson and Bennett, took off from Foynes, in Ireland. The upper aircraft was carrying 600 pounds (272 kg) of freight and mail. After a normal take-off and a gradual ascent to the right altitude using all eight engines, it parted company without any problems, and started off on its transatlantic crossing. *Mercury* arrived at Boucherville (Montreal) after 20 hours and 20 minutes. It covered 2,860 miles (4,600 km) at an average air-speed of almost 177 mph (285 km/h). After a gap of slightly more than two months there was a second attempt, of a more ambitious nature, towards Capetown. Once again piloted by Wilcockson and Bennett, *Maia* and *Mercury* took off from Dundee (on the east coast of Scotland) on October 6. After separating, *Mercury* (which on this occasion carried no payload and just fuel, and had more powerful engines) went on its way and sighted South Africa after 42 hours of flying time. However the final destination was not reached because a shortage of fuel forced the small seaplane to land in the estuary of the Orange river.

The now imminent storm-clouds of war did not, however, permit the project to become fully operational. The 'composite' flights of *Maia* and *Mercury*, therefore, remained as merely extremely useful evidence of a brilliant idea and as remarkable stages in the history of aviation. The two aircraft did not operate together again. The Short S.21 was adapted to 'all passenger' use (with the same capacity as the S.23) and was then handed over to BOAC for it to use with its other flying-boats for wartime services. Its life was, however, a short one: in the course of a bombing raid, on May 11 1941, *Maia* (registered G-ADHK) was destroyed. Two months later the career of *Mercury* also came to an end (this was registered G-ADHJ) in the breaker's yard. This aircraft had also been inherited by BOAC, but they had preferred to hand it on to the Royal Air Force, on June 18, 1940. The R.A.F.

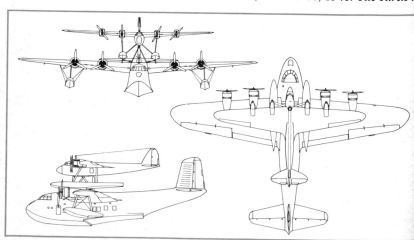

n turn, ear-marked it for a crew-
training unit. Before being handed to
the Royal Air Force the Short S.20 had
been used for a short while on the night-
mail service from Southampton to
Alexandria, thus using its excellent
night capacities when on its own. These
had been well demonstrated on the
latter part of its Atlantic crossing in
1938. On this occasion, having
refuelled at Montreal, *Mercury* flew
down to New York, taking the total
flight time to 22 hours and 31 minutes.

Aircraft: **Short-Mayo S.20/S.21 Composite**
Manufacturer: **Short Brothers Ltd.**
Type: **Civil transport**
Year: **1938**
Weight (S.20): **20,800 lb (9,435 kg) (Loaded)**
Weight (S.21): **27,700 lb (12,565 kg) (Loaded)**
Weight (total): **48,500 lb (22,000 kg) (Loaded)**
Cruising speed: **167 mph at 7,500 ft (269 km/h at 2,290 m)**
Ceiling: **–**
Maximum speed: **195 mph at 7,500 ft (314 km/h at 2,290 m)**
Range: **3,900 miles (6,276 km)**
Payload: **1,000 lb (450 kg)**

Aircraft: **Short S.21 *Maia***
Manufacturer: **Short Brothers Ltd.**
Type: **Civil transport**
Year: **1937**
Engines: **Four Bristol Pegasus XC, radial with 9 air-cooled cylinders, 920 hp each**
Wingspan: **114 ft 0 in (34.75 m)**
Length: **84 ft 11 in (25.88 m)**
Height: **32 ft 8 in (9.95 m)**
Weight: **38,000 lb (17,237 kg) (Loaded)**
Cruising speed: **165 mph at 5,000 ft (265 km/h at 1,524 m)**
Ceiling: **20,000 ft (6,100 m)**
Range: **850 miles (1,368 km)**
Crew: **5**

Aircraft: **Short S.20 *Mercury***
Manufacturer: **Short Brothers Ltd.**
Type: **Civil transport**
Year: **1937**
Engines: **Four Napier Rapier VI, 16 air-cooled cylinders 340 hp, each**
Wingspan: **73 ft 0 in (22.25 m)**
Length: **50 ft 11 in (15.53 m)**
Height: **20 ft 3 in (6.17 m)**
Weight: **12,500 lb (5,670 kg) (Loaded)**
Cruising speed: **180 mph at 10,000 ft (290 km/h at 3,050 m)**
Range: **350 miles (560 km)**
Crew: **2**
Payload: **1,000 lb (450 kg)**

Short S.26 G-Class

The great success in commercial terms of the S.23 Empire Boats and the store of experience gathered in making them were instrumental in the decision by the Short company to focus its production of large flying-boats in the military sector. The S.25 Sunderland made its maiden flight as a prototype on October 16, 1937 and was the first in a long series of 714 aircraft. Throughout the war and beyond they remained in service for some 21 years, and were the last flying-boats to be used by the Royal Air Force. Although committed to the hilt in this military production, Short were also able to branch off into the civil sector. This was with the production in 1938 of the S.26, a successor to the S.23 which was destined for the Imperial Airways fleet. There were just three of these aircraft built, but despite this, they enjoyed a busy career during the war and in the immediate post-war period. The only S.26 to survive the war, christened

Golden Hind and registered G-AFC sank during a storm in May 1954. Wi it the last flying-boat of the 193 vanished.

The project which gave rise to th S.26 was launched in 1938 at th request of Imperial Airways. Imperi wanted an aircraft capable of givir rapid non-stop passenger and freig services across the Atlantic. Three ai craft were ordered and Short were ab to build them in a relatively short tim As the design was based o immediately preceding projects, th first S.26 (the *Golden Hind*) took to th air in June 1939. Even though th general appearance was like that of i predecessor the S.23, the ne aeroplane was considerably larger an heavier. Four Bristol Hercules I engines producing 1,380 hp each gav it a cruising speed of 180 mph (29 km/h) and with the normal fuel reserv a range of at least 3,100 miles (5,00 km). *Golden Hind* was delivered t

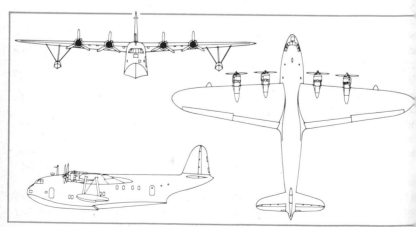

...mperial Airways on September 24, ...939 and was followed by *Golden ...leece* (registered G-AFCJ) and ...olden Horn* (registered G AFCK). ...hese three aircraft thus formed the so ...alled 'G Class'.

Plans for commercial transport to ...e other side of the Atlantic were, ...owever, abruptly cut short by the out-...reak of war. On July 2, 1940 the three ...ying-boats were handed over to the ...oyal Air Force which used them as ...ng-range maritime reconnaissance ...eroplanes. The war claimed one of the ...26s as a victim. This was the *Golden ...leece* which was destroyed during a ...orced landing off Cape Finisterre on ...une 20, 1941. At the end of that year ...e two surviving aircraft were ...ansferred to BOAC and reconverted ...or passenger transport.

The *Golden Horn* crashed at Lisbon, ...n January 9, 1943, and was destroyed ...s the result of a fire in the engines. The ...st survivor, *Golden Hind*, returned ...or a while to domestic service in Great

Aircraft: **Short S.26 G-Class**
Manufacturer: **Short Brothers Ltd.**
Type. **Civil transport**
Year: **1939**
Engines: **Four Bristol Hercules IV, radial with 14 air-cooled cylinders, 1,380 hp each**
Wingspan: **135 ft 4 in (40.95 m)**
Length: **103 ft 2 in (31.40 m)**
Height: **37 ft 7 in (11.46 m)**
Weight: **74,500 lb (33,800 kg) (Loaded)**
Cruising speed: **180 mph at 7,500 ft (290 km/h at 2,290 m)**
Ceiling: **20,000 ft (6,100 m)**
Range: **3,200 miles (5,150 km)**
Crew: **5–7**
Passengers: **40**

Britain and then between September 24, 1944 and August 30, 1945 operated on a long flight between Africa and India, from Mombassa to Ceylon. At the end of the war between September 30, 1946 and September 21, 1947, after the engines had been replaced and the supporting structure that had housed the rear turret had been removed, *Golden Hind* was used between Poole and Cairo. These were its last flights under the BOAC flag. The *Golden Hind* was then sold to private owners, never to fly again.

Heston Type 5 Racer

The Heston Type 5 Racer was perhaps the last example of a classic sporting aircraft before the outbreak of the war. This miniature 'monster' with an engine producing 2,560 hp did not have a happy life. Its one and only flight took place on June 12, 1940 when it only just managed to take off and fly for seven minutes before crashing. The project was got under way towards the end of 1938 by the Heston Aircraft Company. This was a small company founded in 1934 and specializing in the manufacture of light aircraft. The programme was quite an ambitious one, with two aims. Firstly to create an aeroplane which could be used as an airborne testing-ground for the new Napier Sabre engine, and secondly to create an aeroplane that was capable of breaking the world speed record. The designers put a great deal of effort into the idea, but failed to solve the problems of engine-trouble and instability.

Aircraft: **Heston Type 5 Racer**
Manufacturer: **Heston Aircraft Co.**
Type: **Competition**
Year: **1940**
Engine: **One Napier Sabre, with 24 water-cooled cylinders in H-formation, 2,560 hp**
Wingspan: **32 ft 1 in (9.78 m)**
Length: **24 ft 7 in (7.49 m)**
Height: **11 ft 10 in (3.61 m)**
Weight: **7,200 lb (3,266 kg) (Loaded)**
Maximum speed: **480 mph (772 km/h)***
Ceiling: **–**
Range: **–**
Crew: **1**
* Estimated

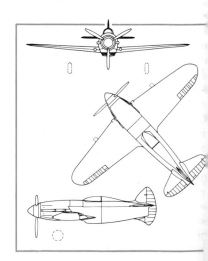

Avro 685 York

Apart from its intensive use by R.A.F.
Transport Command squadrons, the
Avro York also enjoyed a long
operational career as a civil transport
aircraft. This large four-engined type
made its maiden flight on July 5, 1942.
It was derived directly from the
Lancaster bomber and reached a
production total of 257. It was,
therefore, one of the few aircraft that
managed to score successes in both the
military and the strictly commercial
sectors. In fact from 1944 onwards
BOAC had managed to obtain five aircraft destined for the R.A.F. which the
R.A.F. used on flights to Cairo. By the
end of 1945 BOAC had obtained 25
more aircraft. These were fitted with
more powerful Merlin engines and
formed the 'M Class' of civil transport
aeroplanes. A further 12 examples
were then built in 1946 for British
South American Airways, followed by
three for Skyways Ltd and five more
for the Argentinian FAMA company.

Aircraft: **Avro 685 York**
Manufacturer: **A. V. Roe and Co. Ltd.**
Type: **Civil transport**
Year: **1942**
Engines: **Four Rolls-Royce Merlin 502,
water-cooled V-12, 1,610 hp each**
Wingspan: **102 ft 0 in (31.09 m)**
Length: **78 ft 6 in (23.93 m)**
Height: **17 ft 10 in (5.44 m)**
Weight: **70,000 lb (31,752 kg) (Loaded)**
Cruising speed: **210 mph at 10,000 ft (338
km/h at 3,050 m)**
Ceiling: **21,000 ft (6,500 m)**
Range: **2,700 miles (4,345 km)**
Crew: **4**
Passengers: **12–24**

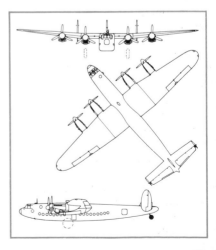

Avro 683 Lancaster
Avro 691 Lancastrian

Just as the Avro 685 York had been derived from the Lancaster bomber, so two other versions of the famous four-engined military aircraft appeared in 1944 and 1945. They were a cargo version which retained the same designation as the bomber, and a version for carrying passengers which was called the Avro 691 Lancastrian. Unlike the York which had used the same wing, undercarriage and engines as the Lancaster and had only a redesigned fuselage for transportation purposes, these two later versions did not undergo substantial modifications as compared with the military model. Obviously, however, the armament and equipment were removed and the original bomb-bay was replaced by a cargo hold or a passenger cabin. Both these aeroplanes were clearly transitional models, used while awaiting the appearance of the first commercial transport models of the new post-war generation. In any event they gave busy and useful service, contributing considerably to the restructuring of British civil aviation in the first years of peace. The first civilian Lancaster was delivered on January 20, 1944 to BOAC. This aircraft, registered G-AGJI, was used for almost three years by the company's experimental division and was extremely useful in airborne engine-testing and the testing of equipment destined for future commercial aircraft then in the process of development. In 1946 another six Lancasters were requested by British South American Airways, which

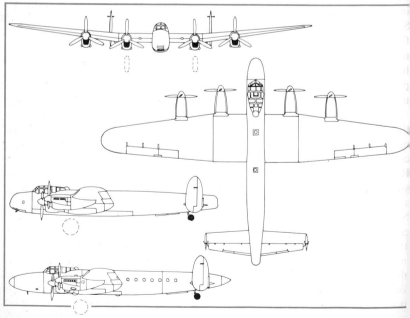

wanted to use them for transporting freight. Unlike the first aircraft, four of these were modified with the addition of a cargo hold in the forward section, thereby resembling the contemporary Lancastrians. These aircraft remained in service for almost one year on the South American routes, being used for the transport of perishable merchandise. The other two were handed back to the R.A.F. after a short period of service which turned out to be uneconomical.

A further four bombers were used in the latter half of 1946 for a rather unusual purpose, flying tankers. The company which bought them, Flight Refuelling Ltd, used them for several years mainly for developing an efficient system of mid-air refuelling on the North Atlantic route. Another seven civilian Lancasters were used until the 1950s, but were mainly used for training airline crews. An Italian company also acquired one in 1947, and used it for training until the Lancastrians were available.

Aircraft: **Avro 683 Lancaster 1**
Manufacturer: **A. V. Roe and Co. Ltd.**
Type: **Civil transport**
Year: **1944**
Engines: **Four Rolls-Royce Merlin 24, water-cooled V-12, 1,640 hp each**
Wingspan: **102 ft 0 in (31.09 m)**
Length: **69 ft 6 in (21.18 m)**
Height: **20 ft 0 in (6.10 m)**
Weight: **65,000 lb (29,484 kg) (Loaded)**
Cruising speed: **210 mph at 20,000 ft (338 km/h at 6,100 m)**
Ceiling: **24,500 ft (7,500 m)**
Range: **2,530 miles (4,070 km)**
Crew: **4**
Payload: **25,000 lb (11,350 kg)**

The Avro 691 Lancastrian made a quite different contribution. Although converted from the bomber in a fairly similar way, it was used in larger quantities and spread to all the most important post-war commercial routes. The first idea of adapting the Lancaster to trans-oceanic transport came during the war. Trans-Canada Air Lines, had a bomber converted and they inaugurated a regular mail service across the Atlantic Ocean on July 22, 1943. The first flight from Dorval to Prestwick was completed in 12 hours and 26 minutes with four tons of mail on board. On the basis of this initial

success, Trans-Canada converted eight aircraft and carried on with this service throughout the war.

BOAC followed Trans-Canada's example and ordered a similar conversion on a batch of 32 models from the latest production batch of the Lancaster bomber. They received the first one, called Lancastrian 1, early in 1945. This aircraft was immediately put through an intense series of experimental flights on the long routes to Australia and New Zealand. It showed itself to be excellent at the job and robbed the glorious Empire Boats of the fastest flying times. BOAC immediately organized a regular service in collaboration with the Australian company Qantas which started on May 31, 1945. The flight lasted three days from Great Britain to Australia and the Lancastrian was only able to carry nine passengers in these operating conditions. However, the financial loss and the inconvenience of the journey was made up for by the return of the former pre-war prestige to the British company.

Aircraft: **Avro 691 Lancastrian 1**
Manufacturer: **A. V. Roe and Co. Ltd.**
Type: **Civil transport**
Year: **1945**
Engines: **Four Rolls-Royce Merlin 24,** **water-cooled V-12, 1,642 hp each**
Wingspan: **102 ft 0 in (31.09 m)**
Length: **76 ft 10 in (23.42 m)**
Height: **19 ft 6 in (5.94 m)**
Weight: **65,000 lb (29,484 kg) (Loaded)**
Cruising speed: **230 mph at 20,000 ft (370** **km/h at 6,100 m)**
Ceiling: **25,500 ft (7,770 m)**
Range: **4,150 miles (6,680 km)**
Crew: **4**
Passengers: **9–13**

On October 9, 1945 the Lancastrians opened up another ambitious route to South America, to Buenos Aires, Santiago and Lima. After a few experimental flights the service was inaugurated in 1946. In the same year a further 12 Lancastrians were completed; three went to Silver City Airways, four to Skyways and five to the newly formed Alitalia. The civil career of the Lancastrians ended in the hands of smaller companies, acting as transporters of liquid cargo. The last one was scrapped in 1951.

Avro Tudor

The impetus behind producing a commercial aircraft capable of ensuring sound service across the Atlantic was quite strong in England in the closing years of the war. The motivation was the prospect of a rapid development of civil aviation. In the early years of peace the British aeronautical industry was forced to give way to the Americans. The Americans had for some time been able to organize themselves for the new production and already had valid and competitive aircraft ready. Many of the efforts made in Great Britain to shake off the American supremacy were thus in vain. The Avro Tudor, one of the most ambitious projects of all, was manufactured in the immediate postwar period and was one of those aeroplanes which failed to compete successfully with American competition. After a lengthy development phase, its use was reckoned to be uneconomical. The large four-engined type which was intended to represent the rebirth of the British airlines thus ended its career in relative obscurity.

The project had been launched in 1943, with the intention of producing a long-range commercial transport aircraft which would be run by BOAC on services across the North Atlantic. As was the case with the two previous civil models made by A. V. Roe and Co., the York and the Lancastrian, so it was decided to use a military aircraft as a basis of the design of the Avro Tudor. Thus, the wing and engine installation of the Avro 694 Lincoln, which was in turn derived from the Lancaster, were adopted. In other respects, the new

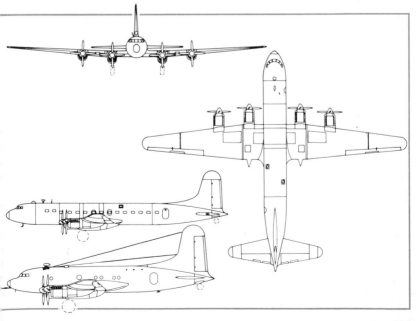

aeroplane was designed with a circular pressurized fuselage and single tailfin. In 1944 the official specifications were laid down: a payload of about 3,750 pounds (1,700 kg); range of about 4,000 miles (6,400 km); and a cruising speed of 235 mph (378 km/h) at an altitude of 25,000 feet (7,600 m). The weight of the aircraft at take-off was to be 80,000 pounds (36,300 kg) with accommodation for 24 passengers in the daytime layout and 12 on night-flights. With the official designation of Avro 688 Tudor 1, the project moved into the operational phase in September with an order for two prototypes. At the same time, after lengthy discussions between BOAC, Qantas and South African Airways it was also decided to develop a second version of the aircraft. This would have a smaller range but a larger capacity and would be designed for the connected routes of all three companies. This version, called the Avro 689 Tudor 2, was to have the same performance as the Tudor 1, except for its capacity which was increased to 60 passengers, and its

Aircraft: **Avro 688 Tudor 1**
Manufacturer: **A. V. Roe and Co. Ltd.**
Type: **Civil transport**
Year: **1945**
Engines: **Four Rolls-Royce Merlin 600, V-12, water-cooled, 1,770 hp each**
Wingspan: **120 ft 0 in (36.58 m)**
Length: **79 ft 6 in (24.23 m)**
Height: **20 ft 11 in (6.37 m)**
Weight: **80,000 lb (36,287 kg) (Loaded)**
Cruising speed: **210 mph (338 km/h)**
Ceiling: **28,800 ft (8,780 m)**
Range: **3,630 miles (5,840 km)**
Crew: **4**
Passengers: **24–32**

maximum range which was reduced to 2,800 miles (4,500 km). Two Tudor 2 prototypes were ordered, followed by orders from the government for ten and 30 aircraft of each series respectively. All of these went to BOAC. In April 1945 a further ten Tudor 1s were requested, while BOAC, Qantas and SAA, ordered another 49 Tudor 2s for joint use.

The large four-engined aeroplane had quite a different fate in store for it than that promised by the original paper design. The Tudor 1 prototype flew for the first time on June 14, 1945. It was then put through a long series of

ests and trials which revealed serious problems with its longitudinal stability, and forced the technicians to design new tail surfaces. These modifications considerably delayed the completion of the aircraft. Further delays ensued after the request by BOAC to make at least 300 changes to the design in order to bring the aircraft completely in line with its requirements. Slightly less than three months after the appearance of the fourth production aircraft on April 11, 1947, the British company decided that the Tudor 1 was unable to meet its requirements on the North Atlantic routes and the order was cancelled. Six production aircraft (modified in versions 4 and 4B, with the payload increased to 32 passengers) were offered to British South American Airways, which used them until early 1949 on its flights to South America. During the latter years of service they were, however, only used for transporting freight and mail.

A version deriving from the Tudor 2 was also developed for BSAA. This aeroplane, which had made its maiden

Aircraft: **Avro 689 Tudor 2**
Manufacturer: **A. V. Roe and Co. Ltd.**
Type: **Civil transport**
Year: **1946**
Engines: **Four Rolls-Royce Merlin 621, V-12, water-cooled, 1,770 hp each**
Wingspan: **120 ft 0 in (36.58 m)**
Length: **105 ft 7 in (32.18 m)**
Height: **24 ft 3 in (7.39 m)**
Weight: **80,000 lb (36,288 kg) (Loaded)**
Cruising speed: **285 mph (459 km/h)**
Ceiling: **28,600 ft (8,720 m)**
Range: **2,200 miles (3,740 km)**
Crew: **2–4**
Passengers: **40–60**

flight on March 10, 1946, also revealed the same serious problems as the Tudor 1. It had been refused by Qantas and SAA, which preferred to equip with American-made aircraft. The order for 79 aircraft was therefore, reduced first to 50 and then to 18 aeroplanes. From these it was decided to produce a version for 44 passengers to be supplied to BSAA called the Tudor 5. Six aircraft were completed and delivered from 1948 onwards. One was soon converted to the transportation of liquid cargo and the other five gradually followed the same path and were used in the Berlin airlift.

105

Auster J/1 Autocrat

Among the first designs for civil light aircraft in the post-war period, the Auster J/1 Autocrat was the forbear of a prolific and widespread family of small aeroplanes. These aeroplanes made a decisive contribution to the rebirth of private flying in post-war Great Britain. The Auster J/1 Autocrat's development got under way in the latter years of the war with the intention of producing a more economical but no less versatile version of the Auster aerial observation model, which was a monoplane that had been made for the armed forces. The prototype made its maiden flight in 1945 and on January 1 of the following year made a symbolic flight between Cardiff and Filton to celebrate the re-opening of private air traffic after the war years. This was fairly similar to its predecessor but with a slightly modified fuselage. The Auster J/1 was very successful in terms of production, and 420 examples were completed by the end of 1947.

Aircraft: **Auster J/1 Autocrat**
Manufacturer: **Auster Aircraft Ltd.**
Type: **Light transport**
Year: **1945**
Engine: **One Blackburn Cirrus Minor 2, with 4 straight cylinders, air-cooled, 100 hp**
Wingspan: **36 ft 0 in (10.97 m)**
Length: **23 ft 5 in (7.14 m)**
Height: **6 ft 6 in (1.98 m)**
Weight: **1,850 lb (839 kg) (Loaded)**
Cruising speed: **100 mph (160 km/h)**
Ceiling **15,000 ft (4,750 m)**
Range: **500 miles (805 km)**
Crew: **1**
Passengers: **2–3**

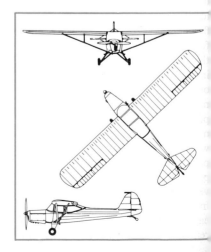

Miles M.57 Aerovan

This small twin-engined light transport aeroplane was one of the most useful all-round models in postwar civil aviation. It was economical, tough, versatile and capable of carrying either passengers or goods. The Miles M.57 Aerovan was designed in 1944 in anticipation of the future demand for short-range aircraft capable of operating in the sector of carrying awkward loads. The prototype made its maiden flight on January 26, 1945 and was followed by a second one in March of the following year. Its success was instant. Seven production aircraft were ordered in 1946 and followed by 39 more in 1947, called Aerovan 4. In practical terms these aircraft were the nucleus of the firm's production and were most widely used by small companies specializing in the transport of passengers or freight. There followed a very small number of series 5 and 6 models, modified respectively in the engines and wing. The Aerovans remained in service until the 1950s.

Aircraft: **Miles M.57 Aerovan 1**
Manufacturer: **Miles Aircraft Ltd.**
Type: **Light transport**
Year: **1945**
Engines: **Two Blackburn Cirrus Major 3, 4 straight cylinders, 155 hp each**
Wingspan: **50 ft 0 in (15.24 m)**
Length: **36 ft 0 in (10.97 m)**
Height: **13 ft 6 in (4.11 m)**
Weight: **5,800 lb (2,631 kg) (Loaded)**
Cruising speed: **110 mph (177 km/h)**
Ceiling: **13,250 ft (4,040 m)**
Range: **400 miles (644 km)**
Crew: **1–2**
Passengers: **6–9**

de Havilland D.H.104 Dove 1

The first post-war de Havilland was linked in its concept to the D.H.89 Dragon Rapide, the last of the successful family of light transport models made in the 1930s. Its immortal predecessor, of which 737 were built and many are still being kept busy after more than 40 years since the maiden flight of the prototype, gave the de Havilland D.H.104 Dove the same usefulness, versatility and commercial success. More than 500 examples of this small twin-engined aeroplane left the production line from 1946 onwards. They were popular not only in Great Britain but also abroad, in transport versions, executive versions and versions for other aerial work.

The Dove made its maiden flight on September 25, 1945, soon after the end of the Second World War. It was a low-winged monoplane of entirely metal construction, with a retractable nose-wheel undercarriage. The broad fuselage could accommodate eight passengers and two crew. It was fitted with a pair of de Havilland Gipsy Queen engines, each of which drove a three-bladed metal propeller which could rotate in reverse. The successor of the renowned Rapide was officially presented on October 29 at Farnborough and subsequently went through the schedule of tests and finishing touches. In the course of these trials it became necessary to modify the tailplane on several occasions, with the aim of eliminating a certain tendency towards instability in specific flying conditions. The appearance of a second prototype allowed mass-production to go ahead. Commercial success was immediate despite the high cost of the aircraft and the adverse effect of two fatal accidents. These accidents caused the second prototype and the first production model to be destroyed, on August 14, 1946 and March 13, 1947 respectively. The Dove was of greatest interest to foreign purchasers, even though initially it was

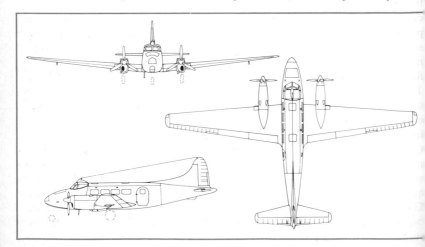

used in small numbers by a few British companies specializing in charter and private flights.

To increase interest on foreign markets an executive version was made in 1948. It was called Dove 2 and fitted out to carry six passengers. This joined the main production line and both versions became the object of a continuous series of improvements, which made them more and more competitive. In particular the modifications concerned the engines which, with their power increased in subsequent versions, gave rise to noticeable improvements in all-round performance. The first modified version was introduced in 1952 and gave rise respectively to series 1B and 2B. Two 70-4 type engines, producing 340 hp, were installed, in the place of the Gipsy Queen 70-3 engines. The second modification made in 1953 was more substantial and produced the series 5 and 6 Doves. These aircraft had new Gipsy Queen 70 Mk.2 engines, each producing 380 hp and were used respectively for passenger transport

Aircraft: **de Havilland D.H.104 Dove 1**
Manufacturer: **de Havilland Aircraft Co. Ltd.**
Type: **Light transport**
Year: **1945**
Engines: **Two de Havilland Gipsy Queen 70-3, 6 straight cylinders, air-cooled, 330 hp each**
Wingspan: **57 ft 0 in (17.37 m)**
Length: **39 ft 4 in (11.99 m)**
Height: **13 ft 0 in (3.96 m)**
Weight: **8,500 lb (3,855 kg) (Loaded)**
Cruising speed: **200 mph at 8,500 ft (322 km/h at 2,590 m)**
Ceiling: **18,500 ft (5,640 m)**
Range: **500 miles (805 km)**
Crew: **2**
Passengers: **8**

and executive purposes. The series 5 and 6 Doves were the best of the entire production, with a weight at take-off increased to 8,800 pounds (3,992 kg) and the payload increased by 20% over distances of about 500 miles (800 km). As a consequence, most of the Doves in the preceding series were modified to these standards.

The success of the D.H.104 was rounded off by a military version, the Mk.4, which was ordered in large numbers by the R.A.F. and called the Devon C.1. From 1948 onwards the R.A.F. used 40 of them in its Communications squadrons.

Handley Page Halifax

The real heyday in the commercial career of the Handley Page Halifax was during the Berlin airlift when more than 8,000 flights were made at an average load of 14,330 pounds (6,500 kg). This aircraft was one of the best strategic bombers in the Second World War and the second most important one in the Royal Air Force. Just as the Lancaster managed to make a considerable contribution to the rebirth of the British airlines in the immediate postwar period, so the Halifax played an important role in civil transportation at the end of the 1940s. It was nevertheless something of a secondary role. The Halifax 8 and 9 models which were the last two mass-produced series developed to meet the demands of R.A.F. Transport Command, were modified for commercial use and used mainly for cargo. Only 12 Halifax 8s, rechristened Halton 1, were actually used for passengers by BOAC. These passenger flights were between summer 1946 and summer 1947 when the delivery delays with the Avro Tudor forced the British company to use everything that was going. On the London–Accra (Ghana) route it used the 'civilianized' bombers for about a year. They had been adapted to carrying ten passengers and about 8,000 pounds (3,600 kg) of freight and mail.

The first flight by a demilitarized Halifax was not made by an aircraft expressly designed for transport, but by a veteran Mk.III adapted for the occasion. This was on May 26, 1946 when it set out to repatriate 12 Australians. Christened *Waltzing Matilda* and bearing the civil registration G-AGXA (though still wearing camouflage) this aeroplane was the forbear of all the civil Halifaxes which were to be used in the next three years. The first Halifax 8s appeared in the autumn of 1946 and six were bought by the London Aero and Motor Service Ltd for transporting cargo, particularly perishable goods. This was the start of a long series of orders by numerous specialized operators, whose com-

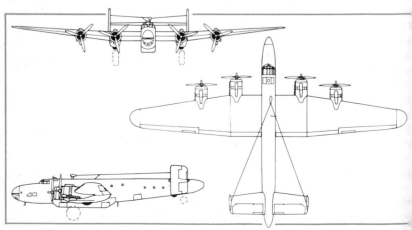

mercial activities fanned out from Great Britain to Africa, Asia and Australia. Among these the major ones were the Lancashire Aircraft Corporation, Bond Air Services Ltd, and Westminster Airways Ltd. The Halifaxes showed themselves very versatile in the role of all-round cargo transporters because of the large freight pannier beneath the fuselage.

In 1948 after a brief period as a passenger aircraft (although carrying freight as well) with BOAC, these aircraft started on their downward path. The huge demand for goods transported by air, which had hallmarked the two preceding years, started to reduce and with it so did the role of the Halifaxes. Its last chance came with the huge concentration of energies entailed by the Berlin airlift. All the available aircraft were brought into use, including 41 Halifaxes called in from a wide variety of sources. They were used quite intensively and in some cases exhaustingly for both men and machines. Nine aircraft were destroyed, but the achievement was a

Aircraft: **Handley Page H.P.70 Halifax 8**
Manufacturer: **Handley Page Ltd.**
Type: **Civil transport**
Year: **1946**
Engines: **Four Bristol Hercules 100, radial with 14 air-cooled cylinders, 1,675 hp each**
Wingspan: **103 ft 8 in (31.60 m)**
Length: **73 ft 7 in (22.43 m)**
Height: **20 ft 8 in (6.30 m)**
Weight: **65,000 lb (29,482 kg) (Loaded)**
Cruising speed: **260 mph at 15,000 ft (418 km/h at 4,570 m)**
Ceiling: **21,000 ft (6,400 m)**
Range: **2,530 miles (4,070 km)**
Crew: **3**
Payload: **10,500 lb (4,763 kg)**
Passengers: **10**

brilliant one and the Halifaxes contributed greatly to the success of the whole operation.

In the latter half of 1949 the surviving models started to be scrapped. One of the last Halifaxes (G-AKEC christened *Air Voyager*) managed to compete in the Daily Express Air Race on September 20, 1950 and came in 24th at an average speed of almost 280 mph (450 km/h). This was a fine performance and a further confirmation of the soundness of these aircraft, born way back in 1937 and used for many different tasks.

Bristol Type 170 Wayfarer/Freighter

Ugly, but extremely tough and versatile. Embodying these features, the Bristol Type 170 made its mark on post-war British air transport, and was much more successful than expected. The service which without doubt made it most popular was as a car ferry across the Channel, which started on July 13, 1948. The idea was to load two vehicles through the convenient front-loading ramp inside the large fuselage of the twin-engined aeroplane and accommodate their passengers in the central cabin. It was an auspicious idea. The prospect of being able to reach the continent in less than half an hour's smooth flying-time, free from the annoyance and uncertainty of crossing the Channel by boat, turned out to seduce many tourists and travellers, and the service got off to a strong start. In 1958, ten years later, the Bristol 170s belonging to Silver City Airways (the company which had thought up and inaugurated this special type of service) had travelled some 125,000 times to and fro across the Channel, carrying 215,000 cars and 759,000 passengers.

The design for the Type 170 had been conceived by Bristol in the last years of the war. The original idea had been to make an aircraft for military transport purposes, with good structural qualities, a large carrying capacity, excellent versatility and low running costs. The end of the war meant that an aircraft of this type was virtually of no use to the Royal Air Force, but the Bristol technicians decided nonetheless to go ahead with the project and converted it to commercial use. This concept was supported by the conviction, which turned out to be well-founded, that the market would be characterized by a huge demand for transport aircraft after the war.

On December 2, 1945, the first Bristol Type 170 prototype emerged from its hangar and revealed itself as a

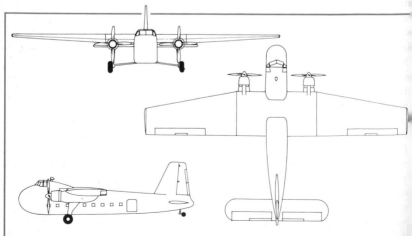

huge high-winged twin-engined type, with a large fuselage with access through a pair of doors at the forward end, and a fixed undercarriage. The second prototype made its maiden flight on April 4, 1946, and unlike the first one, had been fitted out as an all-passenger version with 34 seats. All the subsequent production was born out of these two aeroplanes (170 Freighter 1 and 170 Wayfarer 2A), and divided into cargo and passenger types. The version which was most successful, and went on to corner most of the production line, was the former, however. Only 16 Bristol Wayfarer 2As were built, most of which were exported and many of these were subsequently converted to cargo use. Following this commercial success, Bristol embarked on a programme of constant up-dating of its aircraft so as to keep it competitive. In 1948 the first of the series 21 Freighters appeared with a modified and strengthened wing, and fitted with more powerful engines. These improvements made it capable of being swiftly adapted to freight transportation. It

Aircraft: **Bristol Type 170 Wayfarer 2A**
Manufacturer: **Bristol Aeroplane Co. Ltd.**
Type: **Civil transport**
Year: **1946**
Engines: **Two Bristol Hercules 632, radial with 14 air-cooled cylinders, 1,675 hp each**
Wingspan: **108 ft 0 in (32.93 m)**
Length: **68 ft 4 in (20.83 m)**
Height: **21 ft 8 in (6.60 m)**
Weight: **37,000 lb (16,783 kg) (Loaded)**
Cruising speed: **163 mph at 10,000 ft (262 km/h at 3,050 m)**
Ceiling: **22,000 ft (6,705 m)**
Range: **300 miles (482 km)**
Crew: **3**
Passengers: **32–48**

was these aircraft which, on July 13, inaugurated the car ferry service across the Channel. Total production reached 92 models, and these were followed by a further 93 in series 31, with a considerably modified tailplane. This modification had shown itself to be necessary in order to eliminate a certain structural weakness which, on May 6, 1949 and March 2, 1950, had caused the loss of two Freighter 21s in the Channel. The final version which appeared in 1953 was the series 32, 15 of which were built. They had a lengthened nose, which made it possible to transport a third vehicle.

Vickers Viking

In the postwar years the British aeronautical industry failed to achieve its potential in the sector of commercial aircraft with large capacities and long-range. However, they made up for this in a brilliant way in the field of short-to-medium range transport. The Vickers Viking was one of the most remarkable examples. By the latter months of 1947 a total of 161 aircraft had been completed and they had been put to very intensive use. Not only were they put into service on the European routes handled by BEA, but they were also used by companies in Africa, Argentina, Denmark and Ireland. The major operator was British European Airways which kept the Vikings in service until 1954, when it started to replace them with the turbo-prop Viscounts. In eight years of service the Vikings flew more than 65,000,000 miles (105,000,000 kms) and carried 2,748,000 passengers. Their career continued long after 1954 in the hands of many charter companies which

purchased the models withdrawn b BEA.

The Viking project was launched i 1944 at the request of the Britis government. They wanted a twi engined transport aeroplane bui which could use the most possible par of the Wellington bomber, particular the wings, with their distinctive geodet structure, the engines and th undercarriage. The first of the thre prototypes made its maiden flight o June 22, 1945 and was followed by th other two during that year. The thre aircraft underwent an exhaustive cyc of tests and operational trials afte which an initial order for 19 aircra was placed by BOAC. In the followin year there was another order for 1 units, modified at the request of th company. These aircraft gave rise t the series 1 and compared with the pr vious models (later called Viking 1A they differed mainly in terms of th wing, which was redesigned an covered entirely in metal. On August (

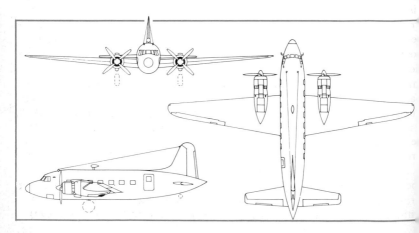

946 the prototype of the most
roduced version, the Viking 1B, made
s maiden flight. It was then modified
y lengthening the forward section of
1e fuselage to increase the capacity by
1ree passengers and 113 of these were
ompleted in all.

BEA quickly put the new aircraft
1to service and by the end of 1947 the
'ikings had replaced the ancient DC-
s on the main routes to France,
3elgium, Switzerland, Holland, Spain,
3ermany, Ireland and Norway. These
ircraft showed themselves to be
replaceable. In their last years of
ervice with BEA colours, the
ompany made a series of modifica-
ons to them, as a result of which it
1anaged to increase the capacity to 36
assengers. In addition to considerably
nproving the running costs, this made
possible to lower the cost of tickets on
ertain flights and thus introduce
roader and more accessible tariffs.

In its long career the Viking had a
pecial moment of glory. It was the first
ritish commercial aeroplane to fly
ith jet propulsion. This modification

Aircraft: **Vickers Viking 1 B**
Manufacturer: **Vickers-Armstrong Ltd.**
Type: **Civil transport**
Year: **1946**
Engines: **Two Bristol Hercules 634, radial
with 14 air-cooled cylinders, 1,690 hp
each**
Wingspan: **89 ft 3 in (27.12 m)**
Length: **65 ft 4 in (19.91 m)**
Height: **19 ft 6 in (5.94 m)**
Weight: **34,000 lb (15,422 kg) (Loaded)**
Cruising speed: **210 mph at 6,000 ft (338
km/h at 1,830 m)**
Ceiling: **23,750 ft (7,240 m)**
Range: **1,620 miles (2,607 km)**
Crew: **5**
Passengers: **24–36**

was made to the 107th model built and
consisted of replacing the two radial
Hercules engines with two Rolls-Royce
Nene turbo-jets, which produced a
thrust of 5,000 pounds (2,270 kg). This
was clearly an experimental aeroplane
but the trials produced excellent
results. Three months after the first
flight (April 6, 1948), on July 25, 1948,
the aircraft flew from London to Paris
in 34 minutes and 7 seconds at an
average speed of 348 mph (560 km/h),
beating all previous records for the
flight. Registered G-AJPH it was later
reconverted to a Viking 1B and used by
the Cunard Eagle charter company.

Handley Page H.P.R.1 Marathon

The Handley Page H.P.R.1 Marathon was certainly not a fortunate aircraft. Its unlucky fate started in 1948 with the bankruptcy of the company which had designed it, Miles Aircraft Ltd. After production had been taken over by Handley Page Ltd there followed a drastic reduction of orders from British airlines, who considered the aircraft ill-suited to their requirements. As a result the career of this small four-engined type ended up as a training aircraft with the R.A.F. and with numerous, mainly foreign, small companies, which used it during the 1950s. One of the outstanding features of the project was the version Marathon 2 which made its maiden flight as a prototype on July 23, 1949 (the first Marathon 1 had made its first flight on May 19, 1946). The Marathon 2 had been modified by the installation of two Armstrong Siddeley Mamba turbo-prop engines each producing 1,010 hp.

Aircraft: **Handley Page H.P.R.1 Marathon 1**
Manufacturer: **Handley Page (Reading) Ltd.**
Type: **Civil transport**
Year: **1946**
Engines: **Four de Havilland Gipsy Queen 71, 6 straight cylinders, air-cooled, 340 hp each**
Wingspan: **65 ft 0 in (19.81 m)**
Length: **52 ft 1 in (15.88 m)**
Height: **13 ft 7 in (4.14 m)**
Weight: **18,800 lb (8,165 kg) (Loaded)**
Cruising speed: **201 mph (323 km/h)**
Ceiling: **18,400 ft (4,710 m)**
Range: **723 miles (1,160 km)**
Crew: **2**
Passengers: **18–22**

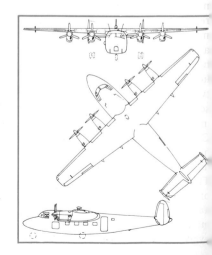

Airspeed A.S.65 Consul

Aircraft: **Airspeed A.S.65 Consul**
Manufacturer: **Airspeed Ltd.**
Type: **Light transport**
Year: **1946**
Engines: **Two Armstrong Siddeley Cheetah 10, radial with 7 air-cooled cylinders, 395 hp each**
Wingspan: **53 ft 4 in (16.25 m)**
Length: **35 ft 4 in (10.77 m)**
Height: **10 ft 1½ in (3.09 m)**
Weight: **8,250 lb (3,742 kg) (Loaded)**
Cruising speed: **156 mph (251 km/h)**
Ceiling: **19,000 ft (5,790 m)**
Range: **900 miles (1,448 km)**
Crew: **2**
Passengers: **6**

In the immediate postwar period the Airspeed company developed from the Oxford military trainer a considerably modified civil version. This new aircraft was redesignated the A.S.65 Consul. The prototype made its maiden flight in March 1946 and was the forbear of more than 150 aircraft. Although it retained the main components of the military trainer, the A.S.65 Consul had a redesigned fuselage capable of holding six passengers with their luggage. In this new form the versatile twin-engined model echoed in the civil sector the great success already earned in the military field. In fact the A.S.65 Consul barely managed to meet the huge demand for light transport aeroplanes in the postwar civil market. The Consuls were purchased by a host of small companies in Great Britain and abroad. With the appearance of more modern aircraft more became available for the domestic market.

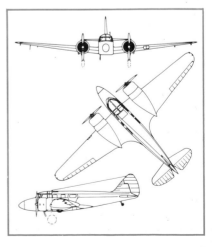

Short S.25/V Sandringham

The flying-boat sector of air transport was saved despite the crisis of reconstruction that afflicted British companies in the immediate postwar period. The long industrial tradition in this sector and the experience gained in the 1930s with the prestigious routes across the Empire managed to keep the concept of the flying-boat alive even in a period of clearly defined decline hallmarked by the powerful expansion of commercial land aircraft. The Short Sandringham was one of the best examples of this policy. It was derived directly from the famous Sunderland maritime reconnaissance aeroplane and enjoyed almost two years of intensive use on the longest routes handled by BOAC. In addition it was used by numerous small specialized companies, notably in Australia and Central America. As late as 1976 a venerable Sandringham 4 was still flying in the Virgin Islands under the flag of the Antilles Air Boats Company.

The first transformation of a Sunderland into a Sandringham took place in 1945. From 1942 onward BOAC had been running a whole fleet of Sunderlands which had been partially demilitarized and adapted to passenger and mail transport. The company now decided to make the fullest possible commercial use of this aircraft's good qualities. The result was that the Short company was given one of the Sunderland Mk.III model (registered G-AGKX and christened *Himalaya*) by BOAC and asked to convert it into a fully fledged civil aeroplane. The aeroplane was to be capable of accommodating 24 passengers by day and 16 on night flights. Thus the Sandringham 1 was born. It was outwardly modified both fore and aft in a way similar to the Short S.26 and inside the hull there were two decks, giving large areas which included a dining-room and a bar. This aircraft was the only one of its kind. It was followed by three 45 passenger capacity Series 2 aircraft

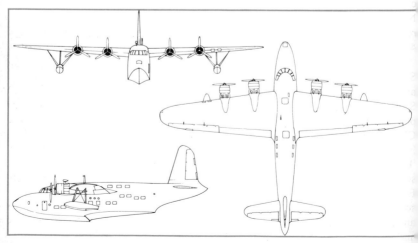

ordered by the Dodero Company of Argentina); two 31 passenger capacity Sandringham 3 models; and three 30 passenger capacity Sandringham 4 models. These aeroplanes were all exported to South America and New Zealand (the three Series 4 going to Tasman Empire Airways Ltd) and most of them were delivered directly with British registration by BOAC crews. During one such flight, on November 25, 1945, Buenos Aires was reached in a remarkable flying time of 45 hours and 47 minutes.

The British firm took charge of the Sandringhams in the last two Series, 5 and 7, from 1947 onwards. The nine Sandringham 5s (which held 22 passengers) formed the 'Plymouth Class' and the three Sandringham 7s (which held 30 passengers) formed the 'Bermuda Class'. They remained in service until 1949 on routes to the Far East and Australia. They were then all sold to various private operators, among which were Aquila Airways and the Australian Ansett Airways.

Aircraft: **Short S.25/V Sandringham 4**
Manufacturer: **Short Brothers Ltd.**
Type: **Civil transport**
Year: **1946**
Engines: **Four Pratt & Whitney R-1830-90D Twin Wasp, radial with 14 air-cooled cylinders, 1,200 hp each**
Wingspan: **112 ft 9 in (34.37 m)**
Length: **86 ft 3 in (26.29 m)**
Height: **32 ft 10½ in (10.00 m)**
Weight: **56,000 lb (25,400 kg) (Loaded)**
Cruising speed: **221 mph (356 km/h)**
Ceiling: **21,300 ft (6,500 m)**
Range: **2,410 miles (3,880 km)**
Crew: **5**
Passengers: **30**

It was in fact from Ansett Airways that Antilles Air Boats purchased the last Sandringham 4 in late 1974. This aircraft was one of the three used by Tasman Empire Airways Ltd and had been transferred to Ansett Airways in 1950. Rechristened *Southern Cross*, this large flying-boat was flown to the Virgin Islands by Charles F. Blair, the chairman of the Antilles Air Boats company. From Rose Bay it went to its new base at St. Croix on December 9 thus ending an historic journey of more than 12,000 miles (19,000 km) with no mishap whatsoever.

Short S.45 Solent

The age of the commercial flying-boat ended once and for all in Great Britain on November 10, 1950. The aeroplane which marked this date and which was also the last flying-boat used for civil transport was the Short Solent. BOAC used it from May 1948 mainly on its routes to South Africa, but the commercial career of the Solent extended well beyond 1950. The private company Aquila Airways which, since 1948 had opened a flight to Madeira, and specialized in services with flying-boats kept the Solent in service until September 30, 1958. Not unlike the Sandringham the Short S.45 Solent was derived from a larger and improved version of the maritime reconnaissance Sunderland model called the Seaford, which had been cancelled in 1945. In 1946 one of the small number of Seafords produced for the Royal Air Force was loaned to BOAC so that it could be put through trials for possible commercial use. There followed an order for 12 aircraft,

to be delivered with more powerfu Bristol Hercules engines and a two-tier interior structure to hold 30 passengers. The first of these aircraft, which were designated Solent 2, made its maiden flight on November 11, 1946 and the last followed less than 18 months later, on April 8, 1948. Although outwardly the Solent did not betray its direct descendance from the illustrious family of Short seaplanes, it incorporated numerous modifications and improvements when compared with its predecessors. Apart from the engines, the principal structural differences lay in the redesigned tailplane and lower section of the hull.

A month after the delivery of the last aircraft ordered, BOAC started using its fleet of Solents by replacing the elderly Yorks which were operating on the route to South Africa with the Solents. It was undeniably a long flight and entailed many stops at Marseilles, Augusta, Cairo and Port Bell on Lake Victoria. However the large flying-boats made it possible to ensure a safer and more comfortable service with the large cabin available to passengers, not

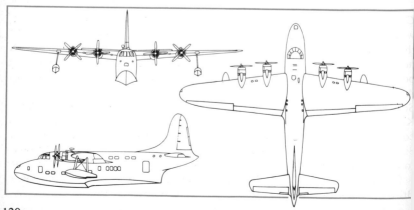

Short S.45 Solent 2 – 1946

to mention the dining-room and bar on board. Its success was such that in 1948 BOAC asked the Short company to convert another six Seafords, built for the Royal Air Force, into Solent 3 models. These aeroplanes were to be used to bolster the service to South Africa and were ordered with an interior design which would accommodate 36 passengers. Outwardly they differed from the Solent 2 solely in the addition of a pair of small rectangular windows in the rear section of the upper level of the fuselage.

The first Solent 3 was christened *City of London* on May 5, 1949 and went into service ten days later. With the arrival of the other aircraft these new aeroplanes not only made it possible to extend and improve the African flights, but also to replace the Sandringhams on the flights to Karachi. Later BOAC decided to convert five Series 2 models to Solent 3s, and these were accordingly added to the revitalized fleet.

Shortly after the decision by the British company to completely stop its

Aircraft: **Short S.45 Solent 2**
Manufacturer: **Short Brothers Ltd.**
Type: **Civil transport**
Year: **1946**
Engines: **Four Bristol Hercules 637, radial with 14 air-cooled cylinders, 1,690 hp each**
Wingspan: **112 ft 9 in (34.37 m)**
Length: **88 ft 7 in (27.10 m)**
Height: **34 ft 3 in (10.44 m)**
Weight: **78,000 lb (35,380 kg) (Loaded)**
Cruising speed: **236 mph (376 km/h)**
Ceiling: **15,500 ft (4,730 m)**
Range: **2,040 miles (3,290 km)**
Crew: **7**
Passengers: **30**

flying-boat service, the aircraft used to date were mostly sold to American and Australian operators. One Solent 3 went to Tasman Empire Airways Ltd which was already using four 44 passenger Solent 4s on the long route between Sydney and Auckland. Two of these aircraft were subsequently purchased by Aquila Airways and added to the other Solents and Sandringhams being used by that company. On September 30, 1958 only three Solents remained in service and despite an attempt to re-open the flight to Madeira, these aircraft too were finally removed from service.

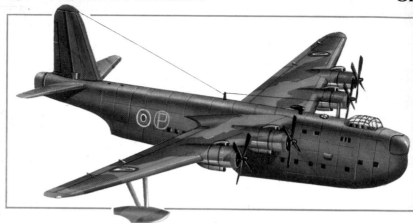

Short S.35 Shetland

This was to have been one of the last great flying-boats but it never managed to get beyond the prototype stage. The Short S.35 Shetland came into being as the result of a specific request issued in 1940 for a very long-range maritime reconnaissance aircraft. However, the progress of the war, together with the long period of time it took to design the aircraft caused this request to be modified. When the prototype took to the air for the first time on December 14, 1944, it had been decided to turn the Short S.35 into a military transport aircraft, but it was destroyed in January 1946 by an accidental fire. Despite this the project went ahead, although it was decided to turn the aeroplane into a civil transport type. A second prototype, called the Shetland 2, took to the air for the first time on September 17, 1947.

Aircraft: **Short S.35 Shetland 1**
Manufacturer: **Short Brothers Ltd.**
Type: **Maritime reconnaissance**
Year: **1947**
Engines: **Four Bristol Centaurus XI, radial with 18 air-cooled cylinders, 250 hp each**
Wingspan: **150 ft 4 in (45.82 m)**
Length: **108 ft 0 in (32.94 m)**
Height: **38 ft 8 in (11.80 m)**
Weight: **130,000 lb (59,020 kg) (Loaded)**
Cruising speed: **183 mph at 8,000 ft (295 km/h at 2,440 m)**
Ceiling: **17,000 ft (5,200 m)**
Range: **4,650 miles (7,440 km)**
Crew: **11**
Payload: **2,000 lb (907.2 kg) bombs/mines/ depth charges**

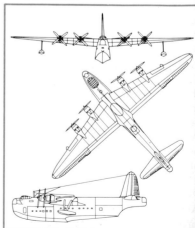

Airspeed A.S.57 Ambassador

Almost six and a half years of service on BEA's European routes, from March 13, 1952 to July 30, 1958, carrying more than 2,500,000 passengers. These are the main achievements of the busy career of the Airspeed A.S.57 Ambassador, which together with the Vickers Viking, made it possible for the British airlines to come to life again in the postwar years in the short-to-medium range sector. The first prototype took to the air for the first time on July 10, 1947 and was followed a little more than one year later by the second. The second, the Ambassador 2, was the principal production type. BEA received the first of the 20 aircraft ordered on August 22, 1951 and inaugurated its service to Paris on March 13, 1952. The Ambassadors were the last piston-engined aircraft to be used by BEA.

Aircraft: **Airspeed A.S.57 Ambassador 2**
Manufacturer: **Airspeed Division of de Havilland Aircraft Co. Ltd.**
Type: **Civil transport**
Year: **1948**
Engines: **Two Bristol Centaurus 661, radial with 18 air-cooled cylinders, 2,625 hp each**
Wingspan: **115 ft 0 in (35.05 m)**
Length: **82 ft 0 in (24.99 m)**
Height: **18 ft 3 in (5.55 m)**
Weight: **52,500 lb (23,814 kg) (Loaded)**
Cruising speed: **288 mph (463 km/h)**
Ceiling: **34,500 ft (10,500 m)**
Range: **1,550 miles (2,494 km)**
Crew: **3**
Passengers: **47–60**

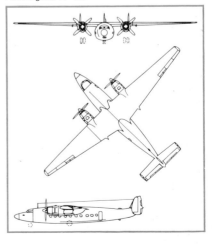

Percival P.50 Prince

In the sector of private aircraft one of the soundest products of the British industry in the late 1940s was the Percival P.50 Prince. This was a fairly tough and versatile aeroplane, despite the fact that it was not made in large quantities. However before it gave way to an improved military version, it enjoyed considerable success particularly on the export market, and proved itself to be an excellent 'all-round' transport type. It was also used for aerial surveys and as an executive aeroplane.

The origins of the P.50 date back directly to a project carried out by Percival Aircraft Ltd in the immediate postwar period. This was the P.48 Merganser, a small twin-engined model with a high wing which could carry five passengers and had been designed with an attentive eye on their comfort. A delay in the delivery of the de Havilland Gipsy Queen engines temporarily stopped the aircraft being completed, but eventually in May 1947, the first and only P.48 took to the air. The

success of the trials encouraged the designers to improve the aeroplane by producing a larger and more powerful version. This was called the Percival P.50 Prince and it made its debut on May 13, 1948. Compared with its direct predecessor the new aeroplane retained the general twin-engined, high wing structure, but was considerably larger in size. It was powered by a pair of radial Alvis Leonides engines producing 520 hp each, almost twice as powerful as the de Havilland Gipsy Queen engines.

The positive results of the tests and trials persuaded the Percival Company to launch a production line for ten aircraft. The first of these was called Prince 1 and registered G-ALFZ. It set off in March 1949 on a long flight across Africa, covering a total of 25,000 miles (40,000 kms). The purpose of this feat was not only to demonstrate the qualities of the aeroplane to potential customers but also to assess its operating features in tropical conditions. A similar flight was made by the second aircraft completed in the direction of the Middle East and India. Shortly afterwards another air

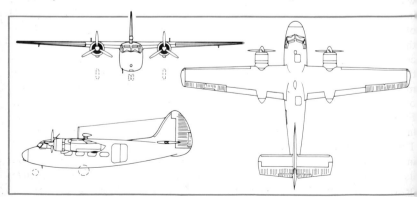

G-ALFZ

craft was fitted out specifically for survcy work and aerial photography.

The experience gained from these testing trial flights led to the production of a second version, called Prince 2, in which the structure was generally reinforced and there were detailed modifications to the forward section of the fuselage. Orders started to arrive: four from a small company operating passenger flights in Brazil; another three from a large oil company. Its commercial success increased in 1952 with the appearance of the Prince 3 which was further strengthened, improved and boosted by the adoption of a more powerful 550 hp version of the Alvis Leonides engine. The oil company which was already using the three previous aircraft ordered five more and a similar number was ordered by other private operators. Further improvements appeared in the last two Series, Prince 4 and Prince 6. These improvements concerned the instruments, engines, and the structure itself, which was reinforced to carry heavier payloads. In addition the

Aircraft: **Percival P.50 Prince 1**
Manufacturer: **Percival Aircraft Ltd.**
Type: **Light transport**
Year: **1948**
Engines: **Two Alvis Leonides 501/4, radial with 9 air-cooled cylinders, 520 hp each**
Wingspan: **56 ft 0 in (17.07 m)**
Length: **42 ft 10 in (13.06 m)**
Height: **16 ft 1 in (4.90 m)**
Weight: **10,650 lb (4,830 kg) (Loaded)**
Cruising speed: **179 mph at 5,000 ft (288 km/h at 1,525 m)**
Ceiling: **24,800 ft (7,560 m)**
Range: **1,260 miles (2,028 km)**
Crew: **2**
Passengers: **8–10**

Percival Prince 6 had its nose considerably modified and lengthened.

More important, for the career of the P.50 Prince than the quantity produced, was the type of use to which it was put. It had a very busy life doing taxing work in extremely harsh areas and climatic conditions. From Europe to Africa, Asia and South America, this versatile twin-engined aeroplane showed itself to be tireless for many years. Although commercial production finished in 1953, production of the Pembroke military descendant, continued until 1958 and the R.A.F. used it throughout the 1960s, and 1970s.

125

Handley Page Hermes

This large four-engined transport aircraft became best-known for the use made of its military version by the Royal Air Force. This version was called the Hastings and 150 were made in all. The role played by the Hermes in the BOAC company in the early 1950s was also important. In fact 25 aircraft were made for the British airline, which started using them in 1950 on its flights to African countries and kept them in service until 1952. The Handley Page H.P.81 Hermes was clearly a transitional aircraft, but after being sold by BOAC, it enjoyed a second busy life in the hands of several private companies specializing in charter flights.

The original design for the H.P.68 Hermes 1 had been started during the Second World War, with the purpose of being used on the commercial routes in the immediate postwar period. The first prototype was not blessed by fate, and on the very day of its maiden flight, December 3, 1945, faulty ailerons caused it to crash and be destroyed. Despite this serious accident which killed Handley Page's chief test-pilot J. R. Talbot, the programme for a military and a civil version went ahead. A second civil prototype, with a distinctively longer fuselage, and designated the H.P.74 Hermes 2, was completed and made its maiden flight on September 2, 1947. This aircraft gave rise to the main commercial production version the H.P.81 Hermes 4. The prototype of the H.P.81 Hermes took to the air a year later on September 5, 1948. BOAC had already ordered 25 aircraft by that time.

While the Hermes 4 prototype was completing its tests and trials, Handley Page prepared two examples of a considerably modified version. This was called the H.P.82 Hermes 5 and was driven by Bristol Theseus turbo-prop engines. It flew for the first time on August 23, 1949. The Hermes 5's were solely experimental aircraft made to test out the new engines and assess

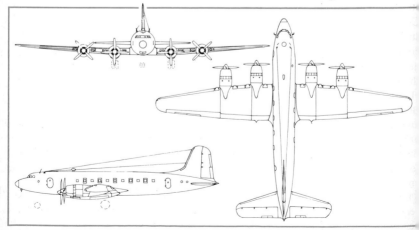

126

heir performance for commercial use nd were the largest turbo-prop aircraft nade to date in Great Britain.

BOAC received its Hermes 4 eroplanes from February 1950 nwards. There followed appropriate rew-training and a series of experimental flights after which they put hem into service, first on the route to Lagos and Accra and then on the route o South Africa. However, their career vas not a long one. In 1952 the Hermes tarted to be replaced by the Canadair C-4. In addition worrying signs of tructural weakness in the wing were coming to light which made it necessary to overhaul and modify all he aircraft in service. Nevertheless the H.P.81 models were transferred from BOAC to various private companies ncluding Airwork Ltd, Skyways Ltd nd Britavia Ltd. Airwork Ltd made he fullest use of these aircraft. The first our aircraft purchased had modified ngines and were called Hermes 4A. They were used to launch regular ervices for military transport in entral Africa. This service was subse-

Aircraft: **Handley Page H.P.81 Hermes 4**
Manufacturer: **Handley Page Ltd.**
Type: **Civil transport**
Year: **1948**
Engines: **Four Bristol Hercules 763, radial with 14 air-cooled cylinders, 2,100 hp each**
Wingspan: **113 ft 0 in (34.44 m)**
Length: **96 ft 10 in (29.51 m)**
Height: **29 ft 0 in (8.84 m)**
Weight: **86,000 lb (39,009 kg) (Loaded)**
Cruising speed: **266 mph at 20,000 ft (428 km/h at 6,100 m)**
Ceiling: **24,500 ft (7,500 m)**
Range: **2,200 miles (3,540 km)**
Crew: **5**
Passengers: **40–78**

quently extended to certain countries in Asia and ended up by carrying some 14,000 passengers a year. A number of the aircraft were lost, some as the result of sabotage.

Among the last services run by the Hermes 4 were those inaugurated by Silver City Airways between Great Britain and France in June 1959. In addition Bahama Airways operated a service between Nassau and Miami. The latter was started at the end of the same year by two H.P.81s converted to carry up to 78 passengers.

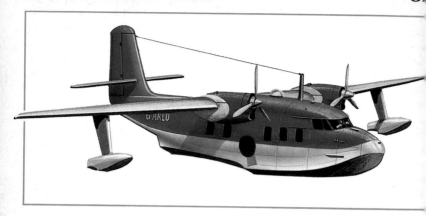

Short S.A.6 Sealand

The only amphibious aircraft manufactured by the British industry in the postwar period, the Short S.A.6 Sealand was destined mainly for the export market. Between 1948 and 1952 just 24 models were built and sold to operators scattered in all four corners of the globe. These operators used them intensively and with great success. The Sealand prototype made its maiden flight on January 22, 1948 and at the end of its trials was joined by the first production aircraft, which were used on long display flights in Europe and in North and South America. On these latter flights they covered more than 50,000 miles (80,000 kms) across the whole of the American continent. Orders arrived from British West Indian Airways, Yugoslovenski Aero Transport, the Norwegian company Vestlandske Luftfartselskap as well as from numerous private operators. They were also used in India and Indonesia.

Aircraft: **Short S.A.6 Sealand**
Manufacturer: **Short Brothers Ltd.**
Type: **Light transport**
Year: **1948**
Engines: **Two de Havilland Gipsy Quee 70–3, with 6 straight, air-coole cylinders, 340 hp each**
Wingspan: **61 ft 6 in (18.75 m)**
Length: **42 ft 2 in (12.85 m)**
Height: **15 ft 0 in (4.57 m)**
Weight: **9,100 lb (4,128 kg) (Loaded)**
Cruising speed: **176 mph (283 km/h)**
Ceiling: **20,800 ft (6,340 m)**
Range: **595 miles (956 km)**
Crew: **2**
Passengers: **5–10**

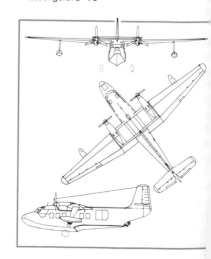

Bristol Type 167 Brabazon

London to New York non-stop, with at least 100 passengers on board, such facts and figures look quite ordinary for any commercial aeroplane today. However, on February 9, 1943, when the technical committee chaired by Lord Brabazon made known its conclusions about the characteristics which British commercial aircraft were to have after the war, such a service was still shrouded in a veil of speculation. It was precisely on the basis of the proposals of the Brabazon Committee that one of the most ambitious and unsuccessful programmes ever carried out by the British aeronautical industry came into being. It led to the construction of the gigantic Bristol 167 Brabazon 1, a technically valid aeroplane, but one which was unusable both in a practical and an economical sense. The only prototype completed flew for at least 400 hours over four years, during which it was used almost exclusively for tests.

The Brabazon Committee was set up on December 23, 1942. Its task was to make a long-term analysis of the civil aeronautical market and define the basic features of future commercial production. Today, more than thirty years later, there are still many historians and technical experts who still criticize the way the technical committee went about its job and consider it superficial. They maintain that of the numerous aircraft produced on the basis of the Committee's recommendations those which were successful were designed in a completely different way from the original specifications. The

Brabazon 1 programme, perhaps because it was launched directly on the basis of the specifications indicated by the committee, was certainly not a success. This was in spite of the wonders worked by the designers and technicians at Bristol to overcome the numerous problems that faced them in the six years which elapsed before the production of the prototype.

The technical committee suggested the construction of the Brabazon 1 basically for two reasons: firstly because of the prestige which would be earned for Great Britain by putting into service the first commercial aircraft capable of flying non-stop from London to New York, and secondly because of the safety and reliability of a service of this type which omitted the need for intermediate landings in Iceland or Newfoundland. In March 1943, with the full backing of the government, the programme was launched and the Bristol company was chosen to carry it out.

This decision was taken with particular consideration of the fact that the Bristol Company had acquired more experience than others in the preliminary studies for a large and very long-range strategic bomber. The range of the bomber was 5,000 miles (8,000 kms) but this project had been abandoned in December 1942. In addition the Bristol Company was producing the most suitable engines and was capable of accommodating the entire construction of the two prototypes requested in its own works. It could also accommodate the future production lines for an anticipated ten aircraft. As a result the Brabazon project was drawn up on the basis of the features already worked out for the bomber: a monoplane with a centrally positioned wing, a long, circular, pressurized fuselage, and engines incorporated within the wing. This last feature was possibly the most radical of the whole project. Eight large Bristol Centaurus radial engines were chosen, each producing 2,500 hp, mounted in pairs with each one driving two three-bladed counter-rotating propellers. With this solution it was calculated that the wind resistance would be reduced by at least 25%. The engines were cooled by means of air intakes on the leading edge of the wing with outlets positioned near the rear edge on the upper and lower surfaces.

The construction of the various structural components and the testing of the numerous systems required a great deal of time. In addition it took a long time to perfect the pressurization plant which entailed complicated tests to check the structure of the fuselage. Further time was needed to design and make the secondary equipment to test the engines. This included the linkage system of the flight instruments and the system which ensured the perfect synchronization of the propellors, so as to avoid any dangerous structural vibration. In addition all the calculations were complicated by the fact that at some future date turbo-props were to be fitted and they involved quite different stresses.

By early 1947, the date that the government's technical authorities had anticipated for the maiden flight, the main components had still not been assembled. Assembly took place in the course of the year, but it was not until January 6, 1949 that the gigantic aircraft was towed out of its hangar to receive the finishing touches and have the last secondary equipment installed. It was still another eight months before the prototype was taken into the air by Bristol's chief test-pilot Bill Pegg. That historic date was September 4, 1949 and during the 25-minute flight there were no technical problems. There was one odd thing in that the huge aeroplane, registered G-AGPW, raised its 95 tons or so into the air at a speed of only about 87 mph (140 km/h) after a run of about 1,500 feet (450 m). The

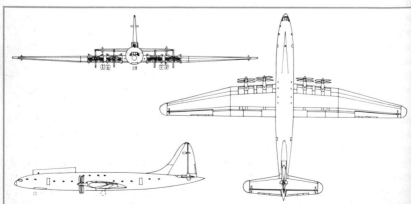

landing was quite smooth at a speed estimated to be slightly faster than that at take-off. Three days later the Brabazon 1 made a second test flight lasting two and a half hours and on September 8 it went on display at Farnborough.

However interest in the aeroplane had already dwindled, not least because of major problems occurring in the construction of the second prototype. These problems were closely linked with the installation of the different engines. The Brabazon 1 was, therefore, used mainly for tests and trials in the air, the results of which were to be used for the model already designated as its successor. It was not until June 1950 that the mighty aircraft made another public flight.

In the meantime the construction of the second prototype had been going ahead, though not without its problems. At the end of 1951 the Brabazon Mk.II had at last reached the stage of final assembly, with the fuselage, central wing section and tailplane already assembled. It was too

Aircraft: **Bristol Type 167 Brabazon 1**
Manufacturer: **Bristol Aeroplane Co. Ltd.**
Type: **Civil transport**
Year: **1949**
Engines: **Eight Bristol Centaurus 20, radial with 18 air-cooled cylinders, 2,500 hp each**
Wingspan: **230 ft 0 in (70.10 m)**
Length: **177 ft 0 in (53.95 m)**
Height: **50 ft 0 in (15.24 m)**
Weight: **290,000 lb (131,544 kg) (Loaded)**
Cruising speed: **250 mph at 25,000 ft (402 km/h at 7,620 m)***
Ceiling: **34,500 ft (10,500 m)**
Range: **5,500 miles (8,850 km)***
Crew: **12**
Passengers: **100**
***Estimated**

late to try to salvage the programme. In February 1952 the government issued its first negative decision which was that work on the Brabazon Mk.II would be temporarily suspended until more favourable conditions occurred. It was now clear that the right conditions would never occur. On July 9 of the following year the cancellation of the entire programme was announced. The Brabazon 1 was taken into the air for the last time on September 20, 1952, thus reaching a total of 382 hours and 15 minutes in the air.

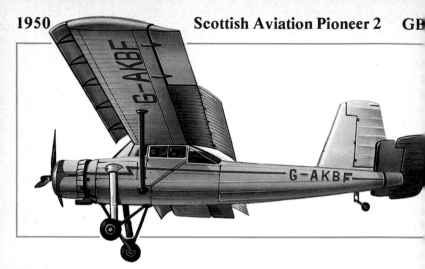

Scottish Aviation Pioneer

The first commercial fruit of the Scottish aeronautical industry was also the first short-take-off transport aircraft constructed in Great Britain. The Scottish Aviation Pioneer was not, however, a very popular aeroplane, because initially it did not receive the attention that it deserved from the military authorities. It was also soon ousted from the assembly lines by the better known Twin Pioneer. The Pioneer 1 prototype was originally powered by a 240 hp de Havilland Gipsy Queen engine and made its maiden flight in September 1947. It soon revealed excellent STOL (short take off and landing) qualities. Due to the lack of interest shown by the R.A.F., it was decided to make a civil version, called Pioneer 2. The prototype made its maiden flight in June 1950. This aeroplane enjoyed a reasonable commercial success, and from 1953 the R.A.F. used 40 of them.

Aircraft: **Scottish Aviation Pioneer 2**
Manufacturer: **Scottish Aviation Ltd.**
Type: **Light transport**
Year: **1950**
Engine: **One Alvis Leonides 501/4, radial with 9 water-cooled cylinders, 520 hp**
Wingspan: **52 ft 6 in (16,00 m)**
Length: **34 ft 7 in (10.53 m)**
Height: **10 ft 2 in (3.10 m)**
Weight: **5,400 lb (2,450 kg) (Loaded)**
Cruising speed: **151 mph (243 km/h)**
Ceiling: **23,000 ft (7,010 m)**
Range: **400 miles (645 km)**
Crew: **1**
Passengers: **4**

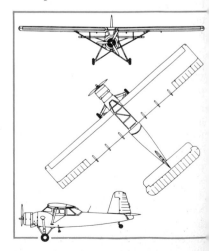

Vickers Viscount

London–Paris, London–Edinburgh. From July 29, 1950, for one month, BEA put into service on these two routes the world's first passenger turbo-prop. The aeroplane was the Vickers Viscount 630 prototype, the forbear of a long series of almost 450 models which flew for many years under the flag of the major airlines of the whole world. The month of experimental service was decisive for the future success of the aeroplane; and no less decisive than the excellent performances of the Viscount was the enthusiastic verdict of the 1,815 passengers carried by it. This fact alone encouraged BEA to push aside any doubts about the validity of the new aircraft and order a first batch of 27 models. These went into regular service on the entire network of European flights from April 17, 1953 onwards. At the end of the 1950s, the Viscounts which were operating with the various European companies monopolized more than a third of the entire air transport in Europe.

After the crisis of the immediate postwar period, therefore, the Vickers Viscount earned, with one fell swoop, a leading position among western nations for the British aeronautical industry. The preliminary project had been launched in the latter months of 1944, when the Vickers technical personnel had already drawn up the specifications of the commercial twin-engined Viking with its piston engines. Given the excellent qualities of this aircraft and the potential it could have on the postwar market (a prediction which

was to be amply backed up by the facts), the designers started thinking about a successor to it. The new aircraft was to be driven not by conventional engines, but by the new turbo-prop engines which at that time were in the development stage in the major aeronautical firms of the sector. The proposal was formalized by the Brabazon Committee and authorized in March 1945.

Consideration was given to various structural solutions and designs before the final plans for the aircraft were drawn up, and alternative solutions were also envisaged for the engines. The most popular engine was the Rolls-Royce Dart, but the possibility of using Armstrong Siddeley Mamba or Napier Naiad turbo-props was considered if the Rolls-Royce Dart did not give the performance required. The final drawing-up of the plans lasted for the whole of 1945, and in March of the following year Vickers signed a contract with the government's technical authorities for the production of four prototypes. The clauses were later altered, with the request for two officially financed prototypes and a third which would be paid for entirely by the Vickers Company.

The two first aeroplanes were made using four Dart turbo-props, and they were called V.630s, while the third, fitted with Napier Naiad engines, was designated the V.640. The first prototype made its maiden flight on July 16, 1948. At this time the Viscount had still not managed to arouse the interest of BEA, the company for which it was mainly destined, because the BEA technicians did not appear to be completely convinced of its capabilities. This reaction put the whole programme into a state of temporary crisis to the point where Vickers, despite the first successful test-flight of the first prototype, abandoned work on the third aircraft and considerably slowed down completion of the second. However, during that year the situation unexpectedly eased. The feature which helped most to solve the problem was the announcement that Rolls-Royce would soon have ready a version of its Dart engine capable of giving 50% more power. In view of this the designers reckoned they could modify the prototype, turning it into a larger and reinforced version, with a basic capacity of 40 passengers. The new proposal turned out to meet with satisfaction from BEA, and Vickers immediately started work on the construction of a new prototype called the V.700.

The first Viscount 700 made its maiden flight on April 19, 1950 and its public debut was immediately followed by an initial order by BEA, although they wanted the capacity increased to 53 seats. This order marked the start of the commercial success of the four-engined Vickers. BEA was followed by Air France, Aer Lingus, Trans-Australia Airlines and other lesser companies. The orders were so diverse, with each one specifying particular requests for equipment and variations, that Vickers decided to allot different design numbers for every single customer. The largest success of all came towards the end of 1952, when the Viscount managed to penetrate the North American market. The company which first ordered it (15 in all) was Trans-Canada Air Lines, and this decision gave the go-ahead to a long series of further orders, the most impressive of which was the one placed by Capital Airlines, for 60 Viscount 745s. In the latter half of the 1950s the success in North America was such that the number of aircraft in regular service was far in excess of those flying with the European companies. During the long production of the series 700, Vickers introduced many modifications to the basic model, in respect of

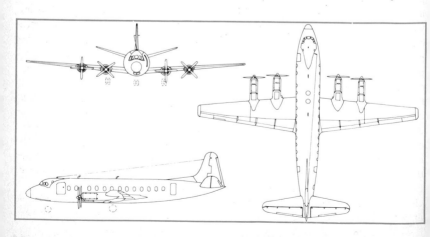

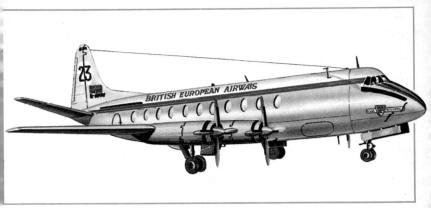

capacity; to the interior design; and to the engines and their different degrees of power. However, in 1952 they started thinking about making a larger, reinforced version with a larger capacity, based on the availability of the latest versions of the Rolls-Royce Dart engine. This gave birth to the design of the series 800 in which the main feature consisted in the considerably longer fuselage which could hold a maximum of 86 passengers. In practice this design turned out to be too ambitious and the production models were restructured as compared with the original plans, and fitted out to hold 65 passengers. On April 14, 1954 BEA placed an initial order for 24 examples of the new Viscount, with the designation 802. The series 800 also got off to a good start in this way, and enjoyed a career not unlike that of its predecessor. Further development gave rise to the Viscount 810, with a strengthened structure to accommodate four Dart turboprops each producing 2,100 ehp, with double the maximum weight at take-off when compared with the

Aircraft: **Vickers Viscount 700**
Manufacturer: **Vickers-Armstrong Ltd.**
Type: **Civil transport**
Year: **1950**
Engines: **Four Rolls-Royce Dart 505 turboprops, 1,540 ehp each**
Wingspan: **93 ft 8 in (28.55 m)**
Length: **81 ft 2 in (24.40 m)**
Height: **26 ft 9 in (8.05 m)**
Weight: **60,000 lb (27,216 kg) (Loaded)**
Cruising speed: **316 mph at 20,000 ft (508 km/h at 6,100 m)**
Ceiling: **27,500 ft (8,380 m)**
Range: **1,690 miles (2,720 km)**
Crew: **3–4**
Passengers: **40–63**

original design. The final stage of development came with the Viscount 840. When the 810 was presented, Vickers announced that it was capable of also using Rolls-Royce Dart R.Da.10 Mk.541 engines, producing 2,350 ehp. All the aircraft ordered to this specification were called Viscount 840s and one of their major features was the cruising speed of 400 mph (643 km/h). Further developments of the Viscount led to the production of its not so successful successor, the Vickers Vanguard.

Production of the Viscount ended at the end of 1959, totalling 444 aircraft.

Saunders Roe S.R.45 Princess

The Princess was the last of the great commercial flying-boats. It made its maiden flight in the summer of 1952, at a time when flying-boats were now definitely on the wane. Even if, technically speaking, it represented the highest expression of its class, reviving the glorious tradition of the Empire Boats of the 1930s, it was also an aircraft produced on the basis of a concept that was now out of date. After a brief series of tests and experimental flights, the two completed prototypes and the third half-built one remained sadly at their moorings for years and were eventually scrapped. The Saunders Roe company, almost as famous as the Short Brothers for its flying-boats, started thinking about making an aircraft of this type, designed for high capacity flights across the North Atlantic, in the latter half of 1945. The official request had come from the government's technical authorities. On the basis of their experience in transcontinental flights using flying-boats bought before and during the war they intended to relaunch this type of transport in the postwar years as well. BOAC itself had shown a degree of interest in the project, although this interest was to wane completely as time passed.

The programme went ahead even though many of the major details still had to be sorted out; for example, no decision had been made about the structure necessary for such a large flying-boat, and the potential future demand for such an aircraft had not been properly assessed. In May 1946 Saunders Roe, which had been chosen as the sole and permanent contractor, received the order for three prototypes. The project, designated S.R.45, started to take shape and before long turned out to be more of an undertaking than had been anticipated. A central hull design was adopted, with a gigantic pressurized fuselage built on two decks, and auxiliary retractable floats at the wingtips. Turbo-props were chosen to power it, and the original idea was to use twelve Rolls-Royce Tweed engines mounted in pairs. Later on, however, after the development of the Rolls-Royce Tweed engines had been

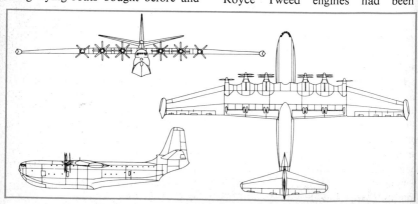

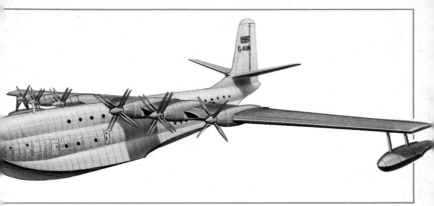

abandoned, ten Bristol Proteus engines were used, eight of which were paired off in the four innermost nacelles, and two single engines were mounted in the outer nacelles.

Construction of the first prototype started in 1947, and almost immediately came up against several technical problems. The Princess was not only the largest flying-boat ever built, but also the largest turbo-prop aircraft. In addition it had the largest ever pressurized structure and it was the pressurization of the immense fuselage which caused a long series of delays, because of the need for continual tests and alterations.

Early in 1951 the initial enthusiasm had cooled off. BOAC, which had by now decided to run a fleet consisting entirely of land aircraft, announced its disinterest in the Princess programme. There followed a muddled series of official directives, the first of which announced that the S.R.45 would be handed to the R.A.F. to be assessed as a military strategic transport aircraft. In this role it had to be capable of

Aircraft: **Saunders Roe S.R.45 Princess**
Manufacturer: **Saunders Roe Ltd.**
Type: **Civil transport**
Year: **1952**
Engines: **Ten Bristol Proteus 600 turbo-props, 3,780 ehp each**
Wingspan: **219 ft 6 in (66.90 m)**
Length: **148 ft 0 in (45.11 m)**
Height: **55 ft 9 in (16.99 m)**
Weight: **315,000 lb (143,000 kg) (Loaded)**
Cruising speed: **360 mph at 37,000 ft (579 km/h at 11,300 m)**
Ceiling: **–**
Range: **5,500 miles (8,850 km)**
Crew: **6**
Passengers: **105**

carrying 200 people instead of the 105 anticipated for the commercial design. However, in March 1952, five months before the prototype flight, it was decided to complete just the first model. The second model, which was almost complete, and the third were to be put into mothballs until more powerful engines had been developed. It was clearly the beginning of the end, not least because of the cost which had risen from £2,800,000 in 1946 to almost £11,000,000 in 1951.

The only Princess to fly (with the marking C-ALUN) made its maiden flight on August 22, 1955.

137

de Havilland D.H.114 Heron

Abiding by the philosophy behind its production during the 1930s, the de Havilland company followed the successful twin-engined D.H.104 Dove with a model derived substantially from the previous aircraft. It was a larger aircraft driven by four engines, called the D.H.114 Heron. The Heron was a medium-range, medium capacity commercial transport model which echoed the success of the Dove. This success was not unlike the case of the D.H.86 in 1934, which was an enlarged version of the famous D.H.84 Dragon.

The D.H.114 Heron project was started in 1949 at a time when the aeronautical market looked ready to accommodate a fairly economical civil transport aircraft which was tough and capable of operating from small airfields. When the first prototype made its maiden flight, on May 10, 1950, it clearly revealed its direct descendance from the D.H.104 Dove. It had the same structure, many of the components were identical and it had fairly similar lines, with the exception of the four engines instead of two. The engines themselves were the same air-cooled six-cylinder de Havilland Gipsy Queens, though in a less powerful version. In addition the structural simplicity and the robustness of the Dove had been improved by the adoption of a fixed tricycle undercarriage, which did away with the need for complicated hydraulic systems for a retractable unit. However, when compared with the Dove, the Heron had practically doubled the capacity of her predecessor.

The prototype was put through a long series of tests and operational trials, both in Britain and in tropical climates. The first model in the initial Heron 1 series was delivered in March 1952 to a company in New Zealand. The seventh aircraft produced became the prototype for the improved Heron 2 series. The Heron 2 was in fact the most successful of the Heron series.

The main difference between the first and second series was in the undercarriage which reverted from

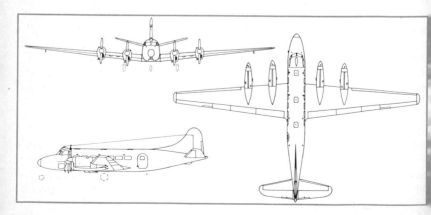

being fixed in the Heron 1 to retractable in the Heron 2. The Heron 2 prototype started its test flights on December 14, 1952 and showed an average increase on speed of about 20 mph (30 km/h) and a noticeable reduction in fuel consumption. In the light of these improvements the technical problems entailed by the adoption of a retractable undercarriage were well worthwhile sorting out.

Commercial success was fairly instant. Numerous private operators chose the Heron as an executive aeroplane and various smaller companies adopted the D.H.114 to replace the old D.H.86 and D.H.89. The first to do this was Jersey Airlines, which first put the Heron into service on the Gatwick–Jersey route on May 9, 1953. It then gradually widened its network of flights to France and Portugal, with the purchase of five more aircraft of the improved 1B and 2B versions. Cambrian Airways was another operator who put the D.H.114 into regular service. BEA also used these versatile

Aircraft: **de Havilland D.H.114 Heron 2**
Manufacturer: **de Havilland Aircraft Co. Ltd.**
Type: **Civil transport**
Year: **1952**
Engines: **Four de Havilland Gipsy Queen 30-2, with 6 straight cylinders, air-cooled, 250 hp each**
Wingspan: **71 ft 6 in (21.79 m)**
Length: **48 ft 6 in (14.78 m)**
Height: **15 ft 7 in (4.75 m)**
Weight: **13,500 lb (6,124 kg) (Loaded)**
Cruising speed: **183 mph (294 km/h)**
Ceiling: **18,500 ft (5,640 m)**
Range: **1,805 miles (2,905 km)**
Crew: **2**
Passengers: **14–17**

and tough four-engined de Havillands on its flights to Scotland and also as flying ambulances.

The subseries 1B and 2B were followed by the Heron 2C and 2D, from 1955 onwards. These were fitted out at the express request of the client and were destined mainly for use as executive aircraft holding between six and eight passengers. The major technical characteristic of these later aeroplanes was the installation of variable-pitch propellers which gave a further overall increase in performance.

139

Bristol Type 175 Britannia

The much coveted non-stop London–New York flight finally became a reality for BOAC from December 19, 1957 onwards. The aircraft which made it possible was the Bristol Britannia, an elegant four-engined turbo-prop which was the first one in the world in its category to make a regular flight across the North Atlantic without stops. While American engineers had focussed all their resources on the production of a commercial transport model powered by pure jet engines, their British counterparts had refused to abandon the development of turbo-prop aeroplanes. After the resounding success of the Vickers Viscount, the Britannia once more revealed the great possibilities of this type of aircraft.

The specifications which gave rise to the Bristol 175 were issued by the British government in December 1946. The authorities wanted a medium-range commercial aeroplane which could carry 32 passengers. Five firms replied to the tender and Bristol were successful. The Bristol design was finally accepted in April of the following year. The programme went ahead with close co-operation from BOAC. BOAC further specified the characteristics of the aeroplane, by increasing the capacity to 48 seats and requiring sufficient range to be able to use it on the route to Cairo and Karachi. On July 5, 1948 there was a further order for three prototypes. On that date the 175 project had already been substantially modified by the Bristol technicians. They had studied the possibility of adopting Proteus turbo-prop engines in place of the original Centaurus radial engines, and this solution won the day. The result was a reduction in the number of prototypes to two, and the first of these made its maiden flight on August 16, 1952. The second prototype made its first flight, on December 23, 1953. These two aircraft were called Britannia 101s. They gave rise to fifteen Britannia 102 aircraft in the first production series ordered by BOAC. The first prototype of this series made its maiden flight on September 5, 1954. The final development of these aircraft was quite tricky, because of problems connected with the formation of ice in

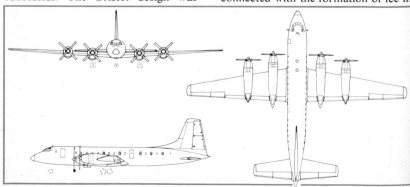

140

the engines. These problems were only solved after lengthy and patient research, and on February 1, 1957 BOAC put its Britannia 102s into service on the route to South Africa.

In the meantime Bristol, being well aware of the potential of the project, had developed a long-range high-capacity version, the major structural feature of which was the lengthening of the fuselage by about ten feet (3 m). This version was called the Britannia 300 and the first prototype took to the air on July 31, 1956. Production was focussed on a further improved version, with an even greater capacity and more efficient fuel tanks. This improved version was called series 310 and turned the Britannia into a fully fledged transatlantic aircraft. Eighteen models were ordered by BOAC under the designation Britannia 312. Deliveries commenced in September 1957 and before the end of the year the first aeroplanes were being used on the prestigious route to New York.

The series 310 Britannias also

Aircraft: **Bristol Type 175 Britannia 102**
Manufacturer: **Bristol Aeroplane Co. Ltd.**
Type: **Civil transport**
Year: **1954**
Engines: **Four Bristol Proteus 705 turbo-props, 3,780 ehp each**
Wingspan: **142 ft 3 in (43.36 m)**
Length: **114 ft 0 in (34.75 m)**
Height: **36 ft 8 in (11.17 m)**
Weight: **155,000 lb (70,308 kg) (Loaded)**
Cruising speed: **375 mph (603 km/h)**
Ceiling: **24,000 ft (7,315 m)**
Range: **3,700 miles (5,954 km)**
Crew: **8**
Passengers: **79–115**

enjoyed a considerable success on the export market. Four were sold to the Israeli El Al company, six to Canadian Pacific, another four to Cubana, and one to Ghana Airways. Two further aircraft were bought by the British charter company Hunting Clan. Towards the end of production all the main modifications adopted in the numerous versions were incorporated in the last series, Britannia 320, eight of which were made. Four of them were purchased by the Canadian company CP Air. The Britannia's success was swollen by the heavy use made of it by smaller airlines and charter companies.

Scottish Aviation Twin Pioneer

After the experience gained with the small Pioneer in 1950, the Scottish Aviation company decided to produce a larger aircraft. This new aircraft echoed the same features of versatility, robustness and straightforward use and maintenance as the previous model. It was called the Twin Pioneer, the prototype made its maiden flight on June 25, 1955. Scottish Aviation set up assembly lines for mass-production after the completion of three pre-production models. The Twin Pioneer was successful above all with small companies operating charter flights, as well as operators specializing in survey work. Orders from abroad were particularly heavy and by the end of 1958, of the 70 aircraft delivered or on order, only 17 were registered in Great Britain. In August the second version appeared. This was the Twin Pioneer 2 driven by two Pratt & Whitney radial engines.

Aircraft: **Scottish Aviation Twin Pioneer 1**
Manufacturer: **Scottish Aviation Ltd.**
Type: **Light transport**
Year: **1955**
Engines: **Two Alvis Leonides 504, radial with 9 air-cooled cylinders, 540 hp each**
Wingspan: **76 ft 6 in (23.32 m)**
Length: **45 ft 3 in (13.79 m)**
Height: **12 ft 3 in (3.73 m)**
Weight: **13,500 lb (6,123 kg) (Loaded)**
Cruising speed: **118 mph (190 km/h)**
Ceiling: **23,000 ft (7,010 m)**
Range: **830 miles (1,336 km)**
Crew: **2**
Passengers: **16**

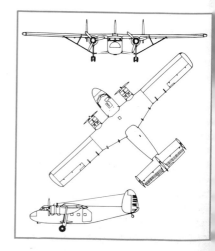

le Havilland D.H.106 Comet

The leading figure behind three important dates in the history of aviation was the de Havilland D.H.106 Comet. The first date, July 27, 1949, was the day of the maiden flight of the prototype, and the first flight of a jet-engined commercial aeroplane. Although the first flight in absolute terms had taken place on April 6, 1948, in the form of a modified Vickers Viking in which two Rolls-Royce Nene turbo-jets had been installed, this had been treated as an experimental aircraft and there had been no follow-up.) The second date, May 2, 1952, was the day of the first regular passenger flight by jet from London to Johannesburg using the Comet 1, registered G-LYP. The third date was October 4, 1958, the day of the first transatlantic flight made by a jet-engined aircraft. This was on the London–New York route and ended the race between BOAC and Pan American, the latter with its Boeing 707-120.

The story started in 1944 when the Brabazon Committee proposed the construction of a civil transport aeroplane powered entirely by jet engines. It was to be designed for short-to-medium range flights and capable of carrying 14 passengers plus a certain amount of mail. The de Havilland company had started studying the possibilities of building an aircraft of this type the year before. They launched a preliminary project and drew up the plans with the collaboration of BOAC, which was also fairly interested in putting up some opposition to the massive onslaught of the North American industry and developing a valid commercial aeroplane for use on the North Atlantic route. The D.H.106 project took shape slowly but surely. Its form differed considerably from that originally proposed by the technical committee, having a larger capacity and a longer range. In February 1945 a provisional preliminary contract was signed authorizing de Havilland to go ahead with its programme and in December BOAC placed a definite order for ten aircraft.

Almost a year was to elapse before the first Comet took on its final form. Various solutions had been chosen by the de Havilland technicians and to start with the most promising one required a sharply sweptback wing and no horizontal tailplane. It was not until the end of 1945 that this idea was dropped because it contained too many unknown quantities for proper and regular commercial use, and the project was modified with a more conventional structure. In May 1946 the contract for the production of two prototypes was signed and the first of these made its successful maiden flight on July 27, 1949 at Hatfield, in the hands of de Havilland's chief test-pilot, John Cunningham. The aircraft was elegant, with a single wing placed low down. It had a circular fuselage holding 36 passengers and four de Havilland Ghost turbo-jets mounted in pairs beside the fuselage and completely embedded in the wing. After its first public presentation at Farnborough the first Comet started a long series of tests and trial flights. These were aimed mainly at studying the characteristics of the engines, the fuel consumption and flying times over the main commercial routes. The first prototype, registered G-ALVG, was joined on July 27, 1950 by the second, registered G-ALZK, and together the two of them continued to be put through the various tests. In the course of these experimental flights the Comet made a good showing, and considerably reduced the flying times between London and the major European capitals. It also made several spectacular non-stop flights on the old routes across the Empire.

In the meantime production of the ten aircraft ordered by BOAC and called Comet 1s went ahead. The first was delivered in January 1951 and the last in September 1952. On April 3, 1953, after the prestigious inauguration of the service to South Africa, BOAC opened a new regular route between London and Tokyo. The average flying time was cut in half when compared with services using conventional aeroplanes. The initial order by BOAC was now joined by substantial orders from numerous other companies. The French UAT company, Canadian Pacific and Air France commissioned various model of the longer range 40 passenger capacity Comet 1A. Australia, Venezuela, Japan and Brazil subsequently ordered models of the Comet 2, a version with a further enlarged passenger capacity. In the autumn o 1952 de Havilland announced the production of the Series 3 which had a lengthened fuselage and was designed for use on the North Atlantic route Orders for this series arrived from Pan American and Air India.

These successes were quickly followed by a series of tragic and apparently inexplicable accidents. On May 2, 1953 the Comet 1 G-ALYV crashed at Calcutta while climbing after take-off. It was totally destroyed and all 43 people on board were killed. On January 10, 1954 the Comet 1 G-ALYP, with 35 people on board. crashed into the sea near the island of Elba, shortly after taking off from Rome. On April 8, 1954 the Comet 1

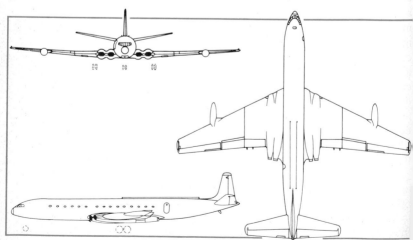

Aircraft: **de Havilland D.H.106 Comet 4**
Manufacturer: **de Havilland Aircraft Co. Ltd.**
Type: **Civil transport**
Year: **1958**
Engines: **Four Rolls-Royce Avon 524 turbo-jets, 10,500 lb (4,763 kg) thrust each**
Wingspan: **114 ft 9 in (34.97 m)**
Length: **111 ft 6 in (33.99 m)**
Height: **29 ft 6 in (8.99 m)**
Weight: **162,000 lb (75,483 kg) (Loaded)**
Cruising speed: **503 mph at 42,000 ft (809 km/h at 12,800 m)**
Ceiling: **42,000 ft (12,800 m)**
Range: **4,330 miles (6,968 km)**
Crew: **4**
Passengers: **56–97**

G-ALYY came to a similar end, with 21 passengers on board, near Stromboli. While the first crash was considered to be due to air traffic and flight procedures and was justified as an inevitable part of the development of this revolutionary aeroplane, the great similarity of the other two crashes dealt a hard blow to the technicians and also greatly affected public opinion. The entire fleet of Comets was grounded and there followed one of the longest, most desperate and dramatic technical investigations carried out in the world of commercial aviation. It was not just a matter of looking for the cause, or causes, which had given rise to two disasters in virtually identical conditions, but also of rebuilding public confidence in this new means of transport. This confidence had been shattered in the short period of just three months.

The public enquiry which followed is now part of the history of the 1950s. Specialized teams managed to recover much of what remained of the Comet that had crashed off Elba. The pieces were examined with the most modern means of scientific investigation. The data gathered were compared with those found in the course of an intensive series of flight tests carried out on board another aeroplane (G-ANAV) and with those obtained by literally destroying G-ALYU in the course of pressure tests carried out in a tank full of water. The technical conclusions were then handed to the official investigating committee in the autumn of 1954. They announced that the fuselage of the Comets had exploded as the result of a structural weakness

145

discovered in the corner of one of the rear windows. This weakness had in turn been caused by metal fatigue resulting from the repeated pressurization of the cabin. The investigating committee's verdict said that the Comet had been developed on the basis of the most valid technical and technological knowledge of the day, but it was clear that there was still much to be learnt about certain sophisticated metallurgical aspects.

The certainty that the crashes of the Comet 1 had not been caused by errors in the design encouraged de Havilland to take the courageous decision to produce a new version of the aircraft into which the firm poured all the bitter experience it had now acquired. This was a valiant demonstration of a resolute determination to go ahead and it earned them the admiration of the whole world.

The new Comet was called the Comet 4 and the prototype made its maiden flight on April 27, 1958. It was a larger capacity, longer range aircraft which, apart from the appropriate structural modifications, derived from the aircraft belonging to the Series 3. Showing admirable confidence, BOAC then ordered 19 models for use on the North Atlantic route. After intensive test-flights carried out by two modified Comet 2s, the service got off to a dazzling start on October 4. The last Comet 4 in the BOAC order was delivered little more than a year later, on January 11, 1960. In the first 24 months of operation the 19 aircraft were used to the full. In all they flew for 68,500 hours, travelling more than 27,000,000 miles (43,000,000 km) all over the world and carried 327,000 passengers.

Shortly after the British company's Comet 4 order, Aerolineas Argentinas ordered six aircraft and East African Airways ordered three aircraft. Another order which might have given great prestige to the British jet was that placed in July 1956 by the North American company, Capital Airlines. They ordered 14 in all. This would have been an historic occasion to penetrate the difficult and very important American market, but because of a series of factors the Capital order was eventually cancelled.

The next version was the Comet 4B, which had a smaller wingspan and a larger capacity, but a smaller range. It was developed after an initial order placed by BEA for six aircraft in April 1958. This number was later increased to fourteen. In fact these aircraft had already been designed to meet the requirements of Capital Airlines and the first of them was delivered to BEA on November 9, 1959. They started a regular service on April 1 of the following year. The Greek company Olympic Airways was another purchaser of the Comet 4B, ordering four aircraft.

The final version of the Comet 4 was the 4C, which combined the large capacity of the previous model with the long range of the basic model. The first of these aeroplanes flew on October 31, 1959 and went into service at the beginning of the following year with the Mexicana company. Other Comet 4Cs were ordered by United Arab Airlines, Middle East Airlines, Aerolineas Argentinas, Kuwait Airways and Sudan Airways. One of the most distinctive of all the Comet 4Cs was the one ordered for the personal use of the King of Saudi Arabia.

Armstrong Whitworth A.W.650 Argosy

The first 'all cargo' aeroplane in the world driven by turbo-prop engines was put into service on January 15, 1961 by the American company Riddle Airlines. This British made aeroplane was an ugly looking four-engined model with twin booms and fins, designed and built exclusively to meet the needs of companies transporting large and varied cargo. The project had been launched in 1956 by Armstrong Whitworth. They were convinced of the commercial potential of the new aircraft and prepared a production line for ten aircraft shortly after the maiden flight of the prototype, on January 8, 1959. This policy was rewarded by the immediate success of the aircraft in North America. The order by Riddle Airlines for seven aircraft was followed in 1961 by an order from BEA for a further three. These aircraft were called, respectively, Argosy 101 and 102. The R.A.F. also ordered 56 aircraft

Aircraft: **Armstrong Whitworth A.W.650 Argosy 100**
Manufacturer: **Armstrong Whitworth Aircraft Ltd.**
Type: **Civil transport**
Year: **1959**
Engines: **Four Rolls-Royce Dart 526 turbo props, 2,100 ehp each**
Wingspan: **115 ft 0 in (35.05 m)**
Length: **86 ft 9 in (26.44 m)**
Height: **27 ft 0 in (8.23 m)**
Weight: **88,000 lb (39,917 kg) (Loaded)**
Cruising speed: **302 mph at 20,000 ft (486 km/h at 6,100 m)**
Ceiling: **22,600 ft (6,890 m)**
Range: **2,500 miles (4,020 km)**
Crew: **2–3**
Payload: **28,000 lb (12,700 kg)**

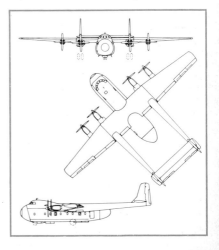

147

Handley Page H.P.R.7 Herald

The Handley Page Herald developed as a short-range piston-engined transport aircraft and was radically altered over a period of two years. It ended up as one of the most versatile of all commercial turbo-prop aircraft. After serving initially with BEA the Handley Page Herald was adopted by numerous companies which used the more powerful versions with a larger capacity which were developed in the course of the 1960s.

The original project was launched by Handley Page in about 1950. The idea was to build a medium capacity, short-range commercial transport aeroplane of great versatility and easy maintenance. In order to check the effective readiness of the civil market to absorb such an aeroplane, the company carried out a survey on an international scale, approaching all the major airlines in Europe, Africa, Asia, Australia and South America. From the results of this survey the aircraft started to take on its basic form: a high winged aircraft, with a maximum capacity of 44 passengers, driven by four, 900 hp Alvis Leonides Major radial engines, with 14 cylinders in a double radial arrangement. The actual construction of the aircraft was then entrusted to the Reading division of Handley Page (the works had previously belonged to Miles Aircraft Ltd and were taken over in 1948). The designation H.P.R.3 was chosen. It was decided to complete the two prototypes on a completely private basis and by the end of 1954 they were already at an advanced stage of construction. At that time there was already a substantial order from the Australian company Queensland Airlines and this was followed early in 1955 by further orders from Australian National Airways and Lloyd Aereo Colombiano, which brought the total number to 29 aircraft. The first prototype made its maiden flight on August 25, 1955.

The aircraft was then put through its various trials and certification tests and it was during this period that the

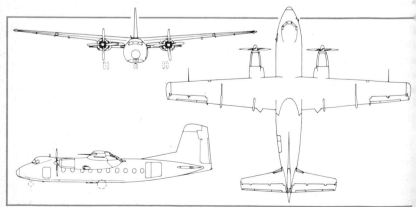

validity of the H.P.R.3 project was cast into doubt. The success of the Vickers Viscount turbo-prop was having a marked effect on the market and eventually the two Australian airlines cancelled their orders. They considered the Herald to be not competitive enough. This forced Handley Page to modify its programme and in May 1957 it announced the imminent production of a version driven by two turbo-prop engines, called the H.P.R.7. The first of these aeroplanes, which was essentially the H.P.R.3 prototype with the new engines, made its maiden flight on March 11, 1958. However, this aircraft was destroyed in a serious accident and was replaced in the next tests by the second prototype which managed to complete all the trials early in 1959. By June the first order for three models arrived from BEA.

These aircraft gave rise to the series 100 which took to the air on October 30, 1959. This series was also soon replaced on the assembly lines by the more powerful Herald 200, with a fuselage which was about 3 feet (1 m)

Aircraft: **Handley Page H.P.R.7 Herald 100**
Manufacturer: **Handley Page (Reading) Ltd.**
Type: **Civil transport**
Year: **1959**
Engines: **Two Rolls-Royce Dart 527 turbo-props, 2,150 ehp each**
Wingspan: **94 ft 9 in (28.88 m)**
Length: **71 ft 11 in (21.92 m)**
Height: **22 ft 4 in (6.81 m)**
Weight: **38,500 lb (17,463 kg) (Loaded)**
Cruising speed: **275 mph at 15,000 ft (442 km/h at 4,570 m)**
Ceiling: **33,000 ft (10,060 m)**
Range: **1,590 miles (2,558 km)**
Crew: **3**
Passengers: **36–56**

longer. This was the first production series and was also the one which became most popular with the airlines. The first Herald 200 produced (of six ordered by Jersey Airlines) took to the air on December 13, 1961. It was followed by aircraft ordered by Itavia, Eastern Provincial, Globe Air, Arkia, Sadia, British Midland Airways, Bavaria and Air Manila, with a total of a further 25 aircraft. Further series included a strengthened military version called the Herald 400 which was designed for transporting troops; the larger, more powerful 1965 version called the Herald 600; and the Herald 700 which could carry 60 passengers.

149

Avro 748

The 748 was the last project to bear the illustrious name of Avro before the name was absorbed by Hawker Siddeley in 1963. It was a project which gave birth to one of the most successful of all commercial British aircraft in the 1960s. By 1970 more than 200 models of this versatile twin-engined turbo-prop had been ordered and by 1976 a total of 310 aircraft in different versions had been sold. Of the total figure, 138 had gone to military operators in 14 countries, while the remaining 172 had been sold to 50 airlines in 36 countries. Even today, along with the Fokker F.27 Friendship, the Avro 748 is possibly the most widespread medium transport aircraft with turbo-prop engines in service.

In 1957 the Avro company, now part of the Hawker Siddeley group decided to reapproach the civil market after an absence of more than ten years. The last commercial aeroplanes produced had all been developed in the immediate postwar period, and after the unsuccessful Tudor no other civil aircraft had carried the name of this

well-established company. Thus the project for the Type 748 got under way. From the beginning it was conceived as a twin-engined, medium range and medium capacity model built with the aim of offering operators a sound replacement for the elderly Douglas DC-3. The project kept the Avro technicians busy for about two years before a definite go ahead was received in January 1959. Using its own funds Hawker Siddeley decided to proceed with the construction of four prototypes, two of which were destined for test flights while two were used for static trials. The features of the Type 748 clearly echoed the need to keep the operating and maintenance costs as low as possible, as well as to keep the levels of use as high as possible. Parts already tested in other aircraft, notably engines and propellers, were utilised.

An immediate confirmation of the validity of the design came six months before the first prototype flight, from the Indian government. Towards the end of 1959 a production licence for the 748 had been acquired, allowing it to be built in India as a military model. This was the first successful attempt to

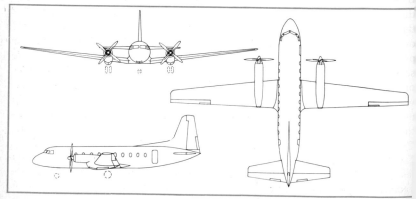

adapt the aircraft to tasks outside the civil market and was followed-up by the R.A.F. which adopted the 748 under the name of Andover.

The first prototype made its maiden flight on June 24, 1960 and was followed by the second one in April of the following year. These two aeroplanes were completed in the basic version and called the Avro 748 Series 1. The certification tests were completed in November 1961 and the aircraft were registered on December 7. By this date Avro had already prepared the first of the three models ordered by the Skyways Coach Air company and on the December 10 the second production model appeared. This second model was one of nine aircraft ordered by Aerolineas Argentinas, which was the first company to put the new turbo-prop into service in April of the following year. Later Skyways Coach Air used its 748s between London and Paris, a service which lasted uninterruptedly for almost 15 years. In the meantime on November 6,

Aircraft: **Avro 748 Series 1**
Manufacturer: **A. V. Roe and Co. Ltd. (Hawker Siddeley Group)**
Type: **Civil transport**
Year: **1960**
Engines: **Two Rolls-Royce Dart 514 turbo-props, 1,740 ehp each**
Wingspan: **98 ft 3 in (29.95 m)**
Length: **67 ft 0 in (20.42 m)**
Height: **24 ft 10 in (7.57 m)**
Weight: **38,000 lb (17,237 kg) (Loaded)**
Cruising speed: **257 mph (414 km/h)**
Ceiling: **24,500 ft (7,470 m)**
Range: **550 miles (885 km)**
Crew: **2–3**
Passengers: **40–52**

1961 the prototype of the second production version, the 748 Series 2, had taken to the air. This aircraft had a considerably increased capacity and adopted the Dart 529 engines each producing 1,910 ehp. This version soon replaced the initial Series 1 and 23 models were built in all, including those made in India. This series gave birth to the remaining 748s designed for military transport. The engines in the 2A were the even more powerful Dart 532 engines each producing 2,280 ehp, which appeared in 1967. This version became the most widespread on the civil market.

Vickers Vanguard

Destined to be the 'big brother' of the successful Viscount, the Vickers Vanguard came on the market at a time when the major airlines were already looking towards commercial jet aircraft. Although it was in every respect an aircraft of the best sort in its category, the Vanguard suffered a great deal from its late arrival and, including the prototype, only 44 models were built in all. These were purchased by just two companies: BEA and the Canadian company TCA. The development of the V.900 project (this was the initial domestic designation) was started even before the Viscount had gone into regular service with BEA. In fact from December 1951 the British company had been putting forward comprehensive plans for a successor to the aircraft which had only just been ordered. However, the project was slow to take shape. Vickers began with the Viscount 850 which had a lengthened fuselage to increase the capacity, and more powerful engines. However, this was only a first step, and there followed no less than 60 provisional designs, in which various structural forms were analysed. These designs differed from each other in the type of wing and the choice of engines. After a lengthy analysis of the market the programme was eventually drawn up, and was called V.950. On June 20, 1956 BEA signed a contract with Vickers for the delivery of 20 series models, called Vanguard 951.

While the assembly lines were being prepared, the Vickers technicians decided to further improve the range and capacity of the Vanguard and announced the production of a second version (the 952) which could increase its passenger load from the initial 93 to 120. This aroused the interest of the Canadian company TCA which in January 1957, ordered 20 aircraft. This order was subsequently increased to 23. A further increase in the payload was announced in July of the following

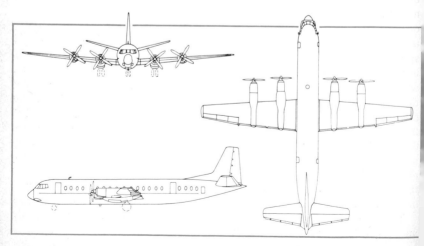

year, together with the proposal for a third version of the Vanguard. This version, called the 953, attracted the attention of BEA which accordingly altered its initial order for 20 Vanguard 951s and specified that 14 were to be of the 953 type.

In the meantime the prototype of the four-engined turbo-prop had already made its maiden flight. The aircraft had been completed as a demonstration model, in the hope of winning new orders. It commenced its tests and trials on January 20, 1959 but in the spring of 1960 the tests were suddenly interrupted because worrying defects were discovered in the compressor of the Tyne engine. As a result all aircraft fitted with this engine were banned from flying. It was not until early July that the Vanguards could resume their activities and continue with the tests, and it was not until December 2, 1960 that they obtained their certificates of airworthiness.

There was thus a considerable delay and when BEA started its first regular

Aircraft: **Vickers Vanguard 953**
Manufacturer: **Vickers-Armstrong Ltd.**
Type: **Civil transport**
Year: **1961**
Engines: **Four Rolls-Royce Tyne 512 turbo-props, 5,545 hp each**
Wingspan: **118 ft 7 in (36.15 m)**
Length: **122 ft 10 in (37.45 m)**
Height: **34 ft 11 in (10.64 m)**
Weight: **146,500 lb (66,452 kg)**
Cruising speed: **425 mph at 20,000 ft (684 km/h at 6,100 m)**
Ceiling: **30,000 ft (9,150 m)**
Range: **1,830 miles (2,945 km)**
Crew: **7**
Passengers: **76–139**

service with the Vanguard 951 on March 1, 1961 the aircraft was already non-competitive. However, the British company could not back down at this stage. On May 1, 1961 the first Vanguard 953 took to the air, and was delivered in the following month. The last one arrived almost a year later, on March 30, 1962. TCA had received the first Vanguard 952 at the end of 1960 which started its service on February 1 of the following year. When jet aircraft took over all the world's major airlines the Vanguard was relegated to transporting cargo.

Soviet Union

For almost two years, and much to the surprise of the western world, Aeroflot was the only company to have a commercial jet in regular service. This historic period started on September 15, 1956, with the inaugural flight of the Tupolev Tu-104 and ended on October 4, 1958 with the resumed service of the British de Havilland Comet. The Soviet Union had managed not only to find a firm footing among the small number of leading nations in the field of air transport, but it had also managed to achieve a very definite advance in terms of quality in its own immense network of air routes. In 1950 this network covered 186,730 miles (300,500 km), and by 1955 had increased to almost 200,000 miles (321,500 km).

As far back as 1932, when it had been established as the State airline, Aeroflot had shown itself to be surprisingly dynamic. In that year it had managed to transport only 27,000 passengers and slightly less than 900 tons of cargo and mail, but growth had been fairly rapid. In 1935 the number of passengers carried had risen to 111,000 and the amount of cargo to 11,000 tons. In addition the network of flights extended across the entire Soviet territory, from Leningrad and Odessa, to Alexandrovsk and remote Siberia. In 1939 the State company had won second place among the major European airlines, surpassed only by Lufthansa which was enjoying its heyday in that period. In the following year, before the German invasion, the network of services had reached 90,910 miles (146,300 km), with the number of passengers carried totalling 395,000 and the amount of cargo 45,000 tons. The outbreak of war abruptly curtailed this flourishing phase of expansion and, although certain vital services remained open, the activities of the State company were concentrated on the task of military transport.

The return to peacetime soon marked the beginning of a new stage of growth. The development of civil aviation in the Soviet Union was considered of prime importance for the consolidation of the entire national economic system. In 1946, a massive programme was launched to revive and strengthen the airline. This programme not only entailed the construction of new aeroplanes, but also the extension of the overall network of services to 108,745 miles (175,000 km). It was in this period that the first entirely new and modern aircraft appeared. This was the twin-engined Ilyushin Il-12 which ended up by becoming the 'cart horse' of the State company, alongside the old Lisunov Li-2, until the mid-1960s. The result of these intense efforts, made under the banner of austerity, was impressive. In 1950 some 1,600,000 passengers and more than 181,000 tons of cargo and mail were transported by Aeroflot. In addition the company had also been allocated tasks not strictly connected with commericial transport. These tasks included fire reconnaissance and agricultural work.

The mid-1950s marked the sudden end of the period of reconstruction in austerity, carried out by using to the full aircraft which were old and non-competitive with the contemporary products of the various industries in the West. The production of the Tupolev Tu-104 was the start of a second phase of expansion which was carried out with unlimited means and has never stopped right up to the present day. The Tu-104 was by no means an economical aircraft, mainly because of its small capacity. It was nevertheless an ultra-modern aeroplane, especially when compared with the obsolete models with twin piston engines which still made up the bulk of Aeroflot's fleet. Its major negative feature was soon remedied by the introduction of the two versions Tu-104 A and Tu-104 B, both with considerably larger capacities. The twin-jet-engined Tupolev was only the first in a line of aircraft which were extremely competitive in the international sector. In addition to pure jet models, the Soviet industries followed the British trend of simultaneously developing excellent aeroplanes powered by turbo-prop engines, such as the Antonov An-10, the Ilyushin I1-18, the gigantic Tupolev Tu-114, and the 'small' Antonov An-24. The contribution of these aeroplanes was immense. In 1959, with a network of flights which had not surpassed 220,000 miles (355,000 km), the number of passengers transported was 12,300,000. In 1965, however, the network had been increased to about 300,000 miles (500,000 km), the number of passengers carried to about 42,000,000, and the cargo and mail transported to 1,000,000 tons. In these same years the consolidation of air transport in the Soviet Union was not limited to just aircraft. The introduction of these new aeroplanes stimulated a vast programme entailing the construction of airports and infrastructures, so as to establish a busy network of fast and efficient services.

In the international field, from the end of the Second World War onwards, Aeroflot was used predominantly as a means of maintaining communications with the satellite countries. In 1949 the Soviet company had managed to create an efficient transport system with all the major cities in eastern Europe and central Europe which were part of the Communist bloc. As far as the western countries were concerned, up until 1954 Aeroflot ran exchange services with the Scandinavian company SAS. Aeroflot used the airport of Helsinki for the change-overs en route to Stockholm, London or Paris, or vice versa. Later a similar agreement was drawn up with Air France, using Prague airport. In 1958, after the start of the Tu-104 service, Aeroflot opened its doors to the other European countries. At the beginning of the 1960s it broadened its range in the international sector by launching services to Africa, Asia, the Middle East and America.

Kalinin K-5

No less than 260 models of this small single-engined commercial aircraft were used on the domestic flights within the Soviet Union. The Kalinin K-5 derived directly from the K-4 built in 1928, echoing the general shape and in particular the elliptically shaped wing patented by the designer K. Alexeivich Kalinin in 1923. The structure of the K-5 was a mixed one, half wood and half metal, as was the outer surface which was made of Duralumin in the forward part of the fuselage and of canvas for the rest of the structure. The State Industries produced two versions of the aeroplane which had different engines and a different forward covering of the fuselage. The first had an M-15 engine constructed under Bristol licence and the second had a Pratt & Whitney Hornet radial engine. This second version of the Kalanin K-5 had a surface covering made of corrugated sheet metal.

Aircraft. **Kalinin K-5**
Manufacturer: **State Industries**
Type: **Civil transport**
Year: **1930**
Engine: **One M-15, radial with 9 air-cooled cylinders, 525 hp**
Wingspan: **67 ft 3 in (20.50 m)**
Length: **51 ft 6 in (15.70 m)**
Height: **–**
Weight: **8,267 lb (3,750 kg) (Loaded)**
Cruising speed: **98 mph (157 km/h)**
Ceiling: **15,680 ft (4,780 m)**
Range: **590 miles (950 km)**
Crew: **2**
Passengers: **8**

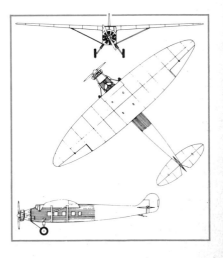

Yakovlev Ya-6 (AIR-6)

Of the three light aircraft produced by the Soviet industries in the 1930s, the Yakovlev Ya-6 was one of the most popular. This was a monoplane with a wing set above the fuselage and a composite covering. It was designed by Alexander Sergeievich Yakovlev in 1932. Yakovlev initially planned the Yakovlev Ya-6 for the specific use of mixed mail and passenger transport over short distances. It was strong, versatile and capable of operating extremely well in poor weather conditions. It was used mainly in Central Asia. A seaplane version was also developed and this was used in areas with lakes and rivers. As is the case with many other Soviet aircraft, the exact number of Ya-6 models built has never been ascertained but it is known that it was produced in large numbers by the State Industries. There is also no doubt that its excellent features fully justified mass production. One of its main features was its ability to take off in a short distance of 80 yards (70 m).

Aircraft: **Yakovlev Ya-6 (AIR-6)**
Manufacturer: **State Industries**
Type: **Light transport**
Year: **1932**
Engine: **One M-11 radial with 5 air-cooled cylinders, 110 hp**
Wingspan: **39 ft 5 in (12.00 m)**
Length: **23 ft 4 in (7.10 m)**
Height: **7 ft 5 in (2.26 m)**
Weight: **2,189 lb (993 kg) (Loaded)**
Cruising speed: **87 mph (140 km/h)**
Ceiling: **14,760 ft (4,500 m)**
Range: **373 miles (600 km)**
Crew: **1**
Passengers: **2**

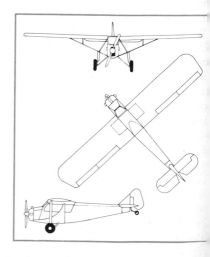

Tupolev ANT-35

Moscow to Leningrad to Moscow — a distance of 787 miles (1,266 km) in slightly more than three and a half hours. This experimental route, tried out in September 1936 by the prototype of the Tupolev ANT-35, is perhaps the best demonstration of the excellent qualities of this small twin-engined commercial aeroplane, one of the first 'modern' civil aircraft made in the Soviet Union. Designed and built in 1935, the ANT-35 was exhibited at the *Salon Aeronautique* in Paris in the following year. After the various tests and trials had been carried out to assess its possibilities on a wide variety of routes, it was put into production. On July 1, 1937 the first ANT-35s were put into service by Aeroflot on the Moscow–Riga–Stockholm route, together with Douglas DC-3s. With a crew of two and ten passengers, its flight specifications and general performances were particularly good, with a cruising speed in the region of 220 mph (350 km/h).

Aircraft: **Tupolev ANT-35**
Manufacturer: **State Industries**
Type: **Civil transport**
Year: **1936**
Engines: **Two M-85 radial with 14 air-cooled cylinders, 850 hp each**
Wingspan: **68 ft 3 in (20.80 m)**
Length: **49 ft 1 in (14.96 m)**
Height: **19 ft 5 in (5.91 m)**
Weight: **14,594 lb (6,620 kg)**
Cruising speed: **218 mph (349 km/h)**
Ceiling: **27,890 ft (8,500 m)**
Range: **1,243 miles (2,000 km)**
Crew: **2**
Passengers: **10**

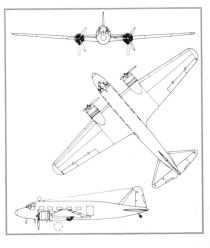

OKO-1

Not unlike the American Northrop Delta of 1934, the OKO-1 was one of several experimental aeroplanes made by the Soviet aeronautical industry in the 1930s both to develop new technologies and to gain experience to match the most advanced western countries. However, compared with the single-engined American commercial transport model, the OKO-1 echoed only the general shape and the appearance of its American counterpart. The structure of the Russian aircraft was totally different, consisting almost entirely of wood, with a wooden covering, while the Delta was built completely of metal. The OKO-1 was designed by Vsevolod K. Tavirov who belonged to the experimental design division of the State Industries. The OKO-1 was completed in early 1937. It first flew in the summer of that year and then underwent trials which revealed that its flight specifications were excellent.

Aircraft: **OKO-1**
Manufacturer: **State Industries**
Type: **Light transport**
Year: **1937**
Engine: **One M.25A, radial with 9 air-cooled cylinders, 730 hp**
Wingspan: **50 ft 6 in (15.40 m)**
Length: **38 ft 1 in (11.60 m)**
Height: **–**
Weight: **7,716 lb (2,500 kg) (Loaded)**
Cruising speed: **174 mph (280 km/h)**
Ceiling: **22,110 ft (6,740 m)**
Range: **430 miles (700 km)**
Crew: **2**
Passengers: **6**

Ilyushin Il-12
Ilyushin Il-14

These aircraft were in use with Aeroflot for almost twenty years and some ,000 were built altogether. These details sum up the role played by a family of modern twin-engined aircraft. Both the Il-12 and the Il-14P were designed by Sergei Vladimorovich Ilyushin during the middle of the war and in the immediate postwar period. The Il-12s and Il-14s showed themselves to be worthy successors to the aeroplane they had been summoned to replace, the American Douglas DC-3. The DC-3 had been built from 1942 onwards under licence by the State Industries with the name of Lisunov Li-2.

It was some time after the start of regular production of the Dakota, of which more than 2,000 were made, that Ilyushin and his colleagues embarked on the project to produce a more modern successor. This, called the Ilyushin Il-12, appeared as a prototype in early 1946 and was displayed in public for the first time at Tushino airport in August of that year. It was an elegant monoplane with a low wing, built entirely of metal and powered by a pair of large radial Shvetsov engines. These engines in turn were derived from the Pratt & Whitney R-1830 which was built under licence in the U.S.S.R. The aeroplane was also fitted with a completely retractable tricycle undercarriage. The inside of the aeroplane revealed its modern design for commercial transport. Its average capacity was 27 passengers, arranged in nine rows of seats in the cabin. The cabin was also fitted out with plenty of windows.

The service was inaugurated on August 22, 1947 and after less than a year, in May 1948, the Il-12s were being used in large numbers on the main domestic and international flights handled by the State company. Throughout the 1950s the Ilyushins were used widely and intensively and the last ones were not withdrawn finally until spring 1965. As well as the version for passenger transport another version designed exclusively for freight transport was operated simultaneously. In addition to being used by Aeroflot, which had on average some two hundred of these aircraft in service, the Il-12s were used by the Czechoslovakian company CSA and the Polish LOT. The latter withdrew them from service in 1959.

In 1953 the prototype of a new version of the twin-engined Ilyushin appeared. It was called the Il-14. Essentially this aeroplane was an Il-12 which had been structurally improved and fitted with more powerful engines. Apart from a general refinement of the aerodynamics, the aircraft had a considerably different wing and fin, modified respectively to obtain greater lift and better directional stability. After the appearance of the prototype, the initial production of the new twin-engined model was destined for the military. The purely commercial version was called the Il-14P and put into service by Aeroflot on November 30, 1954.

The Ilyushin Il-14 had a fairly similar development to that of the previous model even though it was a more successful and popular aeroplane. In 1956 the Il-14M version appeared,

with a fuselage that had been lengthened by a yard (m) and a capacity
increased to a maximum of 32
passengers. The other version was the
Il-14G, which was only used for
freight. However, apart from these aircraft built in the Soviet Union there
were more than a hundred built under
licence in East Germany and in
Czechoslovakia. These latter were
produced by the Avia company which,

Aircraft: **Ilyushin Il-12**
Manufacturer: **State Industries**
Type: **Civil transport**
Year: **1946**
Engines: **Two Shvetsov ASh-82FN, radia**
  with 14 air-cooled cylinders, 1,650 h
  each
Wingspan: **104 ft 0 in (31.70 m)**
Length: **69 ft 11 in (21.31 m)**
Height: **26 ft 6 in (8.07 m)**
Weight: **38,030 lb (17,250 kg) (Loaded)**
Cruising speed: **217 mph at 8,200 ft (35(**
  km/h at 2,500 m)
Ceiling: **21,980 ft (6,700 m)**
Range: **1,243 miles (2,000 km)**
Crew: **4–5**
Passengers: **27–32**

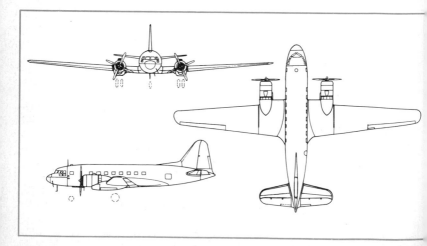

in addition to using its own designations for the versions made in the U.S.S.R. also developed an executive version (the Avia-14 Super) and one equipped with a pressurized cabin called the Avia-14 Salon, with a capacity of 42 passengers.

Overall, even though the figures are approximate, about 3,000 models of the I1-12 were built and almost 3,500 of the I1-14.

Aircraft: **Ilyushin I1-14P**
Manufacturer: **State Industries**
Type: **Civil transport**
Year: **1954**
Engines: **Two Shvetsov ASh-82T, radial with 14 air-cooled cylinders, 1,900 hp each**
Wingspan: **104 ft 0 in (31.70 m)**
Length: **69 ft 11 in (21.31 m)**
Height: **25 ft 7 in (7.80 m)**
Weight: **38,030 lb (17,250 kg) (Loaded)**
Cruising speed: **217 mph at 8,200 ft (350 km/h at 2,500 m)**
Ceiling: **21,981 ft (6,700 m)**
Range: **807 miles (1,300 km)**
Crew: **4–5**
Passengers: **18–32**

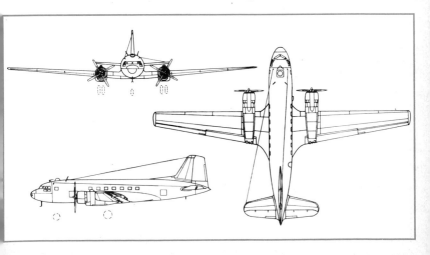

Antonov An-2

The Antonov An-2 was the only transport biplane manufactured in the postwar period and was one of the most popular all-rounders in Soviet civil aviation. With its old-fashioned look and amazing versatility, the Antonov An-2 was used for every conceivable purpose including commercial transport, agriculture, scientific and meteorological research, forestry and for fire-fighting. The great success it enjoyed (in 1960 the U.S.S.R. alone had already built more than 5,000 aircraft and production under licence was also under way in Poland, China and East Germany) was matched by large export orders. Today there are many An-2s still in service in numerous countries in the Communist bloc and in Africa and Asia, and they continue to offer the same safety and reliability as they carry out a host of irreplaceable tasks.

The prototype made its maiden flight in 1947. The aircraft had been designed by the study group headed by Oleg Antonov at the express request of the Soviet Ministry of Forestry and Agriculture. It was a single-engined biplane, with a metal structure and composite covering and a broad spacious fuselage with a fixed undercarriage. From the very first trials in the air the An-2 showed itself to be an extremely sound and reliable aeroplane, capable of flying in any sort of conditions. Mass production was immediately started and the model developed through numerous versions of the basic model, all differing depending on the use for which they were intended. In all there were 17 different versions. The main versions were the An-2P for general transport; the An-2S for agricultural use; the An-2V seaplane; the An-2L, a fire-fighting version of the previous one; the An-2ZA for high altitude meteorological research; and the An-2M, a further improved version for agricultural use.

Each one of these aeroplanes had its own busy operational life. The An-2Ps,

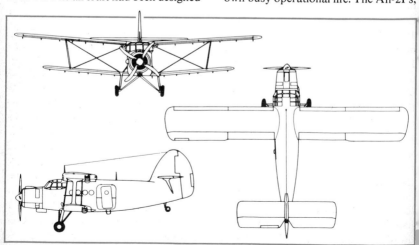

Aircraft: **Antonov An-2P**
Manufacturer: **State Industries**
Type: **Light transport**
Year: **1947**
Engine: **One Shvetsov ASh-621R, radial with 9 air-cooled cylinders, 1,000 hp**
Wingspan: **59 ft 8 in (18.18 m)**
Length: **42 ft 0 in (12.80 m)**
Height: **13 ft 9 in (4.20 m)**
Weight: **12,125 lb (5,500 kg) (Loaded)**
Cruising speed: **108 mph (200 km/h)**
Ceiling: **14,270 ft (4,350 m)**
Range: **560 miles (905 km)**
Crew: **2**
Passengers: **10**

for example, were used in large numbers by Aeroflot for local flights. These flights were especially in remoter and desert areas, carrying out tasks ranging from simple passenger or goods transport to urgent medical rescue work. An idea of the intensity of the use to which these biplanes were put, they were only old-fashioned in appearance, can be given by the date May 15, 1967, when one of the thousands of An-2s in operation had the honour of carrying the 100,000,000th passenger: a remarkable record for an aircraft of this type! However, Aeroflot was not alone in using the An-2Ps, for Russia's example was followed in Czechoslovakia, East Germany, Nepal, Mongolia as well as many African states.

The next most important version was the agricultural one. The An-2S models were appropriately modified for the task of spraying large tracts of cultivated land. They were fitted with a longer undercarriage and a tank capable of holding 310 gallons (1,400 litres) of liquid or powder products.

These were sprayed by means of a tube in the lower wing, which was worked by a pump that was driven aerodynamically. The use of the An-2S was very heavy and the total number of acres (hectares) covered reached tens of millions each year. In order to further improve the capacities of the aircraft to meet increasing needs, the An-2M version was developed in 1964 and this was the only one in the series that differed noticeably from the basic model. As well as having structural reinforcements and a differently shaped fin, these aeroplanes were equipped with more powerful engines and better spraying equipment.

Yakovlev Yak-16

Even though it was modern and capable of giving good allround performances, the Yak-16 was not successful in the Aeroflot ranks immediately after the war. This was basically because of its limited passenger capacity which made it poorly attuned to the precise needs of the Soviet airline, which was at that time busily tackling the problems arising from the rapid growth of air traffic in the U.S.S.R. The Yak-16 was nevertheless completed in 1948. It was a small twin-engined model with a low wing and built entirely of metal. During its trials the aeroplane showed good general features and in spite of the lack of interest from Aeroflot, it was used for a long series of presentations in an attempt to gather orders for it from the satellite countries. It was also exhibited in Czechoslovakia, Poland and Finland, but without success. Few models were used on the commercial routes, although some were used by the Air Force.

Aircraft: **Yakovlev Yak-16**
Manufacturer: **State Industries**
Type: **Civil transport**
Year: **1948**
Engines: **Two Shvetsov ASh-21, radial with 7 air-cooled cylinders, 750 hp each**
Wingspan: **65 ft 7 in (20.00 m)**
Length: **47 ft 7 in (14.50 m)**
Height: **11 ft 10 in (3.60 m)**
Weight: **14,110 lb (6,400 kg) (Loaded)**
Cruising speed: **180 mph at 5,580 ft (290 km/h at 1,700 m)**
Ceiling: **16,400 ft (5,000 m)**
Range: **620 miles (1,000 km)**
Crew: **2**
Passengers: **10**

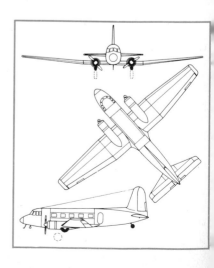

Tupolev Tu-104

The Soviet aeronautical industry slipped almost unnoticed between Great Britain and the United States in the long race for the first commercial jet aircraft. If the de Havilland Comet had the honour of being the first aeroplane of this type in the world to make a regular flight on May 2, 1952, thus beating the Boeing 707 by almost six years, in the Eastern bloc the Tupolev 104 undoubtedly took second place overall. In fact on September 15, 1956 this twin-engined jet, which was also the first civil jet-powered aircraft to be made for Aeroflot, made its inaugural flight on the Moscow–Omsk–Irkutsk route and became for a certain period the only commercial jet flying a regular service in the world. In fact the Comet had been withdrawn two years earlier, after a series of disastrous accidents and it was not until October 1958 that it resumed its activities with BOAC. This followed only a matter of days later by Pan Am's first Boeing 707s.

As is the case with most Soviet aircraft, little is known about the development stages of the Tupolev Tu-104. The project was drawn up in 1953 within the context of a huge programme to reorganize and modernize the Aeroflot company. This programme was vital in order to keep pace with the rapid growth of the demand for air transport in the Soviet Union. It was undoubtedly a great leap forward, especially if one takes into account the fact that in that period the structure of the network of services handled by the State company relied on piston-engined Li-2s and Ilyushin Il-12s and Il-14s. To speed up the phase of development as much as possible, the study group, headed by Andrei Nicolaevich Tupolev, made extensive use of certain structural components from the twin-engined Tu-16 bomber. The bomber was at that time in an advanced stage of production having been shown to the public in 1954. In fact the Tu-104 was designed in such a way that it could be fitted with the wing, tailplane, undercarriage, engine installation and forward section of the fuselage of the bomber. Construction of the civil aeroplane was quite swift, and the Tu-104 prototype made its maiden flight on June 17, 1955. A little more than three weeks later, on July 3, the aircraft was put on display at Tushino airport. However, western observers had to wait for almost eight more months before they were informed of the existence of the new aeroplane. It was not until March 22, 1956 that the prototype landed at London airport on a special flight. The impression created was considerable. The aeronautical industry of the Soviet Union had managed, amidst much secrecy, not only to make up all the time lost but also to step well ahead of the western aeronautical industries.

The Tupolev Tu-104 was an elegant monoplane with a low wing. It was hallmarked by the negative dihedral angle and pronounced swept-back form of the wing which varied between 35° and 40°. The main landing gear was retracted backwards and housed in two conspicuous fairings which extended well beyond the rear edge of the wing. The two Mikulin turbo-jets were mounted alongside the fuselage. The fuselage could hold 50 passengers, who were accommodated in a total of four compartments, the rearmost one being the main one. In the cockpit there was one detail which was to become a feature of many Soviet commercial aircraft and it took western observers somewhat by surprise: the position of the navigator, who was situated in the tip of the nose and at a lower level than the pilot. This position was right behind the glassed-in panel identical to that of the Tu-16 bomber.

The initially produced Tu-104s totalled twenty or so in all. They were followed almost immediately on the assembly lines by the first models of the second version, the Tu-104A, with a larger capacity of 70 passengers, and more powerful engines. The first of these aeroplanes was displayed in June 1957 and immediately proved its mettle by setting up a series of speed and load records for its category: on September 6 the record of the largest load of 44,216 pounds (20,053 kg) at 6,500 feet (2,000 m) and the altitude record of 36,814 feet (11,221 m): on September 11 the circuit speed record at 6,500 feet (2,000 m) with loads of 2,200 and 4,400 pounds (1,000 and 2,000 kg) at 557.7 mph (897.498 km/h).

Aeroflot was quick to put the new version of the twin-engined Tupolev into service and with the new potential of its fleet was in a position to extend and consolidate all its flights, both domestic and international. The Tu-104 made it possible to make an incredible improvement to the company, in terms of both quality and quantity. The traditional Ilyushin I1-12 flight from Moscow to Irkutsk lasted a total of 17 hours and 50 minutes, while the Moscow–Peking service took 32 hours and 10 minutes, including intermediate stops. However, the arrival of the twin-engined jets made it possible to reduce these times, respectively, to 6 hours and 30 minutes, and 10 hours and 5 minutes.

A little more than a year after the appearance of the Tu-104A a third

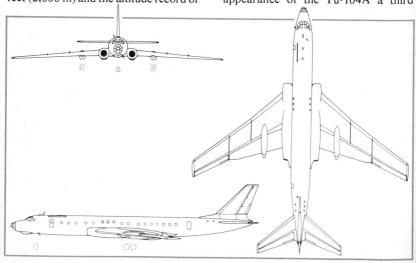

production version, called the Tu-104B, also made its appearance. The Tu-104B was hallmarked by an even larger capacity than the previous version, and was now 100% larger than the capacity of the original model. The accommodation on board for 100 passengers had been made possible by considerably lengthening the fuselage and modifying the structure of the interior. In fact the fuselage was almost the same as that of the four-engined jet, the Tupolev Tu-110 which was presented in summer 1957. The Tu-110 had been developed from the Tu-104 and had four engines and larger overall dimensions. However, the Tu-104B had more powerful engines which were Mikulin engines producing a thrust of 21,400 pounds (9,700 kg).

These last Tupolevs went into service on the Moscow–Leningrad route on April 15, 1959 and within just a few months joined the two previous versions of the aeroplane on the major routes handled by Aeroflot. As a result many Tu-104As were modified so as to

Aircraft: **Tupolev Tu-104A**
Manufacturer: **State Industries**
Type: **Civil transport**
Year: **1957**
Engines: **Two Mikulin AM-3M turbo-jets, 19,180 lb (8,700 kg) thrust each**
Wingspan: **113 ft 4 in (34.54 m)**
Length: **127 ft 5 in (38.85 m)**
Height: **39 ft 0 in (11.90 m)**
Weight: **167,550 lb (76,000 kg) (Loaded)**
Cruising speed: **497 mph at 32,000 ft (800 km/h at 10,000 m)**
Ceiling: **37,700 ft (11,500 m)**
Range: **1,926 miles (3,100 km)**
Crew: **5**
Passengers: **70**

reach the capacity of the last version. In addition many Tu-104Bs had their interior restructured to fit in another 15 seats, thus bringing the total number of passengers carried (although by no means in the lap of luxury) to 115. However, in the course of its long operational career the twin-engined Tupolev underwent numerous modifications with regard to capacity and type of load.

Once again the exact production figures for the Tu-104 are not known, but western technicians and observers estimate the total number to be around 200 aircraft.

Ilyushin I1-18

The Ilyushin I1-18 was conceived as part of the programme to strengthen the Aeroflot fleet in the early 1950s, and made its mark internationally as one of the best available commercial turbo-prop aircraft. Its validity was confirmed by its export successes: no less than 84 aircraft out of about 500 built were bought by Eastern bloc or aligned countries.

The project was launched by Sergei Vladimorovich Ilyushin and his study group towards the end of 1954. It was a completely new aircraft which did not derive from previous models or military aeroplanes. It also had nothing to do with another transport aircraft which had been built by Ilyushin in 1947 and given the same designation of I1-18. In fact this latter aircraft was a large four-engined model with piston engines which after a year of trials had been adjudged unsatisfactory by Aeroflot. It had, therefore, never got beyond the prototype stage. The new project, on the other hand, was radically different and entailed a medium-range, high-capacity four-engined transport model, equipped with a pressurized cabin and powered by four turbo-props. The prototype made its maiden flight on July 4, 1957 and was shown to the public six days later, together with two other commercial aircraft that had been built at the same time. These were the four-engined Tupolev 110 jet and the large turbo-prop transport model, the Antonov An-10. The prototype had the name *Moskva* (Moscow) written in bright letters on both sides of the fuselage and at the end of the flight tests and various other trials the Ilyushin I1-18 was put into mass-production at an ever increasing pace. On April 20, 1959 it went into service with Aeroflot.

In its original version the aircraft had a capacity of 80 passengers, but before too long the first modified versions appeared. These were called I1-18V and they could hold a maximum of 110 people. As is normal with many

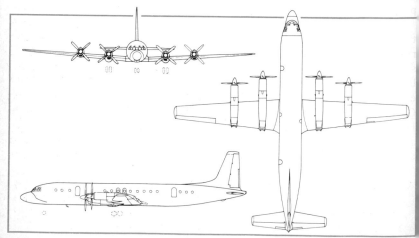

aircraft belonging to the Soviet State airline, the capacity varied according to the time of year, or rather, according to how much space was necessary to accommodate the heavy winter clothing of the passengers. The capacity ranged from 84 in the winter months to 110 for the rest of the year. However the Ilyushin Il-18s were used quite intensively and in 1967 there were 180 Aeroflot flights being served by them. In that year alone they transported more than 10,000,000 people.

The remarkable characteristics of the aeroplane were its safety and reliability, which all favoured its success on the foreign market formed by the satellite countries. The four-engined Ilyushins were purchased by Czechoslovakia, East Germany, Hungary and Poland and put into service in their respective airlines. In addition, Air Guinée, Air Mali, CAAC (People's Republic of China), Ghana Airways and Cubana all purchased the Ilyushin Il-18.

The last two production versions were the Il-18D of 1962 and the Il-

Aircraft: **Ilyushin Il-18V**
Manufacturer: **State Industries**
Type: **Civil transport**
Year: **1959**
Engines: **Four Ivchenko A1-20K turbo-props, 4,000 ehp, each**
Wingspan: **122 ft 8 in (37.40 m)**
Length: **117 ft 9 in (35.90 m)**
Height: **33 ft 4 in (10.16 m)**
Weight: **132,000 lb (61,200 kg) (Loaded)**
Cruising speed: **404 mph at 26,250 ft (650 km/h at 8,000 m)**
Ceiling: **35,000 ft (10,750 m)**
Range: **2,590 miles (4,800 km)**
Crew: **5**
Passengers: **84–110**

18E of 1965. In both cases the aircraft were considerably modified as regards the equipment on board and the size of the passenger cabin. The D version also had a longer range. This increased from 3,000 miles (4,800 km) in the Ilyushin Il-18V and Il-18E, to 4,000 miles (6,500 km) in the Il-18D. The models in the D version also underwent specific modifications to the engines which were Ivchenko A1-20M, which gave a 10% reduction in fuel consumption. In addition this version had modifications to the structure of the central part of the wing. The Ilyushin Il-18D went into regular service with Aeroflot in 1966.

171

Tupolev Tu-114 Rossiya

No less than ten international speed and altitude records were set between 1960 and 1962 by one of the latest giants built by the Soviet aeronautical industry, the Tupolev Tu-114. When it made its appearance on October 3, 1957, this huge four-engined turbo-prop turned out to be the largest and heaviest commercial aeroplane in the world. It was to be surpassed only by the Boeing 747 'jumbo' of the 1970s. With a wingspan of more than 165 feet (51 m), a weight at take-off of 175 tons, and 50,000 hp in its four pairs of counter-rotating propellers, the Tu-114 took a well-deserved place in the well-established family of Soviet giants of the air. These giants had originated back in 1913 with the Sikorsky Ilya Mourometz and had produced aircraft like the Tupolev ANT-14 of 1931.

The project began in 1953 at the request of Aeroflot which wanted to have a long-range, large-capacity com-mercial transport aircraft which it could use on its busiest domestic flights and on its international routes. Here again, as for the twin-engined Tu-104 jet, Andrei Nicolaevich Tupolev and his colleagues were inspired by a military aircraft, the Tu-20, which was a large heavy bomber in an advanced stage of production. As a result the civil project bore a noticeable resemblance to the military one. Apart from the different fuselage, which was redesigned for passenger use, the wing, undercarriage and engine installation were all the same. The four large turbine engines in the original version each produced 12,000 hp and drove pairs of counter-rotating blades with a diameter of more than 18 feet (5.60 m). The cabin could hold 170 passengers, although this number could be reduced to 120 for intercontinental flights. After the completion of the prototype and the end of the trials in June 1959 the Tu-114 was exhibited at the Paris *Salon Aeronautique* where it greatly impressed western aeronautical

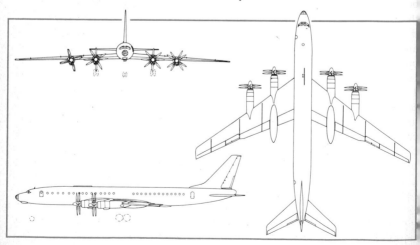

observers. It was subsequently used for a series of experimental flights on some of the major inter-continental routes.

One of the major features of the Tu 114 was its high cruising speed which was quite exceptional for an aircraft with propellers. This feature made it a competitive model, even on the international market. Aeroflot put it into regular service on April 24, 1961 between Moscow and Khabarovsk (on the far-flung Chinese border), covering the 4,225 miles (6,800 km) in 8 hours and 15 minutes. In 1963 the Tu-114s opened flights between Moscow and Havana and Moscow and Delhi, and in 1965 and 1966 they inaugurated services between Montreal and Accra, and Moscow and Montreal. In 1966, in collaboration with Japan Air Lines, attention was given to the possibility of operating on the Moscow–Tokyo route and this service started in April of the following year. This was the last use to which the Tu-114 was put and from autumn 1967 onwards it was gradually replaced by the Ilyushin Il-62 jet.

Aircraft: **Tupolev Tu-114 Rossiya**
Manufacturer: **State Industries**
Type: **Civil transport**
Year: **1957**
Engines: **Four Kuznetsov NK-12MV turbo-props, 12,500 ehp each**
Wingspan: **167 ft 8 in (51.10 m)**
Length: **177 ft 6 in (54.10 m)**
Height: **50 ft 10 in (15.50 m)**
Weight: **385,809 lb (175,000 kg) (Loaded)**
Cruising speed: **478 mph at 29,500 ft (770 km/h at 9,000 m)**
Ceiling: **39,500 ft (12,000 m)**
Range: **5,560 miles (8,950 km)**
Crew: **10**
Passengers: **170**

Not many examples of the Tu-114 were built. The most reliable figures suggest an overall production of around 30 aircraft. Of these, one was completed specifically in the D version, with a fuselage virtually the same as that of the Tu-20 bomber. This aircraft was designed above all for carrying freight, mail and occasionally passengers. Two other models of the Tu-114D were made directly on the military assembly lines. The major feature of this special version of the Tu-114 was its range, which was no less than 6,200 miles (10,000 km).

173

Antonov An-10

As the initial version of the popular series of heavy transport aircraft built by Oleg Antonov in the 1950s and 1960s, the An-10 made its public debut on July 4, 1957, just four months after the maiden flight of the prototype on March 7, 1957. This was a large monoplane with the wing positioned above the fuselage and a spacious pressurized cabin designed expressly for high density transport. It could also operate from rough airfields and strips. After a series of experimental flights Aeroflot put the Antonov An-10 into service from July 22, 1959 onwards. The An-10 was soon joined by the larger version called the An-10A. The Antonov An-10A could carry 100 passengers instead of 85 and had a fuselage about 6 feet 6 inches (2 m) longer. This new and versatile transport model was used intensively and by mid-1967 the 300 or so aircraft of the two versions delivered had managed to carry some 12,000,000 passengers.

Aircraft: **Antonov An-10A**
Manufacturer: **State Industries**
Type: **Civil transport**
Year: **1957**
Engines: **Four Ivchenko AI-20K turbo-props, 4,000 ehp each**
Wingspan: **124 ft 8 in (38.00 m)**
Length: **111 ft 6 in (34.00 m)**
Height: **32 ft 2 in (9.80 m)**
Weight: **119,050 lb (54,000 kg) (Loaded)**
Cruising speed: **422 mph at 32,800 ft (680 km/h at 10,000 m)**
Ceiling: **36,000 ft (11,000 m)**
Range: **758 miles (1,220 km)**
Crew: **5**
Passengers: **100**

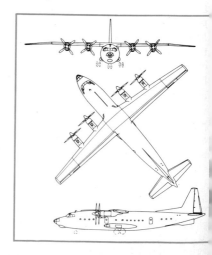

Antonov An-14 Pchelka

Thc Antonov An-14 another versatile all rounder which was produced by Oleg Antonov in 1958, after the renowned An-2 nine years earlier. The An-14 was a small twin-engined model which was christened Pchelka (Bee) and quickly earned popularity not only in the sector of light transport but also for general and agricultural use. The prototype made its maiden flight on March 15, 1958 and was followed by three more aircraft which had modified engines and one or two structural parts, before mass production was started. In all 200 aircraft were built. The An-14 was built in three basic forms: for passenger transport, as a flying ambulance (capable of carrying six people on stretchers plus a doctor) and for agricultural work. In the last case the aircraft was equipped with a tank holding almost 220 gallons (1,000 litres) and a spraying device. The Pchelka was also successful on the export market.

Aircraft: **Antonov An-14 Pchelka**
Manufacturer: **State Industries**
Type: **Light transport**
Year: **1958**
Engines: **Two Ivchenko AI-14RF, radial with 9 air-cooled cylinders, 300 hp each**
Wingspan: **72 ft 2 in (21.99 m)**
Length: **37 ft 1½ in (11.32 m)**
Height: **15 ft 2 in (4.63 m)**
Weight: **7,936 lb (3,600 kg) (Loaded)**
Cruising speed: **109 mph at 6,550 ft (175 km/h at 2,000 m)**
Ceiling: **16,400 ft (5,000 m)**
Range: **400 miles (650 km)**
Crew: **1**
Passengers: **8**

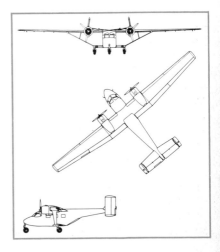

175

Antonov An-24

The Antonov An-24 belonged to the same category as the British Handley Page H.P.R.7 Herald and the Dutch Fokker F.27 Friendship. The twin turbo-prop Antonov An-24 was built with the intention of replacing the old piston-engined Ilyushin I1-12 and I1-14 and the Lisunov Li-2, which were still in service in the early 1960s on many of Aeroflot's domestic flights. Overall the An-24 showed itself to be an excellent aircraft and as well as being used intensively by the Soviet state airline, it was also fairly successful on the export market in many of the Eastern bloc states.

The project was launched by Oleg Antonov's study group in 1957, at the specific request of Aeroflot. The airline wanted a short-to-medium range transport aircraft, with a capacity of 40 seats, which could operate in the most varied of climatic conditions and entailed very low running costs. This was no easy task, but the designers

managed to tackle it brilliantly. In terms of general appearance they chose that of two contemporary aircraft, the twin-engined Herald and Friendship. These aircraft had a high wing, a tricycle undercarriage, propulsion by two turbo-props and a spacious fuselage giving the possibility of further capacity increases. The first prototype made its maiden flight on December 20, 1959, but soon encountered a series of problems to do with stability which made it necessary to make various structural modifications. These were all carried out in the second prototype which passed its various trials with flying colours. At the same time another five pre-production aircraft were also built, two of which were for static fatigue tests and three for flight tests. It was not until April 1962 that the first production An-24 aircraft were finally delivered to Aeroflot. They then had to train crews and make their own experimental technical flights. Various test-flights with freight on board were made in July, followed in September by

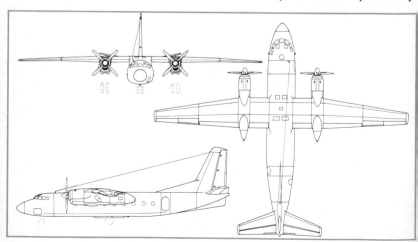

the first passenger services, which were also experimental. Eventually, on October 31, 1962, Aeroflot inaugurated regular services, using An-24s between Kiev and Kherson in the Ukraine. The Ukraine was in some ways the testing ground for the new aeroplane and it lived up to all expectations. By mid-1967 the An-24s in service between the cities of the Ukraine had carried some 2,500,000 passengers and 100,000 tons of cargo, thus achieving a high coefficient in terms of use. In the meantime a no less intensive use was being made on flights in other parts of the Soviet Union which, had just surpassed the figure of 150 different services.

The initial production models were joined by the V version, with a higher carrying capacity. It was in fact the An-24V that attracted the attention of many Eastern bloc or aligned countries. The first orders came from the Lebanon, and these were followed by Poland (which used ten in its LOT airline), and airlines such as Air Guinée, Air Mali, Cubana, Interflug

Aircraft: **Antonov An-24V**
Manufacturer: **State Industries**
Type: **Civil transport**
Year: **1962**
Engines: **Two Ivchenko AI-24A turbo-props, 2,550 ehp each**
Wingspan: **95 ft 9 in (29.20 m)**
Length: **77 ft 2 in (23.53 m)**
Height: **27 ft 3 in (8.32 m)**
Weight: **46,300 lb (21,000 kg) (Loaded)**
Cruising speed: **310 mph at 19,700 ft (500 km/h at 6,000 m)**
Ceiling: **29,500 ft (9,000 m)**
Range: **400 miles (650 km)**
Crew: **3**
Passengers: **50**

(German Democratic Republic), Mongolian Airlines, and other smaller firms.

As well as the all-passenger version, the An-24 was made in four other forms: mixed passenger and freight use (with a capacity of 30 people); all freight; executive (with accommodation for 16 people); and luxury. This last version could accommodate eight passengers in great comfort, and also had two separate cabins with bunks. Towards the end of the 1960s models of a second series production appeared. These had more powerful engines and offered generally better performances.

Antonov An-12

The Antonov An-12 was the direct successor of the An-10 model of 1957. It came into being as a military version of the large heavy transport aeroplane and as such it underwent a series of major structural modifications. These were designed to enlarge its interior capacity and improve and facilitate loading. It became the basic model used by the Soviet Air Force and was supplied in quite large numbers to the air forces of numerous aligned countries. However, for a while it was also used in a civil version and played an important part in the freight division of Aeroflot.

The Antonov An-12 was designed and made at almost the same time as the previous model, compared with which it differed mainly in the rear section of the fuselage which had a large door which was also used as a loading ramp for vehicles or bulky cargo. The first civil use of this aircraft was with aircraft destined for the military. Some military models belonging to the Soviet Air Force were stripped of their armament and other specifically military equipment and handed over to Aeroflot. In addition similar conversions were carried out by Ghana Airways, Cubana and the Polish company LOT. Following these moves it was decided to make a version destined exclusively for the civil market and this was called the Antonov An-12B. Though outwardly similar to the military transport model, this aeroplane differed in the interior of the fuselage and, to a lesser extent, in the tail, from which the gun turret had been removed and replaced by a conspicuous fairing. The inside of the immense hold was over 44 feet (13.50 m) long, 10 feet (3 m) wide, and nearly 8 feet (2.40 m) high. The loading surface was capable of supporting a weight of 1.5 tons (1,500 kg) per square

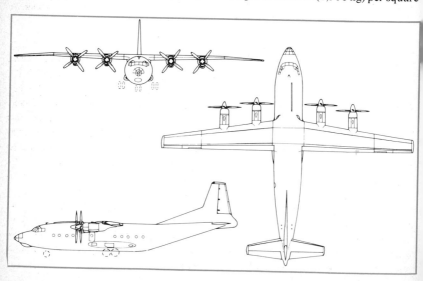

yard (sq m). A small winch was installed above the rear loading bay. It had a capacity of 2.3 tons (2,300 kg) which helped with the job of moving and loading particularly heavy and bulky cargo. In addition, beyond the hold for freight and behind the cockpit, there was a compartment that could hold 14 passengers.

The impressive specifications of this aircraft, plus its safety (which had been amply demonstrated in the task of military transport) and its undoubted versatility encouraged Aeroflot to use it on its commercial services. After a series of experimental flights, on February 3, 1966 an international service was inaugurated between Moscow and Paris, via Riga, in collaboration with Air France. Some time later the international service was extended to the Moscow–Djakarta route. In 1967 the An-12Bs were also used on the longest and most important domestic routes in the Soviet Union and acted as freight transporters on at least 11 of these. In the course of its busy career it was also joined by the

Aircraft: **Antonov An-12B**
Manufacturer: **State Industries**
Type: **Civil transport**
Year: **1960**
Engines: **Four Ivchenko AI-20K turbo-props, 4,000 ehp each**
Wingspan: **124 ft 8 in (38.00 m)**
Length: **108 ft 3 in (33.00 m)**
Height: **34 ft 6 in (10.53 m)**
Weight: **134,500 lb (61,000 kg) (Loaded)**
Cruising speed: **373 mph at 32,800 ft (600 km/h at 10,000 m)**
Ceiling: **33,500 ft (10,200 m)**
Range: **2,110 miles (3,400 km)**
Crew: **5**
Payload: **32,000 lb (14,500 kg) (including 14 passengers)**

An-10, many of which were modified to the same standards as the An-12B.

Oleg Antonov used the vast store of experience gained from the production of the An-10 and An-12 to design what will be remembered as his largest ever transport aeroplane: the gigantic An-22 Antei. When it appeared at the *Salon Aeronautique* in Paris in 1965 it was the heaviest aircraft ever produced up until then. The Antonov An-22 had a wingspan of 211 feet 4 inches (64.40 m), a length of 189 feet 7 inches (57.80 m) and a height of 41 feet 2 inches (12.53 m).

Tupolev Tu-124

In practical terms the Tupolev Tu-124 was a scaled down version of the Tu-104. It was built to meet the requirements of Aeroflot for a new, medium capacity, short-range aircraft with which to replace the last twin piston-engined models still in service. Among the major features which made the Tu-124 successful were its exceptional structural strength, its ability to operate from rough landing strips, its great versatility and the ease with which it could be flown and serviced. The project was launched in 1958 by the study group headed by Andrei Nicolaevich Tupolev. In fact at that time Aeroflot, which had gained two years experience with its first commercial jet, had issued precise requests for the production of a similar aircraft. The original request was, however, for a smaller aircraft and with a lower capacity for use on its short-to medium-range domestic flights. The Tu-124 made its maiden flight in June 1960 and though in many respects it resembled the larger Tu-104, it was hallmarked by an important technical innovation, which made it unique. This was the adoption of turbofan engines, for the first time mounted on a small transport aeroplane which was designed for short to medium-range service. The initial capacity of the Tu-124 was 44 passengers, but this figure underwent many variations in the course of the aircraft's long and busy career. It increased to 56 with the appearance of the V version and ranged from a minimum of 22 to a maximum of 36 in the mixed passenger-cargo versions which were used on many Aeroflot flights.

The Soviet State airline put the new twin-engined Tupolev jet into service on October 2, 1962, between Moscow and Tallinn, and by the end of the year had succeeded in its ambitious

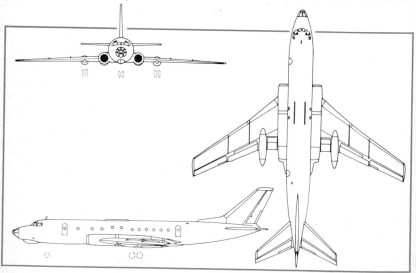

programme to link up all the capitals of the Socialist Republics with turbine-powered transport aircraft. The use of the Tu-124 spread gradually and the network of services covered by these aircraft totalled 22,725 miles (36,570 km) in 1964. Two years later the Tupolev Tu-124s were being used on more than 70 domestic routes and in 1967 alone they carried 2,000,000 passengers.

In addition to the hundreds of models delivered to Aeroflot, a small number were also used by various companies in the satellite countries. CSA of Czechoslovakia, for example, bought three Tu-124s and put them into service in 1964.

The excellent general qualities of the Tupolev Tu-124 and the experience acquired in its production and use gave rise to a somewhat more modern and valid model, which today still represents one of the best aircraft in its category. This was the Tu-134, a twin-engined jet with a larger capacity (on average 72 passengers) which was derived directly from the preceding air-

Aircraft: Tupolev Tu-124V
Manufacturer: **State Industries**
Type: **Civil transport**
Year: **1960**
Engines: **Two Soloviev D-20P turbofans, 11,905 lb (5,400 kg) thrust each**
Wingspan: **83 ft 10 in (25.55 m)**
Length: **100 ft 4 in (30.58 m)**
Height: **26 ft 6 in (8.08 m)**
Weight: **83,775 lb (38,000 kg) (Loaded)**
Cruising speed: **540 mph at 32,800 ft (870 km/h at 10,000 m)**
Ceiling: **38,385 ft (11,700 m)**
Range: **780 miles (1,250 km)**
Crew: **3–4**
Passengers: **56**

craft. The two prototypes of the Tu-134, the first of which flew in 1963, were in fact made by directly modifying two 124s on the production lines. The new aircraft had a series of structural modifications in the fuselage and wing, but its main characteristics were the adoption of a T-shaped tail and the installation of the two engines on both sides of the rear section of the fuselage. In some respects these features were similar to the French Caravelle and the American DC-9. In production the Tu-134s replaced the Tu-124s when about a hundred had been completed.

181

France

Almost 100,000 passengers transported in one year, sixth place among the European airlines after Ala Littoria, KLM, Imperial and British Airways, Aeroflot and Deutsche Lufthansa. This was the rosy situation of Air France in 1939, on the eve of the Second World War. The war dealt a cruel blow to the airline and the entire system of French air transport when it was gathering particular momentum. The consequences of the German occupation were drastic: in 1942 Deutsche Lufthansa appropriated aircraft, buildings, personnel and flight networks. In practical terms metropolitan French aviation ceased to exist as such.

When the war was over the situation changed radically. The surviving airlines were nationalized and on June 26, 1945 they were put under the control of a specific body, the *Réseau des Lignes Aériennes Françaises*. Less than a year later, on January 1, 1946, there re-emerged the famous name that had branded French air transport throughout the 1930s: *Société Nationale Air France*. Things came to life remarkably quickly. As far as aircraft were concerned the French were shrewd enough to follow a fairly diversified policy. On the one hand they encouraged their own industries to produce modern and competitive aeroplanes, and to regain a position of prestige in the international sector; but at the same time they showed no hesitation in acquiring the best means available at that time. In the latter half of the 1940s the French airlines were equipped with the Douglas DC-4 and the Lockheed Constellation and at the beginning of the 1950s British-made aircraft were also bought. In 1953 Air France introduced the Comet and the Viscount alongside the Super Constellation. They combined these models with a sound French one: the Breguet Br.763 Provence.

One of the most successful outcomes of this policy, however, was the production of the Sud-Aviation SE-210 Caravelle. This elegant twin-engined jet gave a lot of momentum to the European aeronautical industry and raised it to the same rung as the North American industry. The Caravelle also made a considerable contribution to its being upgraded. Until recently the Caravelle was perhaps one of the most popular and widely used aircraft in Europe. In 1955 the number one airline in Europe, in the intercontinental sector, was Air France, with more than 450,000 passengers transported, and in 1960 it was second, with almost 700,000 passengers carried.

Mignet M.H.14 Pou du ciel

'Flying Flea' was the nickname given to this tiny and original aeroplane. It gained great popularity during the 1930s in both France and in Great Britain, and was the forbear of all 'home-made' aircraft. Today this category of aeroplane is enjoying a new wave of enthusiasm.

The inventor of the 'Flying Flea' was the Frenchman, Henri Mignet who was keen to build the aircraft which would teach him to fly with his own hands. Mignet first produced this tiny machine in 1933, equipping it with an ingenious system of controls and a motorcycle engine. Mignet failed to obtain official authorization to fly in France, but he won the hearts of British enthusiasts first by writing a small book, in which he described his design and explained how to build his 'Flying Flea' and then by flying directly to English soil. The Pou du ciel started something of a craze in Great Britain. In 1936 its flying activities were banned but by then over 120 aircraft had been built.

Aircraft: **Mignet M.H.14 Pou du ciel**
Manufacturer: **Société des Aeronefs Mignet**
Type: **Do-it-yourself**
Year: **1933**
Engine: **One Aubier and Dunne with 2 straight air-cooled cylinders, 22 hp**
Wingspan: **17 ft 0 in (5.18 m)**
Length: **11 ft 10 in (3.60 m)**
Height: **5 ft 6 in (1.68 m)**
Weight: **550 lb (250 kg) (Loaded)**
Cruising speed: **50 mph (80 km/h)**
Maximum speed: **62 mph (100 km/h)**
Ceiling: **–**
Range: **200 miles (322 km)**
Crew: **1**

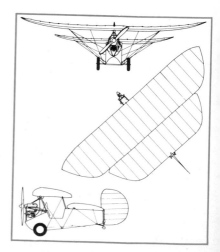

Kellner-Bechereau 28 V.D.

This aircraft was built specially to take part in the 1933 Deutsche de la Meurthe Cup race but it did not have a successful career. The Deutsche de la Meurthe Cup race was limited to aircraft with 8-litre engines and run in two stages each being 620 miles (1,000 km). The Kellner-Bechereau 28 V.D. was a classic product of the sporting spirit of the 1930s. It had extremely pure lines, was quite sophisticated and was capable of high performances with a relatively small engine. The Kellner-Bechereau 28 V.D. was built shortly after the appearance in France of a new Delage engine, with a V-12 arrangement, which lent itself well to a racing aeroplane. The tests and trials started a fortnight before the race which was to be held on May 28, 1933, but the Kellner-Bechereau 28 V.D. soon revealed major problems. On May 14, during the qualifying heats, the aircraft suffered from serious defects, and never actually took part in the race for which it was built.

Aircraft: **Kellner Bechereau 28 V.D.**
Manufacturer: **Kellner-Bechereau**
Type: **Competition**
Year: **1933**
Engine: **One Delage V-12, water-cooled, 370 hp**
Wingspan: **21 ft 10 in (6.65 m)**
Length: **23 ft 6 in (7.16 m)**
Height: **8 ft 8 in (2.65 m)**
Weight: **3,527 lb (1,600 kg) (Loaded)**
Maximum speed: **250 mph (400 km/h)***
Ceiling: –
Range: –
Crew: **1**
* Estimated

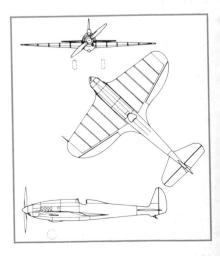

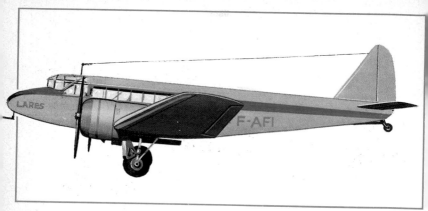

Potez 56

Designed in the mid-1930s and conceived for short-range transport, the Potez 56 was certainly not a very successful aeroplane. Nevertheless the 30 or so examples completed operated up until the very eve of the Second World War. The project was launched in 1933 and the prototype made its maiden flight on June 18, of the following year. Its performance was not exceptional but, despite its shortcomings, it was decided to prepare an assembly line for the Potez 56.

The first Potez 56 models were put into service on May 15, 1935 by the Potez Aéro Service on the Bordeaux—Toulouse – Marseilles – Nice – Bastia route. Two other aircraft followed and these were used in Algeria and Tunisia by the Régie Air Afrique. In addition six aircraft went to Chile and others were bought by Rumania. It was whilst in service in these countries that the Potez had its longest career.

Aircraft: **Potez 56**
Manufacturer: **Société des Aéroplanes Henry Potez**
Type: **Civil transport**
Year: **1934**
Engines: **Two Potez 9Ab, radial with 9 air-cooled cylinders, 185 hp each**
Wingspan: **52 ft 6 in (16.00 m)**
Length: **38 ft 10 in (11.84 m)**
Height: **–**
Weight: **6,569 lb (2,980 kg) (Loaded)**
Cruising speed: **155 mph (250 km/h)**
Ceiling: **19,685 ft (6,000 m)**
Range: **685 miles (1,100 km)**
Crew: **2**
Passengers: **6**

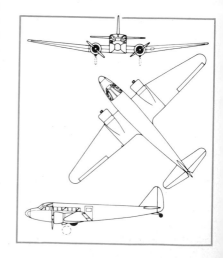

Caudron C.630–C.635 Simoun

From Le Bourget to Tananarive, between December 18 and 21, 1937, in 57 hours and 36 minutes covering a distance of 5,384 miles (8,665 km). This is only one of the numerous and impressive flights made in the latter half of the 1930s by one of the most popular French light aeroplanes of the day.

Shown for the first time at the Paris *Salon Aéronautique* in 1934, this small, elegant single-engined aircraft designed by Marcel Rizzard scored an instant success. Apart from the 70 aircraft built for the civil market, the production of the Simoun was also aimed at the military. A total of 110 models went to the *Armée de l'Air*, and 29 models to the *Aéronavale*. A single model was also built for the American military attaché in France. Although the Simoun had a successful military career, its career as a civil aircraft was the most renowned. The Simoun was also used for carrying mail.

Aircraft: **Caudron C.635 Simoun**
Manufacturer: **Société Anonyme des Avions Caudron**
Type: **Light transport**
Year: **1934**
Engine: **One Renault 6 Pdi Bengali, with 6 straight air-cooled cylinders, 180 hp**
Wingspan: **34 ft 1 in (10.40 m)**
Length: **28 ft 7 in (8.70 m)**
Height: **7 ft 4 in (2.25 m)**
Weight: **2,976 lb (1,350 kg) (Loaded)**
Cruising speed: **174 mph (280 km/h)**
Ceiling: **24,000 ft (7,300 m)**
Range: **764 miles (1,230 km)**
Crew: **2**
Payload: **330 lb (150 kg)**

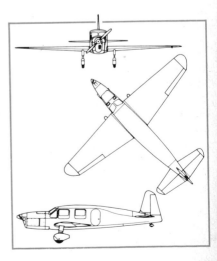

Bloch 220

Just 16 examples of the Bloch 220 were completed but, although the number was so small, this robust, sound commercial twin-engined aircraft enjoyed a long and busy career on the European routes handled by Air France. In fact five of these aircraft managed to survive the Second World War, and after being modified with the installation of American Wright Cyclone engines, they resumed service on the routes from Paris to Geneva, Paris to Zurich and Paris–Strasbourg–Prague.

The 220 project was carried out in 1935, together with that of another commercial aircraft, the model 300. Both these aircraft were designed to meet the needs of Air France for an aeroplane which could be used to the full on European flights. The Bloch 300, with the distinctive three-engined design and a capacity of 30 passengers, had no follow-up. However, the Bloch 220 won the approval of the airline. This was a slender, modern twin-engined model built entirely of metal

with a retractable undercarriage, which could carry 16 passengers which was practically half the capacity of the Bloch 300. The prototype of the Bloch 220 made its maiden flight in December 1935 and immediately afterwards the production lines were prepared for the completion of 14 series aircraft requested by Air France. In building this aeroplane the designers had envisaged considerable use of the components of a military aircraft, the Bloch 210 bomber. The prototype of the Bloch 210 bomber had taken to the air for the first time on November 23, 1934, and was at the time in production for the *Armée de l'Air*. In fact the civil model borrowed both the wing and the tailplane from the 210 but the fuselage was radically different, and had three principal compartments: the forward one which could accommodate six passengers, the central one which accommodated the other ten passengers, and the rear cargo hold for carrying their luggage and any cargo.

The first five Bloch 220 models were not delivered until the end of 1937, and

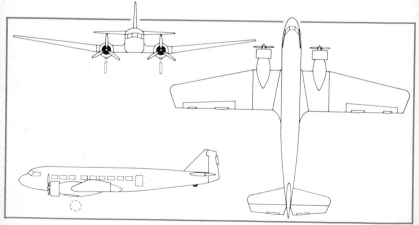

were put into service between December and January of the following year on the route Paris–Marseilles. The aircraft were each given individual names: *Gascogne* (F-AOHB); *Guyenne* (F-AOHC); *Auvergne* (F-AOHD); *Aunis* (F-AOHE) and *Saintonge* (F-AOHF). This practice was followed for the remaining eleven aircraft (the initial order from Air France had been increased by two) which were delivered in 1938. Before long the flight to Marseilles was extended to the first international service, between Paris and London. This service was inaugurated on March 27, 1938 by the Bloch 220 F-AOHE *Aunis* which covered the distance in 51 minutes flat, thus considerably reducing the flight time of the three-engined Wibault belonging to the series 280 T which had operated on this flight up until then.

In the course of that year the new aircraft had been put into service on the main European routes handled by Air France and in particular on the services to Amsterdam, Bucharest, Prague,

Aircraft: **Bloch 220**
Manufacturer: **Avions Marcel Bloch**
Type: **Civil transport**
Year: **1935**
Engines: **Two Gnome-Rhône 14N 16, radial with 14 air-cooled cylinders, 915 hp each**
Wingspan: **74 ft 10 in (22.82 m)**
Length: **63 ft 2 in (19.25 m)**
Height: **12 ft 9 in (3.90 m)**
Weight: **21,000 lb (9,500 kg) (Loaded)**
Cruising speed: **175 mph (280 km/h)**
Ceiling: **23,000 ft (7,000 m)**
Range: **870 miles (1,400 km)**
Crew: **4**
Passengers: **16**

Stockholm and Zurich, completely replacing the Wibault and the Potez 62 which were still in operation.

During the war three Bloch 220 models were requisitioned by Germany and transferred to Lufthansa but when the war came to an end the remaining aircraft still bore their French markings. In 1949 five of them were modernized with different engines and used once again by the French airline, until more modern and competitive aircraft were produced.

1935 – Caudron C-445 Goëland

Caudron Goëland

The Goëland was one of the most successful commercial aircraft produced in Europe in the 1930s. In all more than 1,700 examples of this small twin-engined aeroplane were completed and production carried on well into the postwar years. During the war itself the Goëland was called upon to carry out services for both the French and the Germans. It appeared in 1935 and was developed in numerous versions (which had the factory designations C-440 to C-449). These differed mainly in the adoption of various versions of the Renault engine, and in minor structural modifications. The Caudron C-445 Goëland, for example, was powered by two, 220 hp Renault 6Q-01 Bengali engines.

As a civil type the Goëland became increasingly popular from 1935 onwards in numerous companies operating in France and in Africa, including the Air Bleu mail company and the Régie Air Afrique.

Aircraft: **Caudron C-445 Goëland**
Manufacturer: **Société Anonyme des Avions Caudron**
Type: **Civil transport**
Type: **1935**
Engines: **Two Renault 6Q-01 Bengali, with 6 air-cooled straight cylinders, 220 hp each**
Wingspan: **57 ft 9 in (17.60 m)**
Length: **45 ft 4 in (13.80 m)**
Height: **11 ft 6 in (3.50 m)**
Weight: **7,716 lb (3,500 kg) (Loaded)**
Cruising speed: **162 mph (260 km/h)**
Ceiling: **18,400 ft (5,600 m)**
Range: **350 miles (560 km)**
Crew: **2**
Passengers: **6**

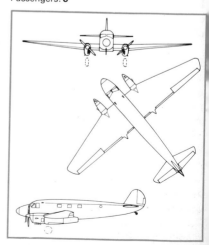

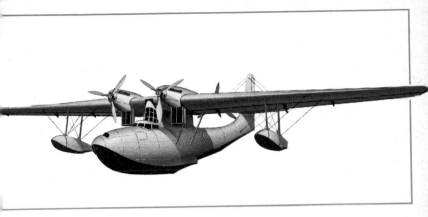

Loiré et Olivier H 47

The Loiré et Olivier H 47 was built at the express request of the French government which wanted to have available a long-range commercial flying-boat capable of ensuring services across the South Atlantic. The tender was issued in 1934 and a year later the design by Loiré et Olivier was selected. It was an elegant flying-boat with a central hull and high wing, built entirely of metal.

The prototype of the Loiré et Olivier H 47 made its maiden flight on July 25, 1936 and showed excellent features which were more than sufficient to give rise to an order for five aircraft from Air France. However, the project was abruptly interrupted by an accident which caused the H 47 prototype to sink in May 1937. There were considerable delays and it was not until July 1938 that the first production aircraft was ready. Unfortunately, however, the war brought the whole programme to a halt.

Aircraft: **Loiré et Olivier H 47**
Manufacturer: **SNCASE**
Type: **Civil transport**
Year: **1936**
Engines: **Four Hispano-Suiza 12 Ydrs, V-12, liquid-cooled, 880 hp each**
Wingspan: **104 ft 4 in (31.80 m)**
Length: **69 ft 6 in (21.18 m)**
Height: **23 ft 7 in (7.20 m)**
Weight: **39,460 lb (17,900 kg) (Loaded)**
Cruising speed: **180 mph at 8,200 ft (290 km/h at 2,500 m)**
Ceiling: **23,000 ft (7,000 m)**
Range: **2,500 miles (4,000 km)**
Crew: **5**
Payload: **3,000 lb (1,320 kg) (including 4–8 passengers)**

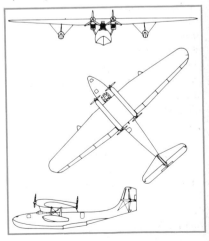

Air Couzinet 10

After the famous Arc-en-Ciel of 1929, another interesting project was embarked upon by René Couzinet in the mid-1930s. This was the Air Couzinet 10, a small twin-engined aeroplane designed to take part in the renowned Istres–Damascus–Paris air-race. This air-race was held in August 1937 and won by the Italian S.M.79C, which took the first five places. Couzinet's ambition, however, was fated not to be fulfilled. On August 16, 1937, just 13 days after the maiden flight, the aircraft had to make a forced landing on a test-flight because one of the flap controls broke. The aeroplane was seriously damaged, and could not be repaired in time for the start of the race. The Air Couzinet 10 was built entirely of wood, and had a top speed of 218 mph (350 km/h). Although it did not fly in the race, after the accident the aeroplane was nevertheless modified at the request of *Aéropostale*, which wanted to use it on the network handled by Air Bleu.

Aircraft: **Air Couzinet 10**
Manufacturer: **Société des Avions René Couzinet**
Type: **Competition**
Year: **1937**
Engines: **Two Hispano-Suiza 9 V16, radial with 9 air-cooled cylinders, 660 hp each**
Wingspan: **59 ft 1 in (18.00 m)**
Length: **41 ft 4 in (12.60 m)**
Height: **–**
Weight: **18,500 lb (8,400 kg) (Loaded)**
Unladen weight: **9,000 lb (4,500 kg)**
Maximum speed: **218 mph (350 km/h)**
Range: **4,350 miles (7,000 km)**
Crew: **3**

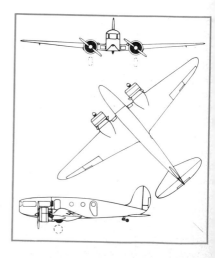

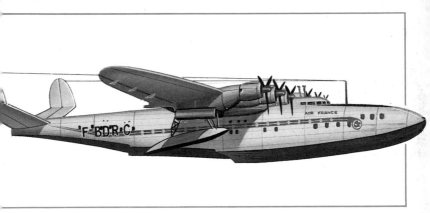

Latécoère 631

Following in its tradition of commercial flying-boats, the well-established Toulouse firm designed its largest and most modern type in 1938. This was the Latécoère 631. The construction of the prototype was interrupted by the outbreak of the Second World War, but resumed after the Franco–German armistice, and concluded in autumn 1942. The maiden flight took place on November 4, but the trials were halted by the Germans who requisitioned the prototype. The prototype was taken to Germany where it was later destroyed during an air-raid. Production started again after the war with an order by Air France for eight aircraft. Only seven aircraft of this order were completed and the first ones were put into service on July 26, 1947. They did not last long with Air France. After the loss of two in August 1948, the Latécoère 631 was withdrawn. One model was converted to cargo transport but the others were all scrapped.

Aircraft: **Latécoère 631**
Manufacturer: **Société Industrielle d'Aviation Latécoère**
Type: **Civil transport**
Year: **1942**
Engines: **Six Wright GR 2600-A5B Cyclone, radial with 14 air-cooled cylinders, 1,600 hp each**
Wingspan: **188 ft 5 in (57.43 m)**
Length: **142 ft 7 in (43.46 m)**
Height: **33 ft 2 in (10.10 m)**
Weight: **157,300 lb (71,350 kg) (Loaded)**
Cruising speed: **185 mph (297 km/h)**
Range: **3,750 miles (6,035 km)**
Crew: **5**
Passengers: **46**

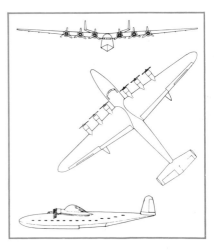

Sud Est SE.161 Languedoc

Although conceived way back in 1936, the Languedoc started its active career in the immediate postwar period and ended up by becoming one of the most popular French civil transport models. One hundred examples of this large four-engined aeroplane were completed altogether, in various versions, and those delivered to Air France remained in service until 1954. An even longer career was enjoyed by the Languedoc aircraft delivered to the *Armèe de l'Air* and the *Aèronavale*, which flew until 1960. By that date five aircraft were still in commercial use with the Spanish company Aviaco, which was the last operator to withdraw these large aircraft from service.

The origins of the Languedoc date back to a request made by Air Afrique in 1936 for a short-range colonial transport aeroplane. On the basis of this specific request, the well-known aeronautical engineer Marcel Bloch developed the model 160. This was a four-engined aircraft with a low wing, capable of carrying 12 passengers, and powered by 690 hp Hispano-Suiza engines. This aircraft never actually went into production, although in 1937 it managed to set two speed records with different loads. It was later replaced by the model 161 which was more powerful and larger, and was developed simultaneously with the project for the unsuccessful Bloch 162 heavy bomber (it flew for the first time on June 1, 1940, just a few days before the armistice with Germany, and was instantly requisitioned by the Germans). In its original form the Bloch 161 was completed in 1939 and made its maiden flight in September of that year. As well as the basic model there were plans for various other versions, including one for 20 passengers (accommodated in bunks) and one for 16 passengers, the latter being aimed at services across the South Atlantic. However, the advent of the war interrupted these programmes. Despite the keen interest shown in this aeroplane by the Germans (they wanted to build 20 aircraft for Lufthansa), production was deliberately slowed down and the SNCASE company (the nationalized group that had fully implemented

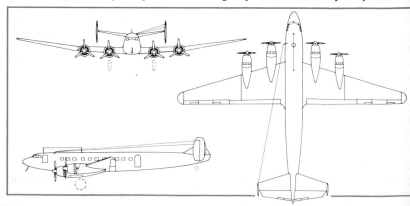

194

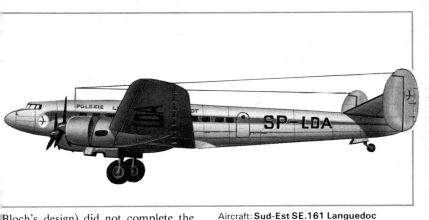

Bloch's design) did not complete the first aircraft until the war was over. The new SE.161, modified when compared with the original model, made its maiden flight on September 17, 1945. Spurred on by the urgent need for reorganization and modernization, Air France showed approval for the aircraft and ordered 40 examples. Thirteen were completed and delivered between late 1945 and early 1946. After a series of experimental services to Great Britain and Africa, they went into service, under the name Languedoc, on May 28, 1946. Initially they were used on the Paris–Algiers route but later on they were also used on flights to Casablanca and Marseilles. By 1946 the Languedocs were also being used on the major European routes.

At the end of that year, however, it became necessary to make a series of improvements to these aircraft, including the installation of de-icing equipment, and interior heating. It was decided at the same time to replace the Gnome-Rhône engines with Pratt &

Aircraft: **Sud-Est SE.161 Languedoc**
Manufacturer: **SNCASE**
Type: **Civil transport**
Year: **1945**
Engines: **Four Gnome-Rhône 14N, radial with 14 air-cooled cylinders, 1,150 hp each**
Wingspan: **96 ft 5 in (29.38 m)**
Length: **79 ft 7 in (24.25 m)**
Height: **16 ft 10 in (5.13 m)**
Weight: **50,500 lb (22,941 kg) (Loaded)**
Cruising speed: **250 mph (405 km/h)**
Ceiling: **23,600 ft (7,200 m)**
Range: **620 miles (1,000 km)**
Crew: **4**
Passengers: **33**

Whitney radial engines. Thus modified, and designated SE.161-P7, the Languedoc aircraft resumed service in March 1947 on flights to North Africa. The new version was also quite successful on the export market. Five aircraft (though still with Gnome-Rhône engines) were bought by the Polish company LOT, which took delivery of them between 1947 and 1948. At the end of that year 62 Languedoc aircraft had been completed, and civil production had been swollen by production for the military.

At the end of 1949, however, Air France started to withdraw the SE.161 from its major passenger services.

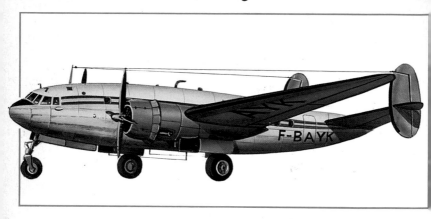

Sud-Ouest SO.30P Bretagne

The origins of the Bretagne date back to 1941 when the SNCASO technicians launched the project of a pressurized twin-engined transport aeroplane to carry 23 passengers. Called the SO.30N, this aircraft was in fact held up by the Armistice authorities, and did not fly until February 26, 1945. This prototype then gave rise to other SO.30R models and eventually production of the definitive version, the SO.30P, started. Christened the Bretagne, the SO.30P took_ to the air on December 11, 1947. It was capable of carrying between 30–37 passengers plus the crew of two. Apart from four aircraft which were used for a while by Air France, the Bretagne was used mainly in Africa. The remainder of the production (consisting of 45 units) was scattered among smaller companies in the French colonies and in the *Armée de l'Air* and the *Aéronavale*.

Aircraft: **Sud-Ouest SO.30P Bretagne**
Manufacturer: **SNCASE**
Type: **Civil transport**
Year: **1947**
Engines: **Two Pratt & Whitney R-2800-B43 Double Wasp, radial, 1,620 hp each**
Wingspan: **88 ft 2 in (26.87 m)**
Length: **62 ft 2 in (18.95 m)**
Height: **19 ft 4 in (5.89 m)**
Weight: **39,881 lb (18,900 kg) (Loaded)**
Cruising speed: **258 mph (416 km/h)**
Ceiling: **21,325 ft (6,500 m)**
Range: **850 miles (1,270 km)**
Crew: **2**
Passengers: **30–37**

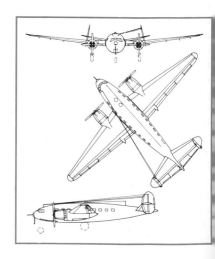

Sud-Ouest SO.95 Corse II

Designed for the French airlines' domestic routes, the Sud-Ouest Corse in fact had another fate in store for it. Sixty aircraft, which was almost all the production, went to the communications and light transport squadrons of the *Aéronavale*. Only two were used for regular passenger services. These two aircraft saw service in India for almost a year, wearing the colours of Air Services which used them on the Bombay–Bangalore and Bombay–Delhi routes until October 1950. Like the project which had given rise to the Bretagne, this project had also been launched in the early years of the war. The first to appear had been the SO.90 model, followed at the end of the war by types SO.93 and SO.94 which all remained at the prototype stage. The first SO.95 made its maiden flight on July 17, 1947. It was built entirely of metal and proved to be a safe and extremely reliable aircraft.

Aircraft: **Sud-Ouest SO.95 Corse II**
Manufacturer: **SNCASE**
Type: **Light transport**
Year: **1947**
Engines: **Two Renault 12 S-02-201, V-12, air-cooled, 580 hp each**
Wingspan: **59 ft 1 in (18.01 m)**
Length: **40 ft 5 in (12.32 m)**
Height: **14 ft 1 in (4.30 m)**
Weight: **12,350 lb (5,600 kg) (Loaded)**
Cruising speed: **205 mph (330 km/h)**
Ceiling: **–**
Range: **810 miles (1,300 km)**
Crew: **2**
Passengers: **10–13**

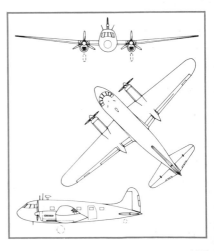

Sud-Est SE.2010
Armagnac

Just nine examples of this large four-engined aeroplane were built and none of them were privileged to fly with Air France, the company for which they had been developed as part of an ambitious programme. Instead of carrying passengers across the North Atlantic, the Sud-Est SE.2010 ended up on the rather more dramatic route to Saigon, during the war in Indochina, carrying troops and military supplies.

The decision to proceed with the project had been reached in 1942 when a request was made concerning a preliminary study for the design of a commercial transport aircraft capable of carrying 87 passengers between Marseilles and Algiers, and capable of crossing the South Atlantic with 32 passengers accommodated in bunks. However it was not until 1945, after the end of the war, that the programme arrived at its operational stage and the SNCASE group designed the model SE.2000. This was a large four-engined aeroplane powered by 2,100 hp Gnome-Rhône engines. In theory this aircraft was also capable of flying on the longer North Atlantic routes. However, even in the initial planning stages the technicians realized that the aircraft would be out-of-date at its anticipated completion date. As a result they considerably modified the design, increasing the size, weight and capacity. The capacity was increased to 64 passengers for the long transatlantic flights and to 107 passengers for shorter services. Called the SE.2010 and christened the Armagnac, this aircraft made its maiden flight on April 2, 1949, powered by four large radial 3,500 hp Wasp Major engines. At the same time a production line was prepared, for fifteen aircraft ordered by Air France, and a development programme was drawn up which envisaged, as from the 16th aircraft made, the adoption of turbo-prop engines. However when the time came for the final decision the French company refused to take the

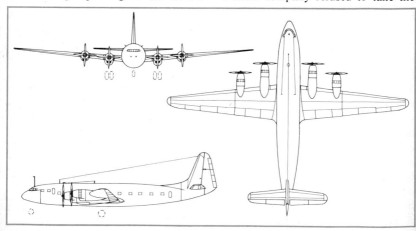

Sud-Est SE.2010 Armagnac — 1949

Armagnac. The official reason for this was that there was excessive space in the fuselage which was not used. The space was intended for the installation of bunks but by that time they were considered obsolete. This made the aeroplane uneconomical and virtually obsolescent, and it was evident that the Armagnac did not match its contemporary products in the United States.

Despite this, the planned production went ahead and after one prototype had crashed, the first series example was delivered to TAI (Transports Aeriens Intercontinentaux). At the end of 1952 this company took a further three aircraft and put them into service. This use of the aircraft, which represented the survival of the entire programme, nevertheless turned out to be decidedly counter-productive. After operating the Armagnac for eight months, TAI realized that the aircraft was not very economical to run and as a result withdrew it from service. The SE.2010s were grounded at Toulouse. A year later it was decided to bring

Aircraft: **Sud-Est SE.2010 Armagnac**
Manufacturer: **SNCASE**
Type: **Civil transport**
Year: **1949**
Engines: **Four Pratt & Whitney R-4360 Wasp Major, radial with 28 air-cooled cylinders, 3,500 hp each**
Wingspan: **160 ft 7 in (48.95 m)**
Length: **130 ft 0 in (39.63 m)**
Weight: **170,858 lb (77,500 kg) (Loaded)**
Cruising speed: **282 mph (454 km/h)**
Ceiling: **22,300 ft (6,800 m)**
Range: **3,180 miles (5,120 km)**
Crew: **4**
Passengers: **84–160**

these hapless four-engined aeroplanes to life again. With the ever-increasing demand for aircraft resulting from the war in Indochina, France required aircraft capable of transporting the huge supplies needed in that part of the world. A special company was set up, called **SAGETA**, consisting of the major French companies. The main purpose of SAGETA was to handle this type of transport operation. The Armagnacs were overhauled and used intensively on the long route from Toulouse to Saigon (via Beirut, Karachi and Calcutta) from the end of 1953 onwards.

199

Breguet 763 Provence

By no means handsome but a very sound product, the Breguet 763 had a long career with Air France, although only twelve aircraft were ever completed. In 1965, twelve years after it first went into service, the six remaining aircraft which had been greatly altered to increase the capacity for carrying heavy, bulky cargo or vehicles, were once again used on short flights between France and England.

The project which gave rise to the Provence was launched in 1944 when the Breguet Company started drawing up plans for a large commercial aircraft to be used for mixed transport. The prototype of the model 761, the outcome of the project, made its maiden flight on February 15, 1949. It was a high-winged four-engined aeroplane, with a distinctively large fuselage built on two levels. It also had a wide rear loading bay. Three more pre-production models, called Br.761S, followed and these successfully concluded the various tests and trials. Although they showed themselves reasonably well suited to the use for which they had been designed, these first models did not attract the attention of Air France. The main reason for Air France's disinterest was that the engines used were all Pratt & Whitney radials left over from the war. The company did not believe that these engines were safe or reliable, and were also concerned about the lack of any official supply. However, the situation was soon sorted out. The Deux Ponts (the name given to the Br.761, meaning Double-decker) were put forward once again in 1951, in a structurally improved version. This new version also had more power, as a result of the use of 2,400 hp Pratt & Whitney engines. These were requested specifically by the French government from the American firm, so as to maintain the production programme. Air France ordered twelve copies of the aircraft, which were rechristened Provence and had the designation

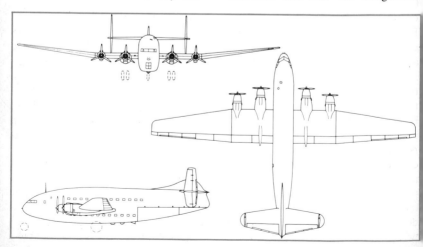

Br.763. The first of these took to the air on July 20, 1951, and was followed gradually by the other eleven.

Before going into regular service the Provence models were put through a gruelling series of trials and test-flights, in various forms. The resulting data, together with that supplied by the similar experimental tests being carried out by Air Algérie with the second pre-production model of the Br.761S (which completed more than 700 hours of trials with this company), led Air France to the conclusion that the aircraft was by this time reasonably acceptable. The inaugural flight on the Algiers–Marseilles–Lyons route and the Lyons–Marseilles–Tunis route took place on March 16, 1953, and before long all twelve Provences went into operation between France and North Africa. Their main task was carrying mainly passengers: some 107 people could be accommodated, 59 in tourist class on the upper deck and 48 in the second class cabin on the lower deck. However, if the whole aircraft was devoted to economy class they

Aircraft: **Breguet 763 Provence**
Manufacturer: **Société Anonyme des Ateliers d'Aviation Louis Breguet**
Type: **Civil transport**
Year: **1951**
Engines: **Four Pratt & Whitney R-2800-CA18 Double Wasp, radial with 18 air-cooled cylinders, 2,400 hp each**
Wingspan: **141 ft 0 in (42.98 m)**
Length: **94 ft 11 in (28.94 m)**
Height: **31 ft 8 in (9.65 m)**
Weight: **113,758 lb (51,600 kg) (Loaded)**
Cruising speed: **209 mph (336 km/h)**
Ceiling: **24,000 ft (7,315 m)**
Range: **1,423 miles (2,290 km)**
Crew: **4**
Passengers: **96–135**

could carry a total of 135 passengers.

With the introduction of more modern aeroplanes, the Br.763's role as a passenger aircraft gradually diminished and Air France sold off six of its Provences to the *Armée de l'Air*. After lengthy tests carried out with the three Br.761S models in 1954, the *Armée de l'Air* had in fact discovered the great potential of the aircraft as a military transporter and had ordered 15 modified for this specific use. These were christened Sahara (the factory designation was Br.765). Air France's last six Provence aeroplanes were later converted to increase their versatility.

Sud-Aviation SE.210 Caravelle

This was the first jet-engined commercial transport aeroplane to be manufactured in France; the first one specifically designed for short-to-medium range use; and the first of its category to have the engines mounted at the rear. In addition, the Sud-Aviation SE.210 Caravelle turned out to be the most successful of all European civil aircraft. Apart from Air France, most of the major European airlines (with the exception of BEA, for obvious reasons of prestige) and the companies in the Mediterranean basin, as well as United Air Lines in the U.S.A. and the Brazilian company Varig, all adopted this swift and safe twin-engined jet in the 1950s and 1960s. On December 30, 1970, shortly after the appearance of the last generation Caravelle 12, production had reached a total of 274 aircraft, and the 267 already in operation had clocked up a total of 4,400,000 flying hours and made 3,100,000 landings.

The historic date of the maiden flight of the Caravelle prototype was May 27, 1955. The plans for its construction had been started in the immediate postwar period by SNCASE. The designers of the nationalized Sud-Est group had in fact drawn up a programme including a wide range of commercial transport models which were to be developed with a view to the future requirements of the civil airlines. The preliminary studies bore the production numbers ranging from X200 to X210. At that time the type of engine chosen had been the turbo-jet. This was because of the considerable development this type of engine had undergone, in comparison with the conventional piston engine. It was one of these designs that, in 1952, was put through assessment trials by the technical authorities of the French government. The original SNCASE project envisaged the installation of three French-made SNECMA turbojet engines at the rear. However, a close study of the market persuaded them to

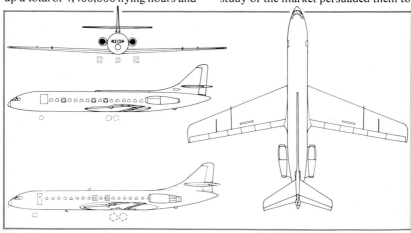

change this arrangement and adopt two Rolls-Royce Avon engines, still mounted by the tail alongside the fuselage, which were more reliable and which, above all, were likely to undergo more rapid development. The SE-210 project was chosen, and with the official name of Caravelle, four prototypes were ordered in July 1953. Later the French government gave the programme its full financial backing.

This policy turned out to be quite effective. At the end of the trials and certification tests, the prototype was delivered to Air France. The French airline in turn subjected the prototype to a busy series of test-flights on some of the most important routes. On February 3, 1956 the company placed an initial order for 12 aircraft, and stipulated an option for 12 more. Production, as a result, got under way and was soon in full swing. The first series Caravelle (Caravelle I) took to the air on May 18, 1958. One year later, on May 12, 1959, these aircraft inaugurated regular services with Air France, on the Paris–Rome–Instanbul

Aircraft: **Sud-Aviation SE.210 Caravelle III**
Manufacturer: **Sud-Aviation**
Type: **Civil transport**
Year: **1959**
Engines: **Two Rolls-Royce Avon 527 turbo-jets, 11,400 lb (5,171 kg) thrust each**
Wingspan: **112 ft 6 in (34.30 m)**
Length: **105 ft 0 in (32.01 m)**
Height: **28 ft 7 in (8.72 m)**
Weight: **101,413 lb (46,000 kg) (Loaded)**
Cruising speed: **484 mph at 35,000 ft (779 km/h at 10,670 m)**
Ceiling: **32,808 ft (10,000 m)**
Range: **1,081 miles (1,740 km)**
Crew: **4**
Passengers: **64–99**

route. Other airlines soon followed the example of the French company: SAS, Varig of Brazil and Air Algérie all ordered the Caravelle I.

With this commercial success there started a long phase in which the basic model was developed, and this lasted right up to the 1970s. The next version was the Caravelle IA whose maiden flight took place on February 11, 1960. The Caravelle IA had modified engines and was used by Finnair, Air France, SAS, Air Algérie and Royal Air Maroc. The maiden flight of the Caravelle III took place on December 30, 1959. This version had still more

powerful engines, a larger capacity, better performance, and went into service first with Alitalia, on May 23, 1960. The Caravelle VI appeared in 1961 in two versions: the VIN and the VIR; the first used Avon 531 engines, producing a thrust of 12,200 pounds (5,535 kg), and had a larger payload and a longer range; the second went to the American company United Air Lines, which had ordered 20 aircraft. The VIR had modifications to the engines, as well as to numerous elements of the equipment (these Caravelles went into service in the United States on July 14, 1961, flying from New York to Chicago). The Caravelle VI was also adopted in both versions by a large number of European, African and South American airlines.

In 1962 the first substantially modified version appeared, using American engines. This version was called the Caravelle 10 and was developed initially in two sub-types, the 10A and the 10B, characterized

Aircraft: **Sud-Aviation SE.210 Super Caravelle**
Manufacturer: **Sud-Aviation**
Type: **Civil transport**
Year: **1964**
Engines: **Two Pratt & Whitney JT8D-1 turbo-jets, 14,000 lb (6,350 kg) thrust each**
Wingspan: **112 ft 6 in (34.30 m)**
Length: **108 ft 3 in (33.01 m)**
Height: **28 ft 7 in (8.72 m)**
Weight: **114,640 lb (52,000 kg) (Loaded)**
Cruising speed: **518 mph (835 km/h)**
Ceiling: **32,808 ft (10,000 m)**
Range: **1,646 miles (2,650 km)**
Crew: **4**
Passengers: **68–105**

respectively by the installation of General Electric and Pratt & Whitney engines. However, only the 10B got beyond the prototype stage. With the Pratt & Whitney engines the 10B subsequently gave rise to the Caravelle 10R (in practical terms a Caravelle VIR with different engines) and the Caravelle Super B, which was renamed the Super Caravelle. This latter flew on March 3, 1964 and was put into service for the first time by Finnair on August 16, 1964, on the Helsinki–Milan route.

Nord M.H.260

The Nord M.H.260 was the first production model of a successful light turbo-prop aircraft which, in its final N.262 version, enjoyed wide commercial success especially in the United States. The original M.H.250 project had been started in 1957 by Avions Max Holste. It was a high-winged, twin-engined model with a capacity of 22 passengers. It was powered by a pair of Pratt & Whitney 600 hp radial engines. After the maiden flight of the prototype, which took place on May 20, 1959, the engineer decided to develop a turbo-prop version. This version appeared as the M.H.260 slightly more than a year later, on July 29, 1960. The Max Holste firm started a small production line, but initially they found no customers. At the end of the year, however, they managed to sign an agreement with Nord-Aviation for ten aircraft. These were completed, but later models were considerably modified.

Aircraft: **Nord M.H.260**
Manufacturer: **Nord-Aviation**
Type: **Civil transport**
Year: **1960**
Engines: **Two Turboméca Bastan IV turbo-props, 986 ehp each**
Wingspan: **71 ft 8 in (21.85 m)**
Length: **59 ft 2 in (18.04 m)**
Height: **21 ft 7 in (6.59 m)**
Weight: **21,605 lb (9,800 kg) (Loaded)**
Cruising speed: **236 mph at 10,000 ft (380 km/h at 3,050 m)**
Ceiling: **31,988 ft (9,750 m)**
Range: **988 miles (1,590 km)**
Crew **2**
Passengers: **23**

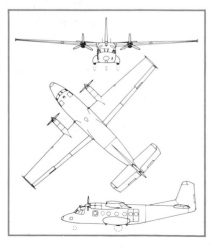

ALA LITTORIA S.A.
ROMA

LINEA DELL'IMPERO ROMA-ASMARA
ADDIS ABEBA · MOGADISCIO

Italy

The countries emerging defeated from the Second World War found themselves having to start again as far as air transport was concerned. However, when compared with Germany, Italy was in a considerably better situation due in particular to the way the last two years of the war had taken their course. By the early months of 1946 considerable thought had already been given to reconstruction in this sector, and together with various private undertakings, the foundations were laid for the establishment of two major and official companies. In September 1946 Alitalia and Linee Aeree Italiane came into being (the latter known as LAI). BEA and TWA had respectively a 30% and 40% interest in the new Italian companies. To begin with the two airlines launched a network of domestic flights but later they extended their range abroad.

At more or less the same time numerous other independent companies also emerged. These included Aerea Teseo, Airone, Salpanavi, Transadriatica, Società Italiana Servizi Aerei (SISA), Gruppo Siculo, ILAM, Aereo Espresso, and Avio-Linee Italiane (ALI). The development of these smaller airlines was quite dynamic. Although some soon disappeared, in 1949 four of them merged under the main group, ALI, and took on the title of ALI-Flotte Riunite. The activities of ALI-FR enjoyed a period of great success. With its combined fleet of DC-3s, Fiat G.212s and G.12s it managed to operate numerous international flights and compete well with the two official companies. However, in the end its undertaking proved too much for ALI-FR and on March 31, 1952 the company went bankrupt and was absorbed by LAI. The activity of this airline and its direct rival went ahead with increasing success until the mid-1950s: LAI and Alitalia battled it out for control of the market, both to secure the best stock available and to win more and more remunerative routes. By 1957 the time seemed ripe for a merger: having two national companies operating as direct rivals, with the consequent sqandering of energies, seemed an uneconomical situation and it was decided to liquidate LAI and transfer its organization and operating structure to Alitalia. This took place in August 1957 and the new company called Alitalia-Linee Aeree Italiana came into being on September 1, 1957. About a month later it started to operate on the old LAI routes.

Macchi M.C.94

The world altitude record of 21,102 feet (6,432 m), with a load of 2,200 pounds (1,000 kg), for amphibious aircraft was set on April 15, 1935 by the Macchi M.C.94 bearing the registration I-NEPI. In the following month the same aeroplane, again piloted by Macchi's chief test-pilot, Giuseppe Burei, set two more records but this time speed records: on May 6 over a circuit of 1,250 miles (2,000 km), at 154.67 mph (248.917 km/h); and on May 9 over a circuit of 625 miles (1,000 km); this time with a load of 2,200 pounds (1,000 kg), at 159.78 mph (257.138 km/h). These records were set during a series of test-flights carried out to check the real possibilities of using the amphibious version of this aeroplane. However, it was subsequently replaced by the version which was only a flying-boat, but which offered overall better performances and greater reliability. Twelve examples of the Macchi M.C.94 were built and they flew for many years on the Mediterranean routes handled by Ala Littoria. They also saw service

during the war years. In addition, three of them were exported in 1939 to Argentina.

The designer of the M.C.94 was Mario Castoldi, the famous 'father' of the racing flying-boat. In 1935 he proposed his last creation in the field of commercial transport to Ala Littoria: a 12-seater twin-engined model, which could be made in the amphibious or flying-boat version, and was designed to replace the ageing CANT.10 aircraft on the Northern Adriatic and Mediterranean routes. The prototype, registered I-ARNO and fitted out as an amphibious model, made its official debut at the Milan *Salone Aéronautico Internazionale* in October 1935. It was an elegant high-winged monoplane with a central hull and lateral floats, with the two Wright Cyclone engines mounted in nacelles positioned on a frame above the wing. The structure and covering were made almost entirely of wood, and the undercarriage supplied in the amphibious version was installed so that it could be retracted upwards, until the wheels reached their housing in the leading edge of the wing. The rear wheel, on the other hand,

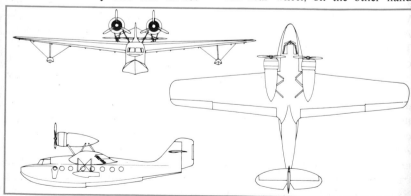

could be retracted in a backward direction and was housed in the base of the vertical tail structure. The solution chosen for the main undercarriage was certainly not perfect, especially in view of the aerodynamic drawbacks it entailed.

At the end of the trials, with an initial order for six aircraft already placed by Ala Littoria, the Macchi M.C.94 started to be delivered to the airline, which put them into service from the summer of 1936 onwards. Subsequently the company ordered six more aircraft, powered this time not by Wright engines but by Alfa Romeo A.R.126 R.C.10 800 hp radial engines. These went into service from June 1938 onwards.

Until the start of the war the Macchi M.C.94s operated over the Northern Adriatic and on the route from Brindisi to Haifa via Athens and Rhodes. Later only two remained in the northern Adriatic and the six remaining models used the Roma-Lido hydroport as their base; from here they made flights to Sardinia and Spain. All eight aircraft

Aircraft: **Macchi M.C.94**
Manufacturer: **Aeronautica Macchi**
Type: **Civil transport**
Year: **1935**
Engine: **Two Wright SGR-1820 Cyclone, radial with 9 air-cooled cylinders, 770 hp each**
Wingspan: **74 ft 9 in (22.79 m)**
Length: **50 ft 11 in (15.52 m)**
Height: **17 ft 10 in (5.45 m)**
Weight: **17,195 lb (7,800 kg) (Loaded)**
Cruising speed: **155 mph at 3,280 ft (250 km/h at 1,000 m)**
Ceiling: **19,030 ft (5,800 m)**
Range: **855 miles (1,375 km)**
Crew: **3**
Passengers: **12**

were then converted to military use, operating in the *Nucleo Communicazioni* (Communications Unit) of Ala Littoria; they flew regularly and without incident throughout the duration of the war. At the end of July 1943, they were still in existence and perhaps the only serious threat to them came shortly after the armistice, when the Germans, who considered the Macchi M.C.94s of no use to the Luftwaffe, ordered them to be demolished. However, the twin-engined flying-boats managed to survive and flew for several more months.

Fiat G.18

Clearly influenced by the contemporary Douglas production (the DC-1 had flown on July 1, 1933 and the DC-2 on May 11, 1934), the Fiat G.18 was designed and built by Giuseppe Gabrielli in 1934. It was to equip the Avio Linee Italiane fleet with a new aircraft. The prototype made its maiden flight on March 18, 1935 and was followed by two other production aircraft. Two years later on March 11, 1937 these were followed by the first of the G.18Vs, fitted with more powerful engines and certain structural modifications. In all, six examples of this latter version were completed. Avio Linee Italiane used the G.18 both on its domestic routes and on its international services. From 1938 onwards services with London and the other major European capitals were also opened. At the outbreak of war the G.18s were all militarized and used widely to transport troops.

Aircraft: **Fiat G.18V**
Manufacturer: **Fiat S.A.**
Type: **Civil transport**
Year: **1937**
Engines: **Two Fiat A.80 RC 41, radial with 18 cylinders, air-cooled, 1,000 hp each**
Wingspan: **82 ft 0 in (25.00 m)**
Length: **61 ft 8 in (18.81 m)**
Height: **16 ft 5 in (5.01 m)**
Weight: **23,809 lb (10,800 kg) (Loaded)**
Cruising speed: **211 mph (340 km/h)**
Ceiling: **28,500 ft (8,700 m)**
Range: **1,040 miles (1,675 km)**
Crew: **3**
Passengers: **18**

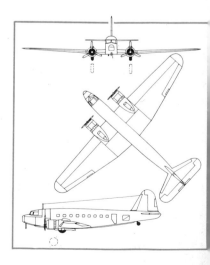

SIAI Marchetti S.M.75
SIAI Marchetti S.M.87

Between July 30 and August 1, 1939 a SIAI Marchetti S.M.75, appropriately modified, set the world distance record on a closed circuit: 8,038 miles (12,935 km) in 57 hours and 35 minutes flying time, covered on the circuit Fiumicino – Capo, Palinuro – Livorno (Leghorn). Compared with the series models, this aircraft had Alfa Romeo 128 RC 21 1,000 hp engines and fuel tanks capable of giving it this exceptional range. Six months earlier (January 10, 1939) the same S.M.75, registered I-TALO, had set the world speed record over 1,250 miles (2,000 km) with a load of 22,000 pounds (10,000 kg) at the average speed of 205.6 mph (330.972 km/h). The development of the special S.M.75 PD (*Primato Distanza* – Distance Record) had been requested by the General Staff of the *Regia Aeronautica*, in view of the excellent characteristics of the civil version in production from 1937

Aircraft: **SIAI Marchetti S.M.75**
Manufacturer: **SIAI Marchetti**
Type: **Civil transport**
Year: **1937**
Engines: **Three Alfa Romeo A.R.126 RC 34, radial with 9 cylinders, 350 hp each**
Wingspan: **97 ft 5 in (29.68 m)**
Length: **70 ft 10 in (21.60 m)**
Height: **16 ft 9 in (5.10 m)**
Weight: **31,967 lb (14,500 kg) (Loaded)**
Cruising speed: **202 mph (325 km/h)**
Ceiling: **23,000 ft (7,000 m)**
Range: **1,420 miles (2,280 km)**
Crew: **4**
Passengers: **18–24**

onwards; they were keen to have a version for military use.

SIAI Marchetti launched the S.M.75 project with the aim of making a successor to the S.M.73 which had a fixed undercarriage. This was the forebear of the long series of three-engined models made by Alessandro Marchetti. They had branded a whole era in Italian aviation and, from 1935 onwards, gave excellent service on mid-European routes. Compared with its predecessor, the new model retained the general features but was larger, decidedly more modern with its up-to-date retractable

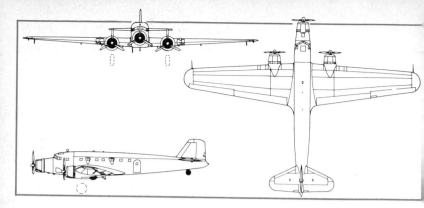

undercarriage, and capable of better performances. The prototype made its maiden flight on November 6, 1937 and at the end of the trials was delivered to Ala Littoria on February 15 of the following year. At the rate of almost one a month the other five aircraft followed in its wake, making up the initial order placed. Subsequently, between July and December, the production of this new three-engined aircraft was suddenly speeded up, with the delivery of six more S.M.75 machines to Ala Littoria and five examples fitted with Weiss engines (Gnome-Rhône K.14 engines built under licence) instead of the Alfa Romeo A.R.126 RC 34 engines, to the Hungarian company Malert. These aeroplanes were followed by a further 18 aircraft for the Italian company, delivered from the end of December 1938 onwards.

This aircraft considerably bolstered the European and African services handled by Ala Littoria: its capacity was 24 passengers on flights of 950 miles (1,500 km), and 18 on longer flights of up to 2,100 miles (3,400 km). Early in 1939 the S.M.75 went into operation on some of the remotest African routes, including the Rome–Benghazi–Addis Ababa route. Until the outbreak of war Ala Littoria

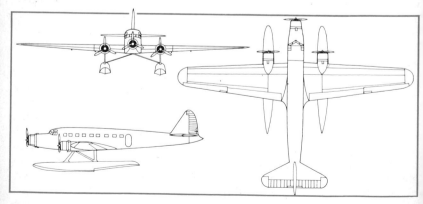

continued to increase its S.M.75 fleet, this aircraft having now become its basic type: by June 1940 it had taken delivery of 34 aircraft and was awaiting the delivery of four more, three of which were to replace aeroplanes lost in flying accidents. When Italy entered the war all the aircraft in service were militarized and added to the *Nucleo Communicazioni* (Communications Unit). The long war years saw the S.M.75 operating busily as transport aircraft on all fronts and occasionally even as bombers. Some aircraft survived the war and remained in service until 1949. The total production reached 90 aircraft. Just four examples of the seaplane version of the S.M.75 were completed, on the other hand, and this was called the S.M.87. It was announced by Ala Littoria in mid-1938 and was designed to replace the Macchi M.C.94 flying-boats in service in South America with the Brazilian Corporacion Sud-American de Transportes Aereos, a company which was affiliated to Ala Littoria. An initial production lot of five examples of the

Aircraft: **SIAI Marchetti S.W.87**
Manufacturer: **SIAI Marchetti**
Type: **Civil transport**
Year: **1939**
Engines: **Three Fiat A.80 RC 41, radial with 18 cylinders, air-cooled, 1,000 hp each**
Wingspan: **97 ft 5 in (29.70 m)**
Length: **73 ft 2 in (22.30 m)**
Height: **19 ft 11 in (6.06 m)**
Weight: **38,360 lb (17,400 kg) (Loaded)**
Maximum speed: **227 mph at 13,450 ft (365 km/h at 4,100 m)**
Ceiling: **20,500 ft (6,250 m)**
Range: **1,370 miles (2,200 km)**
Crew: **4**
Passengers: **20–24**

S.M.87 had been planned, but this original figure was never reached because of the outbreak of war, which brought an abrupt halt to the collaboration between the Brazilian airline and Ala Littoria. The four seaplanes completed (it was decided to abandon work on the fifth) were all fitted with Fiat A.80 RC 41 engines, instead of the originally envisaged Pratt & Whitney Twin Wasp engines, and delivered to the *Regia Aeronautica*. When war was declared the S.M.87s were converted to military use and allocated to the Communications Unit of Ala Littoria.

SIAI Marchetti S.M.83

In effect the S.M.83 Marchetti was the civil version of the famous S.M.79 three-engined bomber. It was developed in 1937 on the basis of the valuable store of experience gained from the sporting achievements of the military model, culminating in the Istres–Damascus–Paris race. The first S.M.83 was presented in October 1937 at the Milan *Salone Aeronautico Internazionale.* The new aircraft was virtually the same as the bomber as far as the wing and engines were concerned, but its fuselage was substantially different, being designed to accommodate ten passengers. A total of 23 aircraft were completed in three different versions: the basic model; the S.M.83A designed for the South Atlantic routes, with a smaller capacity of only six passengers and 2,200 pounds (1,000 kg) of cargo and mail, to give greater range; and finally the S.M. 83T which was used between Rome and Natal and was capable of carrying 1,100 pounds (500 kg) of mail.

Aircraft: **SIAI Marchetti S.M.83**
Manufacturer: **SIAI Marchetti**
Type: **Civil transport**
Year: **1937**
Engines: **Three Alfa Romeo A.R. 126 RC 34, radial, air-cooled, 750 hp each**
Wingspan: **69 ft 7 in (21.20 m)**
Length: **53 ft 2 in (16.20 m)**
Height: **15 ft 1 in (4.60 m)**
Weight: **23,000 lb (10,400 kg) (Loaded)**
Cruising speed: **250 mph (400 km/h)**
Ceiling: **23,000 ft (7,000 m)**
Range: **3,000 miles (4,800 km)**
Crew: **4**

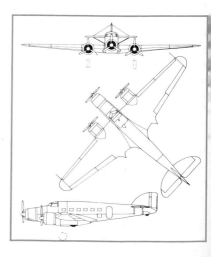

Nardi F.N.305

From Guidonia to Addis Ababa, on a non-stop flight of approximately 2,800 miles (4,500 km), at the average speed of 150 mph (240 km/h) in 18 hours and 49 minutes. This was the most renowned sporting feat by a small single-engined training aircraft called the Nardi F.N.305. It was carried out between March 5 and 6, 1939 by Giovanni Zappetta and Leonardo Bonzi and the Nardi F.N.305 was to become the forbear of a long series of light aircraft which reached a total number of 350 aircraft. The aeroplane used for this long flight, called the F.N.305 D and christened the 'Flying Can', was derived directly from the series model. The prototype had made its maiden flight on February 19, 1935 but the 'Flying Can' included a series of structural modifications, the most conspicuous of which consisted of lengthening the fuselage by almost 3 feet (1.05 m) in the section forward of the leading edge of the wing, so as to install supplementary fuel tanks.

Aircraft: **Nardi F.N.305 D**
Manufacturer: **Fratelli Nardi**
Type: **Competition**
Year: **1938**
Engine: **One Walter Bora, radial with 9 cylinders, air-cooled, 200 hp**
Wingspan: **27 ft 9 in (8.47 m)**
Length: **25 ft 11 in (7.90 m)**
Height: **6 ft 10 in (2.10 m)**
Weight : **–**
Maximum speed: **211 mph (340 km/h)**
Ceiling: **19,685 ft (6,000 m)**
Range: **2,800 miles (4,500 km)**
Crew: **2**

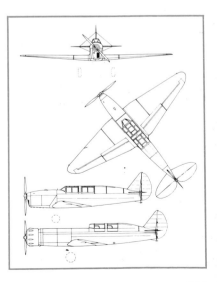

Macchi M.C.100

The direct successor to the Macchi M.C.94 of 1935, the M.C.100 did not enjoy the same success. Even though larger and with a bigger capacity, more powerful, and capable of higher all-round performances, it suffered from the outset from a series of production problems which were never completely put right. The three examples of this aeroplane which were completed were used briefly as civil aircraft by Ala Littoria on the Rome–Alghero–Barcelona route. They were then converted to military use and used intensively in the early years of the war, especially on flights to Africa and, in particular, to Libya. When the armistice came, however, only one of the three aircraft was still operating, the others having been destroyed.

The designer of the Macchi M.C. 100 was the same Mario Castoldi who had created the previous model. The plan was launched in 1938, with the aim of supplying Ala Littoria with an aircraft which could properly replace the M.C.94. The maiden flight by the prototype took place on January 7 1939. The aircraft was a large three-engined flying-boat with a central hull and lateral floats, built entirely of wood. There was a double fin and rudder and, as on the Macchi M.C.94, the engines were mounted on metal frames situated on top of the wing and the fuselage. The engines were Alfa Romeo A.R.126 RC 10 radial engines, each producing 800 hp, driving metal three-bladed propellers, the pitch of which was variable. The hull was built on two levels. The radio operator's small cabin was situated in the nose; immediately behind it, on the upper deck, was the cockpit, with dual controls set side-by-side, and below the cockpit there was a cargo hold; the central part of the hull contained the passenger area, divided into three compartments, accommodating 26 people; lastly, at the very rear, there were the washrooms and a baggage hold. The Macchi M.C.100 combined this rational interior design, which was markedly better than that of its pre-

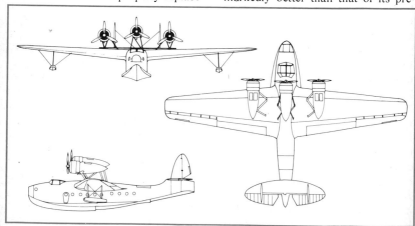

decessor, with good features where both range and speed were concerned: in particular, during the trials, a top speed of 193 mph (310 km/h) at an altitude of 4,600 feet (1,400 m) was recorded. This aeroplane would have been quite an impressive one had it not been for a series of drawbacks which came to light strictly to do with its aerodynamic performance: the major problem here was the need for an exceptionally long area for take-off, especially when fully laden, and this made things difficult in small or crowded expanses of water.

After the delivery of the first aircraft, the second and third were subsequently delivered, but these were withdrawn by Ala Littoria on May 6 and June 29, 1940, respectively. The aircraft were registered I-PLIO, I-PACE and I-PLUS in that order. The outbreak of the Second World War cut short their career on the civil flights run by Ala Littoria quite dramatically. As early as August 1940 the three Macchi M.C.100 aircraft in the *Nucleo Communicazioni* (Communications Unit) started to

Aircraft: **Macchi M.C.100**
Manufacturer: **Aeronautica Macchi**
Type: **Civil transport**
Year: **1939**
Engines: **Three Alfa Romeo A.R. 126 RC 10, radial with 9 cylinders, air-cooled, 800 hp each**
Wingspan: **87 ft 7 in (26.71 m)**
Length: **58 ft 1 in (17.69 m)**
Height: **20 ft 1 in (6.12 m)**
Weight: **29,100 lb (13,200 kg) (Loaded)**
Cruising speed: **163 mph (263 km/h)**
Ceiling: **21,325 ft (6,500 m)**
Range: **870 miles (1,400 km)**
Crew: **3**
Passengers: **26**

operate between Italy and Libya, transporting supplies and troops on the outward flight and bringing back, for the most part, wounded men. These flights went ahead and became particularly intensive in January and February of 1941. As from the summer of that year the Macchi M.C.100s were withdrawn from the services to Africa and used on the shorter flight to Sardinia. It was during this period, in fact, that two of the aircraft crashed and were lost. The first M.C.100, on the other hand, I-PLIO, managed to survive until the armistice.

Campini Caproni CC.2

The first Italian jet aircraft made its maiden flight on May 28, 1940 and for a while this was considered to be an historic date for the whole of aviation. In fact on that day it seemed that the Camprini Caproni CC.2, which took off from the Taliedo airfield without difficulty at the hands of Mario de Bernardi, had managed to outdo the intense efforts of the far more seasoned German and British industries which had been working for years on engines and aircraft of this type. In reality, however, this was not the historic event it was first thought to be. This was because the first flight by a jet aircraft had already taken place in great secrecy, in Germany a year earlier: on August 27, 1939 with the first major trial of the Heinkel He 178. Secondly, the Italian experiment took on a very specific dimension, and remained something of a shot in the dark. Not only was there no follow-up, but also technologically speaking the Italians did not tackle the major problems attaching to the production and development of a real jet engine, as had

been the case in the other two European countries. There was, of course, still the satisfaction of having outmatched Great Britain (the first flight by an experimental Gloster E.28/29 jet aircraft took place there as late as May 15, 1941.

The engineer Secondo Campini had started the preliminary plans for his revolutionary aeroplane in the latter half of the 1930s. Rather than designing an aeroplane, it was more a question of producing a turbine engine capable of providing the necessary thrust for making the aircraft airborne, and Campini opted for a compromise solution: in his engine, the function normally carried out by the turbine in a turbo-jet was carried out by a normal piston engine. In effect the system of propulsion consisted of three parts: the forward-mounted, three-stage compressor capable of 18,000 rpm; the piston engine, in this case a V-12 Isotta-Fraschini producing 900 hp, which worked the compressor; and the dynamic duct with the ring-burner and outlet nozzle, in which the air-flow from the compressor was accelerated before passing ·through combustion

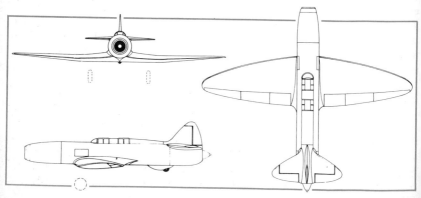

218

Campini Caproni CC.2 – 1940

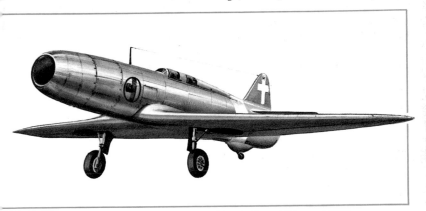

chambers where it was further expanded.

The '*motoreattore*' (moto-jet), which was the term used to define the engine developed by Campini, was mounted in a specially designed monoplane-type body with a low wing and retractable undercarriage, built entirely of metal; the wing was distinctively elliptical in shape, and the aeroplane could seat two people. After its maiden flight the Campini Caproni CC.2 prototype went through an initial series of trials, in the course of which the entire range of the aircraft's features and the engine's characteristics was explored. The major limitations, which soon became evident, were the low speed and the low altitude it could reach. This was because of the relatively poor performance of the Isotta-Fraschini engine installed.

On November 30, 1941, at the end of the trials, Mario De Bernardi flew the second Campini Caproni prototype on its first long-distance flight, which was also the first of its kind in the world. This flight was from Milan to

Aircraft: **Campini Caproni CC.2**
Manufacturer: **Società Italiana Caproni**
Type: **Experimental**
Year: **1940**
Engine: **One Campini motor-jet, 1,650 lb (750 kg) thrust, worked by an Isotta-Fraschini L.121 MC40 Asso, V-12, water-cooled, 900 hp**
Wingspan: **48 ft 0 in (14.63 m)**
Length: **39 ft 8 in (12.10 m)**
Height: **15 ft 5 in (4.70 m)**
Weight: **9,300 lb (4,217 kg) (Loaded)**
Maximum speed: **223.4 mph at 10,000 ft (359.5 km/h at 3,000 m)**
Ceiling: **13,120 ft (4,000 m)**
Range: **–**
Crew: **2**

Rome, landing at Guidonia airport, where the aeroplane was to be handed over for the official trials at the experimental centre of the *Regia Aeronautica*. The flight took place without a hitch and the aircraft also carried a bag of mail on that occasion. However, the series of tests at Guidonia marked the beginning of the end of the Campini Caproni. The combination of scepticism shown by many people and the delays caused by a series of minor technical setbacks and minor accidents, caused the tests to drag on right up to September 1942.

CANT Z.511

The CANT Z.511 went down in history as the largest seaplane on floats ever built. However apart from this distinction it was overall an unsuccessful aeroplane. It came into being in 1937 on the basis of an ambitious project of Ala Littoria which wanted to re-open flights to South America. The programme underwent a series of substantial changes in the following year, when it was decided to abandon the seaplane form in favour of a land-based model. But by that time Filippo Zappata had already drawn up his 511 design which, because of its advanced features, was also authorized. The prototype's maiden flight (the prototype was the only aircraft ever completed) took place in October 1940. The next phase of its development dragged on slowly, with various ups and downs and alterations to the programme, until the armistice when the aircraft was deliberately sunk to prevent it falling into German hands.

Aircraft: **CANT Z.511**
Manufacturer: **Cantieri Riuniti dell'Adriatico**
Type: **Civil transport**
Year: **1940**
Engines: **Four Piaggio P.XII RC 35, radial with 18 cylinders, air-cooled, 1,350 hp each**
Wingspan: **131 ft 3 in (40.00 m)**
Length: **98 ft 1 in (29.90 m)**
Height: **35 ft 4 in (10.77 m)**
Weight: **75,400 lb (34,200 kg) (Loaded)**
Maximum speed: **263 mph (424 km/h)**
Ceiling: **25,000 ft (7,550 m)**
Range: **3,170 miles (5,100 km)**
Crew: **6**
Passengers: **16**

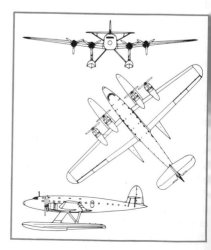

Piaggio P.108

From the Italian 'Flying Fortress', the nickname of the four engined Piaggio P.108 bomber of 1939, the designer Giovanni Casiraghi also designed a version for civil transport. This was called the P.108C and went alongside the two other military versions made, the P.108T for military transport and the P.108A, armed with a 102 mm cannon in the nose. The commercial version of the four-engined Piaggio was advanced in 1940, in response to market analyses which were being carried out at that time by both military and civil aeronautical authorities. The purpose of these was to single out a modern transport aircraft with good performance and adequate capacity, with which to equip the national airlines. The P.108C was made privately by Piaggio and even though the events of the war blocked any further development, it showed itself to be a first-rate aeroplane. It was the first pressurized Italian commercial aircraft.

Aircraft: **Piaggio P.108C**
Manufacturer: **S.A. Piaggio and C.**
Type: **Civil transport**
Year: **1942**
Engines: **Four Piaggio P.XII RC 35, radial with 18 cylinders, air-cooled, 1,350 hp each**
Wingspan: **108 ft 5 in (33.05 m)**
Length: **81 ft 6 in (24.85 m)**
height: **18 ft 8 in (5.70 m)**
Weight: **62,830 lb (28,500 kg) (Loaded)**
Cruising speed: **250 mph (400 km/h)**
Ceiling: **22,000 ft (6,700 m)**
Range: **1,555 miles (2,500 km)**
Crew: **5**
Passengers: **32**

SIAI Marchetti S.M.95

The S.M.95 was the last commercial transport aeroplane built by SIAI Marchetti to go into regular service, and it was also the second type of four-engined aeroplane produced by the Sesto Calende works, after the S.M.74 in 1934. In all fifteen aircraft were completed, and these were used up until 1951 by Alitalia and LATI, and up to 1952 (three aircraft) by the Egyptian company SAIDE.

The origins of the S.M.95 date back to the early stages of the war, when SIAI Marchetti started the preliminary studies for the production of a large long-range transport model, capable of being used as both a military and civil aircraft, designed, in the latter case, for use across the South Atlantic. The design and development stage continued until the spring of 1943 when the first of the four aircraft ordered by the *Regia Aeronautica* as strategic transport aircraft made its maiden flight, in May. However the war slowed down the production programme and only two aircraft were completed durin that year. These were requisitioned b the Germans and moved to German where they were assigned to two uni of the Luftwaffe, which was alread using the transport models of the fou engined Piaggio P.108. The other tw S.M.95s ordered did not appear unt the latter half of 1945: one wa requisitioned by the Royal Air Forc and the other managed to remain i Italy and pass its military tests an trials. It was officially shown a Guidonia in April 1946, an immediately included in 240 Squadro of Transport Command (*Storm Trasporto*). This aircraft was used as military mail transporter an inaugurated the flight from Milan t Rome on April 10, 1946. In th meantime SIAI Marchetti had pre pared a production line for six mor aircraft, with structural modification and a shortened nose, designed for th Air Force (*Aeronautica Militare*). Th first of these took to the air in Decem ber 1946. It was in fact with these air craft that the civil career of the S.M.9

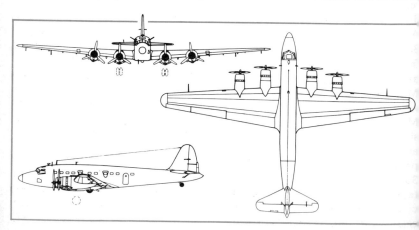

SIAI Marchetti S.M.95C – 1947

egan, after the cancellation of the rder by the military.

The newly established Alitalia was he first to acquire these large four-ngined aeroplanes which, in the now ermanent civil version, took on the lesignation S.M.95C. The first four of he six aircraft which were to form the nost prestigious fleet belonging to the talian company went into service luring 1947. On August 6, the .M.95C christened *Marco Polo* and egistered I-DALM inaugurated the irst international service run by Alitalia, from Rome to Oslo. On April 3, 1948 the first flight to Great Britain, rom Rome to Northolt, was started, and four days later the Rome–Milan–London–Manchester service was also inaugurated. The SIAI Marchetti four-engined aeroplanes showed themselves to be quite robust and had good all-round features. In particular, their capacity ranged from 30 to 38 passengers. One particular technical characteristic of these air-craft was the interchangeability of the engines: there was a transition from the

Aircraft: **SIAI Marchetti S.M.95C**
Manufacturer: **SIAI Marchetti**
Type: **Civil transport**
Year: **1947**
Engines: **Four Bristol Pegasus 48, radial with 9 cylinders, air-cooled, 990 hp each**
Wingspan: **112 ft 5 in (34.28 m)**
Length: **81 ft 3 in (24.77 m)**
Height: **18 ft 8 in (5.70 m)**
Weight: **48,500 lb (22,000 kg) (Loaded)**
Cruising speed: **196 mph at 10,000 ft (315 km/h at 3,000 m)**
Ceiling: **22,300 ft (6,800 m)**
Range: **1,250 miles (2,000 km)**
Crew: **5**
Passengers: **38**

original Alfa Romeo A.R.131 engine with 1,140 hp at take-off, to the English Bristol Pegasus 990 hp radial engine, and then to the American Pratt & Whitney R-1830-SIC3-G 1,215 hp engine. The second Italian airline inaugurated a weekly flight to Caracas in July 1949, using three S.M.95C models christened *Sant' Antonio*, *San Francesco* and *San Cristoforo*. This was a fairly testing flight, the last leg of more than 2,450 miles (4,000 km) being made non-stop; these aircraft nevertheless showed themselves to be well up to the task.

223

Fiat G.212

The last example of the three-engined formula, which was typical of Italian aeronautical engineering from the 1930s onwards, was the Fiat G.212. Although clearly a weak rival to contemporary American and British aircraft, this aeroplane gave useful commercial service between 1948 and the early 1950s, together with its direct forerunner, the G.12, which had been built after the war in the larger capacity L version. Nine models of the civil version of the G.212 (the CP) went into service: six with ALI, three with the Egyptian company SAIDE, which also used the four-engined SIAI Marchetti S.M.95C. The Egyptian aircraft had possibly the most dramatic career. Appropriated by the Air Force they were used in 1957, at the time of the Arab–Israeli war, for the exchange of prisoners. However a military version of the G.212 was also built, and these were used by the Italian Air Force (AMI) from 1948 onwards.

The G.212 project was launched by Giuseppe Gabrielli towards the end of 1943, with the aim of producing larger and more powerful successor t the three-engined G.12, which ha made its maiden flight in the civ version in the autumn of 1940, and ha been followed a year later by th military version. However, the desig and development stage was con siderably delayed both by the way th war was going, and by a ban impose by the German military authorities. was not until January 20, 1947 that th new three-engined model, called th G.212 CA, managed to make it maiden flight. In its general design th aircraft echoed that of its direct pre decessor, even though it had been con siderably replanned, especially wit regard to the fuselage which could no accommodate 30 passengers. After th initial trials, which revealed no majo defects, the prototype was delivered t the Air Force which in turn conclude its own tests. In the meantime, Fiat which had envisaged an initial produc tion series of 25 aircraft, found itsel obliged to reduce this estimate quite considerably in view of the meagre demand for the type on the civi

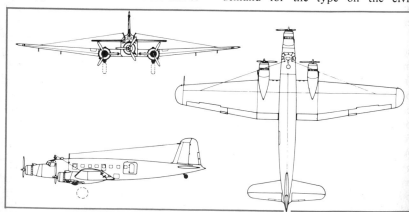

market. The version destined for commercial use, called the G.212 CP Monterosa, differed from the prototype principally in terms of the engines; instead of the Alfa Romeo A.R. 128 they had three Pratt & Whitney R-1830-S1C3-G Twin Wasp engines, producing a constant 1,065 hp and 1,215 hp at take-off and in emergency conditions. The normal capacity was 26 passengers; baggage could be stored in the lower part of the fuselage and in special compartments beneath the leading edge of the wing, outside the engine nacelles.

The Fiat G.212 CP went into service with ALI in 1948, operating mainly on international flights, starting from Milan. The aircraft did not have a particularly lengthy career with this company. The following year ALI took over various minor companies and formed with these the group called ALI-Flotte Riunite. However, this group failed to match up to the two major airlines and did not survive beyond March 1952 when it was taken over by LAI. At least four G.212s were

Aircraft: **Fiat G.212 CP**
Manufacturer: **Fiat S.A.**
Type: **Civil transport**
Year: **1948**
Engines: **Three Pratt & Whitney R-1830-S1C3-G Twin Wasp, radial with 14 air-cooled cylinders, 1,065 hp each**
Wingspan: **96 ft 3 in (29.34 m)**
Length: **76 ft 9 in (23.40 m)**
Height: **26 ft 8 in (8.14 m)**
Weight: **39,700 lb (18,000 kg) (Loaded)**
Cruising speed: **199 mph (320 km/h)**
Ceiling: **24,600 ft (7,500 m)**
Range: **1,555 miles (2,500 km)**
Crew: **5**
Passengers: **26–30**

used by ALI-Flotte Riunite in this period. At the same time the three-engined Fiat went into service with the Egyptian company SAIDE, which used it until 1950 on the Cairo–Benghazi–Tripoli–Tunis route.

It is interesting to note that, with the production of the G.212, Fiat interrupted its activities in the field of air transport for many years. These activities were not resumed until the early 1960s, in the form of the preliminary studies which were to lead to the project for the twin-engined turbine-driven Fiat G.222.

Breda B.Z.308

This could well have been a worthy rival to the DC-6 and the Constellation, had its development not been hampered by the war. In fact, although conceived originally in 1942, the prototype of the Breda B.Z.308 did not make its maiden flight until August 1948 after a long gap imposed by the terms of the armistice. Although the tests and trials revealed to the full the excellent characteristics of this large four-engined transport aircraft, they also further delayed the start of production. As a result there was just one example of the B.Z.308. It saw service with the Air Force, which used it for several years in the General Staff Flying Unit (*Reparto Volo Stato Maggiore*) until it was declared beyond repair after an accident that occurred while it was taxiing at Mogadiscio airport.

Filippo Zappata had started work on his project at the height of the war, and carried on with it even after the armistice of 1943. He started from the very same idea which had urged him, in

the late 1930s, to work on the production of the large passenger seaplane, CANT Z.511: his aim was to design a modern civil aircraft capable of being used to advantage on both European and transatlantic routes. The B.Z.308 immediately appeared to be capable of meeting in full the requirements demanded of it. It was a large four-engined type, built entirely in metal, with a tricycle undercarriage and a maximum capacity of 80 passengers. The performance worked out envisaged a minimum cruising speed of 250 mph (400 km/h) and an average range of 3,000 miles (5,000 km). In the initial design, there was no provision for a pressurized cabin. Construction of the prototype went ahead in the Breda works at Sesto San Giovanni in 1946, but work was immediately interrupted by the intervention of the Allied supervising committee which banned further activities. The ban was not lifted until January 1947, and at this time the engines to be installed in the prototype were also selected: the large Bristol Centaurus 568 British-made radial engines, each producing

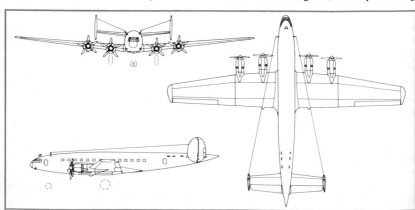

2,500 hp, and driving five-bladed Rotol propellers. Although at a technical level this turned out to be a reasonably good decision, it caused further delays because the first of the engines ordered direct from the British industry did not arrive until May, with the others following shortly after. As a result the schedule had to be extended still further and the flight tests had to be programmed for the latter half of the following year. During this time lapse the Breda authorities launched an advertizing and promotional campaign, aimed at potential customers, which was concentrated mainly in South America. This move was successful, at least at the time, with an order for three examples of the B.Z.308 placed by the Argentinian Air Force, and the establishment, again in Argentina, of an associated company, the Gruppo Aeronautico Italiano, which was to produce Zappata's four-engined model under licence.

In practice, however, all these efforts turned out to be in vain. Trials started

Aircraft: **Breda B.Z.308**
Manufacturer: **Società Italiana Ernesto Breda**
Type: **Civil transport**
Year: **1948**
Engines: **Four Bristol Centaurus 568, radial with 18 cylinders, air-cooled, 2,500 hp each**
Wingspan: **138 ft 1 in (42.10 m)**
Length: **110 ft 0 in (33.52 m)**
Height: **23 ft 7 in (7.20 m)**
Weight: **102,500 lb (46,500 kg) (Loaded)**
Cruising speed: **275 mph at 14,100 ft (441 km/h at 4,300 m)**
Ceiling: **24,100 ft (7,350 m)**
Range: **4,800 miles (7,700 km)**
Crew: **3–4**
Passengers: **80**

after the maiden flight by the prototype, but it was realized that the preparation of a production line would be uneconomical, especially in view of the fierce rivalry from American commercial aeroplanes which were at that time already fully operational. There had been too much delay. Affected by the general postwar crisis, Breda was forced to declare itself bankrupt. The only B.Z.308 was bought in 1949 by the Italian Air Force, which as a result possessed the largest aircraft available since the end of the war.

Macchi M.B.320

Of the light aircraft produced after the war by Macchi, perhaps the least fortunate was the M.B.320. Just six examples of this small twin-engined aeroplane were completed, and three of these were used for a short time on commercial flights by East African Airways, before being replaced. The Macchi M.B.320 was a low-winged twin-engined type, built entirely of wood, capable of carrying four passengers, plus the pilot and co-pilot. The undercarriage was of the tricycle type, completely retractable, and the engines were a pair of 6-cylinder, Continental E.185 models, air-cooled and capable of producing 185 hp each; they drove metal twin-bladed propellers, with variable-pitch. The prototype made its first flight in 1949 and at the end of the various tests and trials, was followed by the small production series aircraft. The Macchi M.B.320 had no specific faults, and in fact its good all-round features aroused the interest of

Aircraft: **Macchi M.B.320**
Manufacturer: **Aeronautica Macchi**
Type: **Light transport**
Year: **1949**
Engines: **Two Continental E.185, 6 straight cylinders, air-cooled, 185 hp each**
Wingspan: **42 ft 8 in (13.00 m)**
Length: **28 ft 5 in (8.66 m)**
Height: **10 ft 6 in (3.19 m)**
Weight: **5,500 lb (2,720 kg) (Loaded)**
Cruising speed: **157 mph at 6,550 ft (252 km/h at 2,000 m)**
Ceiling: **18,500 ft (5,600 m)**
Range: **1,000 miles (1,600 km)**
Crew: **2**
Passengers: **4**

the African company, East African Airways, which ordered three examples. These were bought in 1951 and, registered VP-KJD, VP-KJG and VP-KJJ, were instantly put into operation wearing the colours of this company. They were, however, less than satisfactory. The specific climatic conditions had adverse effects on the behaviour of the small twin-engined aeroplanes, especially because of their structure and covering, which were both all wood and suffered from the high humidity. After a brief period the M.B.320s were put up for sale.

Piaggio P.136
Piaggio P.166

Piaggio resumed its activities, after the gap created by the war, with the production of the small amphibious aircraft the P.136. This light aircraft scored a huge commercial success, especially on the North American market. The design turned out to be the forerunner of a successful series of aeroplanes. In fact, from the P.136, Giovanni Casiraghi developed the larger P.166; this appeared in more than 120 examples and today is still competitive on international markets, because of the P.166-DL3 turbo-prop version which made its maiden flight on July 3, 1976.

Giovanni Casiraghi, the Piaggio designer who between 1936 and 1972, was head of the technical division of this Ligurian firm and who, among others, created the large four-engined P.108 aeroplane, launched the P.136 programme in the immediate postwar period. The aim was to design a small

Aircraft: **Piaggio P.136-L1**
Manufacturer: **Industria Aeronautica e Meccanica Rinaldo Piaggio S.p.A.**
Type: **Light transport**
Year: **1955**
Engines: **Two Lycoming GO 480-B1A6, 6 horizontal cylinders, 270 hp each**
Wingspan: **44 ft 5 in (13.53 m)**
Length: **35 ft 5 in (10.80 m)**
Height: **12 ft 4 in (3.76 m)**
Weight: **6,000 lb (2,720 kg) (Loaded)**
Cruising speed: **170 mph (273 km/h)**
Ceiling: **18,500 ft (5,600 m)**
Range: **715 miles (1,150 km)**
Crew: **2**
Passengers: **3**

amphibious executive type, hallmarked by great versatility and capable of carrying five people in all. The prototype made its maiden flight on August 29, 1948. It was a high-winged monoplane, with a distinctive gull wing, powered by a pair of 215 hp Franklin engines, driving pusher propellers. During its tests and trials the aeroplane did not reveal any particular development problems and in 1949 it was officially ratified and the initial production line was set in motion. In addition to replacing the Franklin engines with 260 hp Lycoming engines, these air-

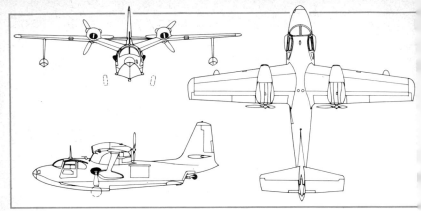

craft had structural modifications to the rear section of the fuselage and to the air-intakes on the engine nacelles. The first order was placed by the Italian Air Force which, after carrying out lengthy tests on a 1950 model of the P.136, subsequently ordered a series of 18 aircraft which were to be used for air-sea rescue, communications and training. This initial order was followed by an order for a further 15 aircraft of the second production version, the P.136-L. These were followed in 1955 and 1957 by the versions P.136-L1 and P.136-L2, with more powerful Lycoming engines and a consequent all-round improvement in performance and load. It was in effect these aeroplanes which were most successful on the export market: called respectively Royal Gull and Royal Gull Super 200, at least 23 examples of the P.136-L1 and P.136-L2 were sold in the United States.

Given the success of the P.136, Piaggio decided to produce another model which would incorporate its excellent characteristics. Unlike its direct predecessor, the P.166 was an exclusively land-operating model, although fairly similar in appearance and general structure to the P.136. This

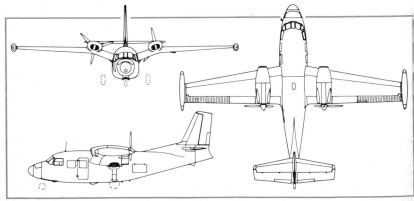

project was started towards the end of 1955 by Giovanni Casiraghi and Alberto Faraboschi, and the prototype made its maiden flight on November 26, 1957. It was larger and heavier than the P.136, but just as robust, versatile and practical, with a capacity of eight passengers, plus pilot and co-pilot. Trials were carried out throughout 1957 and for part of 1958, and it was certificated on July 31 of that year. Production got under way with the P.166-A, an executive and light transport version, of which 32 aircraft were completed. It was followed by the P.166-M version, designed for the Italian Air Force.

Civil production continued with the versions P.166-B (which was christened Portofino) and P.166-C, which appeared respectively in 1962 and 1964. The first, with an increased weight at take-off and more powerful engines, was built in six aircraft, five of which were exported. Only three of the second were built; these had the largest capacity of all and could carry 12 passengers plus the pilot. In 1966, with

Aircraft: **Piaggio P.166-B Portofino**
Manufacturer: **Industria Aeronautica e Meccanica Rinaldo Piaggio S.p.A.**
Type: **Light transport**
Year: **1962**
Engines: **Two Lycoming AGSO-540-A1C, with 6 horizontal cylinders, air-cooled, 360 hp each**
Wingspan: **46 ft 9 in (14.25 m)**
Length: **39 ft 1 in (11.90 m)**
Height: **16 ft 5 in (5.00 m)**
Weight: **8,400 lb (3,800 kg)**
Cruising speed: **223 mph (359 km/h)**
Ceiling: **29,100 ft (8,870 m)**
Range: **1,500 miles (2,410 km)**
Crew: **2**
Passengers: **6–9**

the appearance of the P.166-S, there was a further development of the military version: this version was ordered specifically by the South African Air Force for coastal patrols, and 20 were completed.

In the version P.166-DL3 there was a radical development of the air-frame; this model was fitted with a pair of Avco Lycoming LTP-101 587 ehp turbo-prop engines. The adoption of these new engines made it possible not only to increase performance and carrying capacity, but also to extend the operational life of the aircraft in service.

DEUTSCHE LUFTHANSA

Germany

The rebirth of commercial aviation in Germany after the war was a lengthy process. The last flight by the renowned Deutsche Lufthansa company had taken place in Berlin on April 21, 1945, in the thick of the final defeat, and just a few days before the unconditional surrender to the Allies. This date marked the end of a long upward path, which had taken the German airline to the number one rank amongst European airlines: in 1938 Lufthansa aircraft had flown more than 9,000,000 miles (15,000,000 km) and carried more than 254,000 passengers and close on 7,000 tons of cargo, baggage and mail. In the following year the number of passengers had risen to almost 280,000. The immediate postwar period saw a total ban imposed on all commercial activities in Germany, now divided up between the victorious powers. In 1951 the old airline was put into liquidation, but rather than marking a mood of final resignation and defeat, this move marked the start of nothing less than a rebirth. Thanks to the zeal of a group of enthusiastic men who resolutely backed the formation of a new national company, the agenda for an air transport company, called Luftag and backed principally by the German railways and by private individuals, was drawn up on January 6, 1953. A little more than a year and a half later, on August 6, 1954, the company changed its title, and readopted the old name of Deutsche Lufthansa; it also considerably increased its own company capital. Thanks to the close collaboration of BEA and TWA as far as crew training was concerned, the new Lufthansa was able to start regular services on its domestic network on April 1, 1955. Reaction was immediate. A fortnight later the first international route was inaugurated, and on June 8, 1955 a flight to New York was opened. Within the year Lufthansa was also operating a network of European flights.

Expansion thereafter took on an impressive pace. Not only, over the years, did the German company manage to secure a growing number of competitive routes, but it was also in a position to offer its own service as one of the best in the world, in terms of quality, and became a fierce rival to the far more consolidated companies in both Europe and the United States. Pursuing this policy, Lufthansa spared no effort to secure the best available aircraft on the market, from Super Constellations to Viscounts to Boeing 707s. The introduction of the first jets took place at the end of 1959, giving the company new momentum.

Junkers Ju 160

The Junkers Ju 160 was fairly popular in Germany immediately before the war, and it was also one of the few commercial aeroplanes built by the German industry not to be developed for the military. A total of 48 aircraft were completed, twenty or so of which went into service with Deutsche Lufthansa in 1935. These small, swift single-engined aircraft were used mainly on domestic routes linking German cities until the outbreak of the Second World War.

The Ju 160 prototype made its maiden flight in 1934. This aircraft represented a direct development of the model Ju 60, which had been made two years earlier, of which only three aircraft were ever completed. The Ju 60 aeroplane had been directly influenced by the American light transport model, the Lockheed Orion which had been ordered by Swissair in 1932, and its general appearance was quite similar to the American aircraft. The Ju 60 was a low-winged monoplane, capable of carrying six passengers and built

entirely of metal. Initially it had a fixed undercarriage, but the third version was built with a retractable undercarriage. It was powered by one 600 hp B.M.W. radial engine and its all-round performance was quite satisfactory. It had a top speed of 175 mph (283 km/h), a cruising speed of 150 mph (240 km/h); and an average range of nearly 700 miles (1,100 km). Deutsche Lufthansa had initially put the Ju 60 into service as a cargo transporter in 1933 and the following year had used it for passenger transport on the various domestic services.

The technical experience acquired by Junkers (the Ju 60 had been designed on the basis of completely different constructional principles than those traditionally adhered to by the large German industry) and the operative experience of Deutsche Lufthansa gave rise to the production of an improved version of this aeroplane. This was the Ju 160 which, though retaining the general shape and structure of its predecessor, appeared considerably modified in many details of its construction. The wing, for example, was

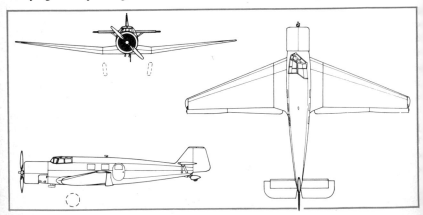

designed to give a better performance. The undercarriage was completely retractable, unlike that of the Ju 60 where the wheels did not disappear completely inside the wing; the fuselage, and in particular the cockpit, had an improved aerodynamic design; and lastly, the entire metal skin was made of polished aluminium sheet, whereas in the Ju 60 the wing covering was still made of the typical corrugated metal used by Junkers from its early production models. However, the capacity of six passengers was identical and the new aircraft could transport them considerably faster than its predecessor. The B.M.W. 132 E engine installed in the Ju 160 gave the aircraft a top speed of 211 mph (340 km/h).

Deutsche Lufthansa took the prototype in hand for a series of test flights and subsequently took delivery of a further 20 of the 48 production aircraft. These aeroplanes were used from 1935 onwards and the German company used them for transporting

Aircraft: **Junkers Ju 160**
Manufacturer: **Junkers Flugzeug und Motorenwerke A.G.**
Type: **Light transport**
Year: **1934**
Engine: **One B.M.W. 132 E, radial with 9 cylinders, air-cooled, 660 hp**
Wingspan: **47 ft 0 in (14.32 m)**
Length: **39 ft 5 in (12.00 m)**
Height: **12 ft 10 in (3.92 m)**
Weight: **7,286 lb (3,550 kg) (Loaded)**
Cruising speed: **196 mph at 6,500 ft (315 km/h at 2,000 m)**
Ceiling: **17,060 ft (5,200 m)**
Range: **620 miles (1,000 km)**
Crew: **2**
Passengers: **6**

both passengers and cargo on the main domestic routes.

This intensive use of the Ju 160 turned out to be quite satisfactory for Deutsche Lufthansa. The characteristics of the small single-engined aeroplane were such as to ensure great regularity, safety, and low running costs, despite its small capacity. When war was declared 16 Ju 160 models out of the 21 originally delivered to the German airline were still in service.

Heinkel He 111

The Hein kel He 111, which was one of the Luftwaffe's bombers during the Second World War, came into being as a civil aircraft in the years when Germany was trying to reorganize its air force in great secrecy. The project was launched in 1934 and the first prototype made its maiden flight on February 24 of the following year. In just a few days another two prototypes appeared, the first of which was adapted superficially to commercial transport. This was followed by the true forbear of the very few civil He 111s made which flew towards the end of 1935 and was officially presented on January 10, 1936. These aircraft were designated He 111C and production started in the spring. The Heinkel He 111C had a cruising speed of 190 mph (305 km/h) and a range of 620 miles (1,000 km). Deutsche Lufthansa took delivery of seven aircraft which, together with the two prototypes, were put into service from summer 1936.

Aircraft: **Heinkel He 111 C**
Manufacturer: **Ernst Heinkel A.G.**
Type: **Civil transport**
Year: **1935**
Engines: **Two B.M.W. VIu, V-12, liquid-cooled, 750 hp each**
Wingspan: **74 ft 2 in (22.60 m)**
Length: **57 ft 5 in (17.50 m)**
Height: **14 ft 5 in (4.39 m)**
Weight: **17,350 lb (7,870 kg) (Loaded)**
Cruising speed: **190 mph (305 km/h)**
Ceiling: **15,750 ft (4,800 m)**
Range: **620 miles (1,000 km)**
Crew: **2**
Passengers: **10**

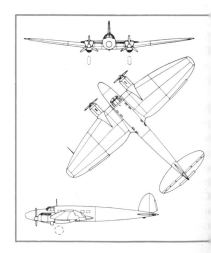

Blohm und Voss Ha 139

Designed in 1935, the Blohm und Voss Ha 139 was intended expressly for transatlantic mail transport. Three examples of this four-engined seaplane were completed and christened respectively *Nordwind*, *Nordmeer* and *Nordstern*. They were used from the summer of 1937 onwards in an interesting series of test-flights across the North Atlantic. Powered by four 600 hp Junkers Jumo engines, the Blohm und Voss Ha 139A had a cruising speed of 162 mph (260 km/h) and a range of 3,300 miles (5,300 km).

Later, and before being requisitioned by the Luftwaffe and used for maritime reconnaissance and for mine-laying and mine-detection, the Ha 139s carried out a regular mail service for a while on the transatlantic route between Africa and South America. One of the main features of the Blohm und Voss Ha 139 was that it could be used from support ships and launched by catapult.

Aircraft: **Blohm und Voss Ha 139A**
Manufacturer: **Blohm und Voss Schiffs-werfts, Abteilung Flugzeugbau**
Type: **Civil transport**
Year: **1936**
Engines: **Four Junkers Jumo 205 C, with 6 straight cylinders, 600 hp each**
Wingspan: **88 ft 7 in (27.00 m)**
Length: **64 ft 0 in (19.50 m)**
Height: **14 ft 9 in (4.50 m)**
Weight: **38,580 lb (17,500 kg) (Loaded)**
Cruising speed: **162 mph (260 km/h)**
Ceiling: **11,500 ft (3,500 m)**
Range: **3,300 miles (5,300 km)**
Crew: **4**

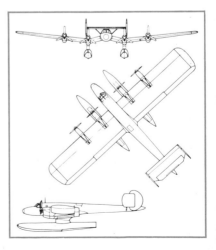

Focke-Wulf Fw 200 Condor

Berlin to New York non-stop. The age-old dream of Lufthansa became a reality on August 10, 1938, when a special Focke-Wulf Fw 200, christened the *Brandenburg* and registered D-ACON (it was the first Fw 200 V-1 prototype) covered the distance of more than 4,070 miles (6,550 km) in 24 hours and 55 minutes at an average speed of 164 mph (264 km/h). On the return flight this first FW 200 V-1 prototype covered the distance in 19 hours and 47 minutes, recording an average speed of 205 mph (330 km/h). On November 28 the same aircraft took off for Tokyo and arrived in less than 48 hours overall, including three stops for refuelling.

The Condor was designed early in 1936 at the explicit request of Deutsche Lufthansa, which, in view of the rivalry of the Douglas DC-3 which had just gone into service, wanted to replace the three-engined Junkers Ju 52 with a more modern aircraft with a larger capacity and better all-round performance. Kurt Tank came up with an elegant low-winged four-engined design, built entirely of metal and with a retractable undercarriage, which could operate on the transatlantic routes. The project was put into gear with considerable speed. In the summer of 1936 a mock-up of the fuselage was prepared and after the approval of Lufthansa, construction of three prototypes got under way. At the same time an assembly line was prepared for the construction of nine pre-production models. The first prototype (originally registered D-AERE and christened *Saarland*) made its maiden flight on July 27, 1937, piloted by the chief designer in person. Just 12 months and 11 days had elapsed since the date of the order from Lufthansa. This was a truly remarkable feat. Powered by four Pratt & Whitney Hornet S1E-G engines each producing 760 hp, the aircraft showed itself to be sound, and after the initial trials it underwent no more than a slight modification to the tail surfaces. Before long it was followed by the other two prototypes (D-AETA, christened *Westfalen*, and D-2600 *Immelmann 111*, which

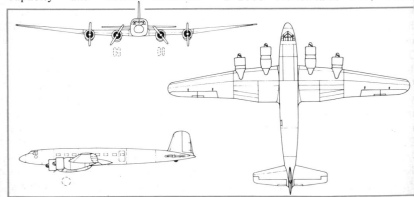

ecame Adolf Hitler's personal ircraft). In these aeroplanes the riginal Pratt & Whitney engines were eplaced by different ones built under cence by B.M.W.

The first Condor to go into regular ommercial service with an airline did ot, however, fly the flag of the German ompany. It was in fact the Danish DDL (Det Danske Luftfartselskab) vhich first used this large four-engined eroplane on its major flights, from the ummer of 1938 onwards. The DDL ought two Fw 200s, the second and he fifth in the pre-production series, nd after registering them respectively DY-DAM and OY-DEM, it christened hem, respectively, *Dania* and *utlandia*. Another two Condors also vent abroad; these were the seventh nd eighth in the pre-production series nd were purchased by the Sindicato Condor Limitada for use in Brazil.

Deutsche Lufthansa took on one of he prototypes and the other five Condors in the initial production series. n 1939 these were accompanied by

Aircraft: **Focke-Wulf Fw 200A Condor**
Manufacturer: **Focke-Wulf Flugzeugbau GmbH**
Type: **Civil transport**
Year: **1937**
Engines: **Four B.M.W. 132G, radial with 9 cylinders, air-cooled, 720 hp each**
Wingspan: **108 ft 3 in (33.00 m)**
Length: **78 ft 3 in (23.85 m)**
Height: **20 ft 8 in (6.30 m)**
Weight: **32,000 lb (14,600 kg) (Loaded)**
Cruising speed: **202 mph at 10,000 ft (325 km/h at 3,000 m)**
Ceiling: **22,000 ft (6,700 m)**
Range: **775 miles (1,250 km)**
Crew: **4**
Passengers: **26**

four examples of the Fw 200 B series, which had an overall increase in weight and capacity, as well as more powerful engines. Commercial operation in the German company started shortly after the opening of the Danish service, and was focussed mainly on domestic routes. The ten Condors in commercial service at the outbreak of war were immediately used for the transportation of troops during the invasion of Norway. However two of them were later handed back to Lufthansa and the last flight with the company took place on April 14, 1945.

Heinkel He 116

The formidable record of 6,000 miles (10,000 km) non-stop in 46 hours and 18 minutes flying time, at an average speed of 140 mph (215.6 km/h) was set in June 1938 by an appropriately modified Heinkel He 116. The aircraft was part of an initial production batch ordered two years earlier by Deutsche Lufthansa, which wanted to operate an aeroplane capable of ensuring very long range mail services. However, this project was not altogether a successful one, in so far as Heinkel did not receive in time the special high-altitude versions of the Hirth engine which was to be mounted on the aircraft. These engines were vital to meet Lufthansa's requirements as the flight to Asia entailed flying over the mountains of Afghanistan. The Heinkel He 116A was actually powered by four 250 hp Hirth engines and two of the aircraft built did eventually manage to go into regular service. They were bought by the Japanese Manchurian Air Lines.

Aircraft: **Heinkel He 116A**
Manufacturer: **Ernst Heinkel A.G.**
Type: **Civil transport**
Year: **1937**
Engines: **Four Hirth HM 508B, V-8, air cooled, 250 hp each**
Wingspan: **72 ft 2 in (22.00 m)**
Length: **44 ft 11 in (13.70 m)**
Height: **10 ft 10 in (3.30 m)**
Weight: **15,275 lb (6,930 kg) (Loaded)**
Cruising speed: **186 mph (300 km/h)**
Ceiling: **14,435 ft (4,400 m)**
Range: **2,800 miles (4,500 km)**
Crew: **4**
Payload: **1,200 lb (550 kg)**

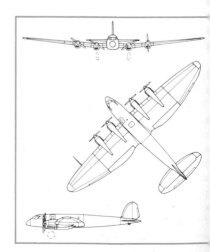

Dornier Do 26

The North Atlantic route has always been the most prestigious and was especially so in the 1930s. Deutsche Lufthansa used up plenty of energy in the attempt to secure a route between Europe and the United States. One of the aircraft which was to give this service was the Dornier Do 26 flying-boat, an elegant aircraft hallmarked by the adoption of four engines mounted in pairs. This aircraft made its maiden flight on May 21, 1938.

The project had been put to Dornier by Deutsche Lufthansa after the first test-flights made with the Blohm und Voss Ha 139 the year before. Among the features specified was the range necessary to fly non-stop from Lisbon to New York. The Do 26A had a range in excess of the 3,600 miles (5,800 km) and could carry a payload of 1,100 pounds (500 kg). Before the outbreak of war Lufthansa only managed to use the Do 26 on one series of mail services across the South Atlantic.

Aircraft: **Dornier Do 26A**
Manufacturer: **Dornier Werke A.G.**
Type: **Civil transport**
Year: **1938**
Engines: **Four Junkers Jumo 205 C, with 6 straight cylinders, 600 hp each**
Wingspan: **98 ft 5 in (30.00 m)**
Length: **80 ft 9 in (24.60 m)**
Height: **22 ft 6 in (6.85 m)**
Weight: **44,100 lb (20,000 kg) (Loaded)**
Cruising speed: **193 mph (310 km/h)**
Ceiling: **15,750 ft (4,800 m)**
Range: **5,600 miles (9,000 km)**
Crew: **4**
Payload: **1,100 lb (500 kg)**

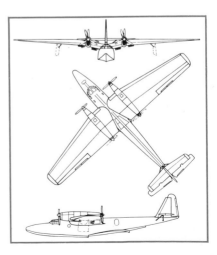

Junkers Ju 90

Out of the unsuccessful Ju 89 military bomber (developed from 1935 onwards as part of the ambitious 'Urals bomber' programme) Junkers developed a large four-engined transport type which, after a brief period in civil use, was then developed exclusively for use in the Luftwaffe. There was a whole series of versions which became steadily more powerful and improved. Four prototypes of the Ju 90 were completed, plus ten production aircraft and it was clearly a transitional type which gave rise to the numerous military versions of the later Ju 290. However, even in its brief operational career the Junkers Ju 90 managed to make a significant contribution to Deutsche Lufthansa in the last year before the outbreak of war, and before the entire output of the German aeronautical industry was focussed on the country's warmongering needs.

Towards the end of 1936 when the programme for the production of a strategic bomber had definitely fallen through, Junkers asked for authorization to use certain structural components, already built for the third prototype of its military model, the Ju 89, with which to build a transport aeroplane. This was granted, and the development of the new aircraft was subject to one condition. This was that provision be made for the installation in the series models of alternative engines to the Jumo 211 or the Daimler Benz DB 600, whose use had been requested for the original bomber. Work on the first Ju 90 prototype started early in 1937 and the designer Ernst Zindel simply combined the wing, undercarriage, engine and tailplane of the previous model with a new fuselage, designed expressly for transport purposes. The prototype made its maiden flight on August 28 and immediately aroused the interest of Deutsche Lufthansa. In order to have a new, modern aircraft with a large capacity, Deutsche Lufthansa was prepared to accept the lower performance of the considerably less powerful B.M.W. 132H radial engines. As a result Junkers started building three

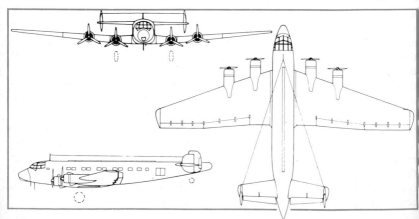

other prototypes fitted with different engines and ten production aircraft, called Ju 90B. The second and third prototypes (Ju 90 V2, registered D-AIVI and christened *Preussen* and Ju 90 V3, registered D-AURE and christened *Bayern*) appeared early in 1938 and took the place of the first prototype (D-AALU, christened *Der Grosse Dessauer*), which had been destroyed on a flight made on February 6, in the various tests and operational trials. After a busy publicity campaign, in which the Ju 90 was also credited with various weight and altitude records set up by the first prototype of the Ju 89 bomber, Lufthansa confirmed its own order for eight production aircraft, while the other two were ordered by South African Airways, (although they never took delivery because of the outbreak of war).

The German airline started its regular service during 1938, using the third prototype, on the Berlin–Vienna route. In the following year, after the arrival of the first Ju 90 production air-

Aircraft: **Junkers Ju 90B**
Manufacturer: **Junkers Flugzeug und Motorenwerke A.G.**
Type: **Civil transport**
Year: **1938**
Engines: **Four B.M.W. 132H, radial with 9 cylinders, air-cooled 830 hp each**
Wingspan: **114 ft 11 in (35.02 m)**
Length: **86 ft 3 in (26.30 m)**
Height: **23 ft 11 in (7.30 m)**
Weight: **50,700 lb (23,000 kg) (Loaded)**
Cruising speed: **200 mph at 10,000 ft (320 km/h at 3,000 m)**
Ceiling: **18,000 ft (5,500 m)**
Range: **1,300 miles (2,092 km)**
Crew: **4**
Passengers: **40**

craft services were extended and one even flew to Great Britain. However the war hampered any regular use of all the aircraft ordered and at the outbreak of war they were requisitioned by the Luftwaffe.

The Junkers Ju 90 was a fairly spacious and comfortable aircraft. There were two internal arrangements: five equal compartments, the forward two being reserved for smokers; or two large compartments, the first of which had 16 seats for smokers, and the second of which had place for 22–24 passengers.

243

Dornier Do 27

This project was developed in Spain, in the technical offices set up in Madrid at the time in which activities of this type were still prohibited in Federal Germany. The study outlined a high-winged monoplane with the same exceptional performance as the famous Fieseler Fi 156 Storch, made during the war. The aircraft was built by the Oficinas Technicas Dornier and called the Do 25, but when the aeronautical industry was authorized to resume its activities in Germany, it was considerably modified and called the Do 27. The prototype made its maiden flight on June 27, 1955 and impressed onlookers so much with its excellent qualities that it was ordered in large numbers by the military. Powered by a single 270 hp Lycoming engine, the Do 27Q-1 had a range of 500 miles (800 km). The new Luftwaffe and the Army took most of the production output of 600 aircraft but the Do 27 also saw civil service.

Aircraft: **Dornier Do 27Q-1**
Manufacturer: **Dornier A.G.**
Type: **Light transport**
Year: **1955**
Engine: **One Lycoming GO-480-B1A6, with 6 horizontal cylinders, 270 hp**
Wingspan: **39 ft 4 in (12.00 m)**
Length: **31 ft 6 in (9.60 m)**
Height: **11 ft 6 in (3.50 m)**
Weight: **4,075 lb (1,850 kg) (Loaded)**
Cruising speed: **109 mph (175 km/h)**
Ceiling: **11,000 ft (3,300 m)**
Range: **500 miles (800 km)**
Crew: **1**
Passengers: **6–7**

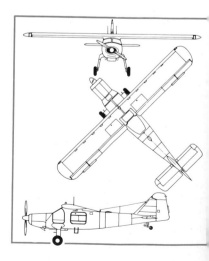

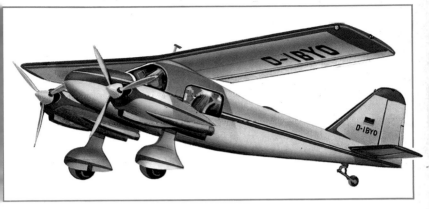

Dornier Do 28

After the successful Do 27 Dornier developed the no less useful model 28. When the prototype of this model made its maiden flight on April 29, 1959, it looked essentially similar in outline to the Do 27, but had engines mounted in nacelles at the side of the fuselage. However with the second prototype various structural modifications were introduced which gave rise to the first production series, the Do 28A-1. As had been the case with the previous model, the Do 28A-1 was also used by small companies. The first one to buy the Do 28 was the German Deutsche Taxiflug, in the autumn of 1960.

In 1963 the second production version, the Do 28B appeared. This version had more powerful engines. In 1966 there was a considerable departure from the basic model, with the prototype of the Do 28 D Skyservant. This was a redesigned and larger version, with a larger capacity and improved features.

Aircraft: **Dornier Do 28A-1**
Manufacturer: **Dornier A.G.**
Type: **Light transport**
Year: **1959**
Engines: **Two Lycoming 0-540-A1D, with 6 horizontal cylinders, air-cooled, 250 hp each**
Wingspan: **45 ft 3 in (13.80 m)**
Length: **30 ft 1 in (9.18 m)**
Height: **9 ft 2 in (2.80 m)**
Weight: **5,400 lb (2,450 kg) (Loaded)**
Cruising speed: **146 mph (235 km/h)**
Range: **715 miles (1,150 km)**
Crew: **1**
Passengers: **6–7**

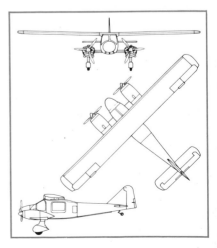

日本の翼　皆様の翼

日本航空

Other Countries

After the war the expansion of air transport became a worldwide phenomenon. Growth was exceptionally fast and involved both the countries traditionally in the forefront in the field of aeronautical engineering as well as those countries which had hitherto been virtually overshadowed by the leading nations.

In particular the Old Continent was able to demonstrate its excellent capacity of recovery in the air transport sector. In effect, every nation felt the need to organize an efficient national airline, and the almost unrivalled supremacy of the British and French airlines was soon under siege on all sides. The Scandinavian company SAS was formed on July 31, 1946, although it did not become fully operational until February 8, 1951. From that date onwards SAS incorporated the organization and operative structure of the three Scandinavian airlines, the Swedish Aktiebolaget Aerotransport (ABA), the Danish Det Danske Luftfartselskab (DDL) and the Det Norske Luftfartselskap of Norway. No less effective was the expansion of the Dutch KLM, with its ancient and renowned tradition; the Belgian SABENA and the Swiss Swissair. Although short of aircraft and funds, the Spanish company Iberia was also able to take advantage of the mood of the moment. The Finnish company Finnair inaugurated its services on April 15, 1951, and was shortly followed by the Icelandic Loftleidir.

In Eastern Europe, Poland was the first East Bloc country to reorganize an air transport company, LOT, on March 6, 1945; Rumania followed a year later with TARS (later called TAROM); and Czechoslovakia reopened its CSA services on March 1, 1946. These airlines, as well as those belonging to the other Communist countries, all operated under the wing of the U.S.S.R. and Aeroflot. In other parts of the world the revival of air transport was particularly strong in Canada, Australia and Japan. Trans-Canada Airlines (TCA), Canadian Pacific Airlines (CPA) and Quantas were soon among the world's leading airline companies. Similarly, the Japanese Japan Air Lines (JAL), which was finally restored to its former self in 1953, is now recognised as a major international airline.

SAAB 90 Scandia

Swedish aeronautical production has always tended to focus on military rather than civil aeroplanes. Among the few commercial projects to have seen the light of day, the 1946 project which gave rise to the SAAB 90 Scandia was one of the most important, especially as it was up against a market which was at that time in full swing: the short-to-medium range and medium-capacity transport category. The Scandia was conceived to replace the omni-present DC-3 and it would surely have succeeded in doing so if its production had not been greatly slowed down because of the major commitments undertaken by SAAB in the military sector. As a result only 18 aircraft, including the prototype, were completed between 1948 and 1954. Eight of these were purchased by the Scandinavian company SAS, while nine served under the flag of the Brazilian airline VASP. In 1957 VASP

also bought the SAS Scandia aircraft and the entire fleet remained in service until the mid-1960s.

The project was started by the engineers of Svenska Aeroplan AB (SAAB) during the Second World War in 1944. The idea was to produce a twin-engined commercial transport aeroplane with good all-round performance which would be capable of competing with the DC-3. A fairly modern shape was chosen: twin engines, with a low wing, built entirely of metal, with a retractable tricycle undercarriage. The oval fuselage could accommodate four to five crew members plus 24–32 passengers, although the capacity was often increased to 36. Originally the engines were a pair of Pratt & Whitney R-2000 Twin Wasp radials producing 1,450 hp at take-off, but the production models designated SAAB 90A-2 were all fitted with 1,800 hp Twin Wasp engines.

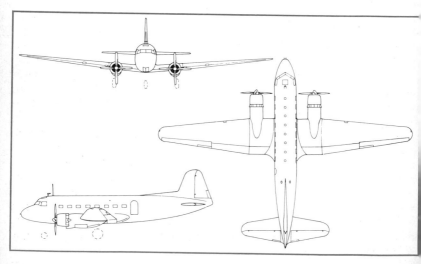

The Scandia prototype made its maiden flight on November 16, 1946 (it had distinctive oval engine cowlings, but these were soon replaced by circular ones), and after the various tests and trials it was used on a long publicity tour to various European states. This commercial effort to launch the new aircraft on the international market did not, however, have the success expected, especially since SAAB could not make any deliveries before 1948, burdened as it was by the production of military aeroplanes. In 1946 there was only one order for ten aircraft, which was placed by the domestic company AB Aerotransport. The creation of SAS (Scandinavian Airlines System, which took over AB Aerotransport) subsequently caused the order to be reduced to six. The remaining four aircraft were sold to Aerovias Brasil, the company which was later taken over by VASP.

The Scandia aeroplanes first went into service with SAS in November 1950. They were used mainly on

Aircraft: **SAAB 90A-2 Scandia**
Manufacturer: **SAAB**
Type: **Civil transport**
Year: **1950**
Engines: **Two Pratt & Whitney R-2180-E1 Twin Wasp, radial with 14 cylinders, air-cooled, 1,800 hp each**
Wingspan: **91 ft 10 in (28.00 m)**
Length: **69 ft 11 in (21.30 m)**
Height: **23 ft 3 in (7.08 m)**
Weight: **35,275 lb (16,000 kg) (Loaded)**
Cruising speed: **243 mph at 10,000 ft (391 km/h at 3,050 m)**
Ceiling: **24,600 ft (7,500 m)**
Range: **920 miles (1,480 km)**
Crew: **4–5**
Passengers: **24–36**

domestic routes and proved themselves to be so efficient that the company ordered two more. There was a similar success in South America where VASP, which was using twin-engined SAAB models on its domestic Brazilian routes, also ordered five additional aircraft. Because SAAB was unable to build them, all these aircraft, except one, were built by Fokker.

The basic design also gave rise to a version with a pressurized cabin, called SAAB 90B, but this was in fact never constructed.

Mitsubishi Hinazuru

Christened Hinazuru (Young Crane) by Mitsubishi, this twin-engined light transport aeroplane was a version, built under licence, of the successful British aircraft, the Airspeed A.S.6 Envoy.

The extension of manufacturing rights to Japan represented a huge success in the intense campaign carried out by Airspeed to put its twin-engined model on the various foreign markets. Compared with the British-made original, the Hinazuru differed in only very few details. It was essentially identical as far as the structural components were concerned and was fitted with a pair of 240 hp Mitsubishi Lynx IV-C radial engines, also built under British licence. The Hinazuru had a cruising speed of 150 mph (240 km/h). Mitsubishi built an unidentified number of Hinazuru models, although at that time it was certainly not quantity that interested the Japanese aeronautical industry, whose efforts tended to be directed at acquiring advanced technological knowledge.

Aircraft: **Mitsubishi Hinazuru**
Manufacturer: **Mitsubishi Jukogyo K.K.**
Type: **Light transport**
Year: **1934**
Engines: **Two Mitsubishi Lynx IV-C, radial with 7 cylinders, air-cooled, 240 hp each**
Wingspan: **52 ft 4 in (15.95 m)**
Length: **34 ft 6 in (10.52 m)**
Height: **9 ft 6 in (2.90 m)**
Weight: **5,855 lb (2,656 kg) (Loaded)**
Cruising speed: **150 mph (240 km/h)**
Ceiling: **16,500 ft (5,030 m)**
Range: **650 miles (1,045 km)**
Crew: **1**
Passengers: **8**

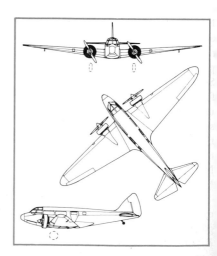

Nakajima AT-2

This was the first twin-engined commercial transport aircraft built in Japan to an entirely original design. The Nakajima AT-2 appeared on the drawing-board in 1935, shortly after Nakajima had acquired manufacturing rights for the American Douglas DC-2. It was after closely studying the constructional methods and technology used in the Douglas DC-2 that the Nakajima technicians started on the design of a smaller aircraft for short-range commercial flights. The prototype made its maiden flight on September 12, 1936 and apart from a few problems caused by the undercarriage and the engine cooling system, it turned out to be without any major faults. At the end of the trials mass production was started. The Nakajima AT-2 was powered by Nakajima Kotobuki 41 radial engines.

Between 1937 and 1940 a total of 32 examples of the civil version were completed. These went to Dai Nippon Koku K. K. and Manchurian Air Lines.

Aircraft: **Nakajima AT-2**
Manufacturer: **Nakajima Hikoki K.K.**
Type: **Civil transport**
Year: **1936**
Engines: **Two Nakajima Kotobuki 41, radial with 9 cylinders, air-cooled, 710 hp each**
Wingspan: **65 ft 4 in (19.91 m)**
Length: **50 ft 2 in (15.30 m)**
Height: **13 ft 7 in (4.15 m)**
Weight: **11,575 lb (5,250 kg) (Loaded)**
Cruising speed: **193 mph (310 km/h)**
Ceiling: **23,000 ft (7,000 m)**
Range: **745 miles (1,200 km)**
Crew: **2**
Passengers: **10**

1938 – Mitsubishi G3M2

Mitsubishi G3M

Even though used on a massive scale as a bomber and military transport by the Imperial Navy during the Second World War, the Mitsubishi G3M also had a brief commercial career in the years immediately leading up to the war. In fact, in 1938 twenty examples of the second major production series were converted to civil use. Most of these G3M2 aircraft were used by Nippon Koku K.K. and later by Dai Nippon Koku K.K., the major Japanese airlines. The renown in the civil sector of the Mitsubishi twin-engined aeroplanes was linked with a series of spectacular intercontinental flights. These flights consisted of one from Tokyo to Teheran, made by the aircraft registered J-BEOA; the flight from Tokyo to Rome, carried out by J-BEOC; and lastly the round-the-world flight by J-BACI, christened *Nippon*, made between August 26 and October 20, 1939. On this flight more than 32,840 miles (52,850 km) were covered in 194 flying hours.

Aircraft: **Mitsubishi G3M2**
Manufacturer: **Mitsubishi Jukogyo K.K.**
Type: **Civil transport**
Year: **1938**
Engines: **Two Mitsubishi Kinsei 41, radial with 14 cylinders, 1,075 hp each**
Wingspan: **82 ft 0 in (25,00 m)**
Length: **53 ft 11 in (16.45 m)**
Height: **12 ft 1 in (3.68 m)**
Weight: **17,640 lb (8,000 kg) (Loaded)**
Cruising speed: **174 mph (280 km/h)**
Ceiling: **26,250 ft (8,000 m)**
Range: **2,175 miles (3,500 km)**
Crew: **2**
Passengers: **8**

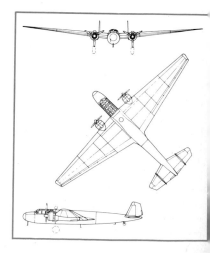

Koken

Between May 15 and 16, 1938 an elegant Japanese aircraft managed to set the world closed-circuit distance record. This aeroplane, called Koken, flew a total of 7,240 miles (11,651 km), and remained airborne for 62 hours and 23 minutes. The leading characters in this amazing feat were Y. Fumita (an officer of the Japanese Imperial Army) and F. Takashi (an NCO in the Imperial Army), together with an anonymous mechanic who also went on the flight to carry out minor emergency repairs if needed. The Koken, which was built by Tokyo Gasu Denki K.K., a small firm which had started building aeroplanes in 1933, had been designed specifically for this attempt at the record by the Institute of Aeronautical Research at Tokyo University. The aircraft was built entirely of metal, and had exceptionally pure lines which were not even disturbed by the huge wing. The wing had a span of almost 92 feet (28 m) and was in effect a huge fuel tank.

Aircraft: **Koken**
Manufacturer. **Tokyo Gasu Denki K.K.**
Type: **Competition**
Year: **1938**
Engine: **One Kawasaki, V-12, liquid-cooled, 800 hp**
Wingspan: **91 ft 8 in (27.93 m)**
Length: **53 ft 4 in (15.96 m)**
Height: **13 ft 2 in (4.00 m)**
Weight: **21,000 lb (9,510 kg) (Loaded)**
Maximum speed: **152 mph (245 km/h)**
Ceiling: **–**
Range: **9,325 miles (15,000 km)***
Crew: **3**
* Estimated

There were in fact, in each wing section, seven tanks with an overall capacity was about 1,550 gallons (7,000 litres). The single engine had been expressly built by Kawasaki: it was a V-12 model, liquid-cooled, capable of producing 800 hp, and driving a twin-bladed metal propeller with variable-pitch. Lastly, the completely retractable undercarriage had an extremely simple structure and had very large wheels. Although, on this record-beating flight, the Koken flew for 7,240 miles (11,651 km) without stopping, this range was well below the theoretical maximum range of 9,325 miles (15,000 km).

Pander S-4 Postjager

The Pander S-4 Postjager was designed and built with one sole aim in mind: to give swift mail service between Holland and the Dutch East Indies. However the aircraft never managed to fulfil its mission and the Postjager was unable to exploit the one chance it had to ensure certain commercial success: a demonstration flight from Amsterdam to Djakarta, with the aim of checking the practical possibilities of setting up the flight in four days instead of the nine days used by KLM.

The Pander S-4 started from Schiphol at dawn on December 9, 1933. However, it was forced to touch down at Grottaglie (Brindisi) because of damage to one of the engines. The aeroplane did not take off again until December 28 and arrived at Djakarta three days later. Mechanical problems also dogged the homeward flight. The one example of the Postjager was destroyed during the London to Melbourne race in October 1934.

Aircraft: **Pander S-4 Postjager**
Manufacturer: **Pander**
Type: **Civil transport**
Year: **1933**
Engines: **Three Wright R-975-E2 Whirlwind, radial with 9 cylinders, air-cooled, 420 hp each**
Wingspan: **54 ft 5 in (16.60 m)**
Length: **41 ft 0 in (12.50 m)**
Height: **10 ft 10 in (3.30 m)**
Weight: **12,550 lb (5,700 kg) (Loaded)**
Cruising speed: **186 mph (300 km/h)**
Ceiling: **20,000 ft (6,050 m)**
Range: **–**
Crew: **2–3**

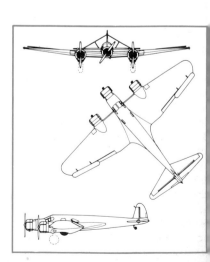

Koolhoven F.K.50

ust three examples of the Koolhoven F.K.50 were built between 1935 and 1938, but two of them managed to survive the war and resume commercial service in the postwar period. The last aircraft was still flying in the early 1960s. The Koolhoven echoed the general form of two previous models, the F.K.48 and the F.K.49, made in 1934. However it was heavier and larger, and had more powerful engines. It was a twin-engined, high-winged monoplane, with a fixed undercarriage and mixed structure and covering. The first aircraft was delivered to the Swiss company Alpar Bern towards the end of 1935 and was followed, again for the same company, by the second in early 1936 and the third in 1938. But the last F.K.50 differed considerably from its forerunners: as well as modifications to the fuselage, it had twin rudders and had been generally improved both structurally and aerodynamically.

Aircraft: **Koolhoven F.K.50**
Manufacturer: **N.V. Koolhoven Vliegtuigen**
Type: **Civil transport**
Year: **1935**
Engines: **Two Pratt & Whitney R-985-T1B Wasp Junior, radial, 400 hp each**
Wingspan: **59 ft 0 in (18.00 m)**
Length: **45 ft 11 in (14.00 m)**
Height: **12 ft 1 in (3.70 m)**
Weight: **9,000 lb (4,100 kg) (Loaded)**
Cruising speed: **162 mph (260 km/h)**
Ceiling: **17,000 ft (5,200 m)**
Range: **620 miles (1,000 km)**
Crew: **2**
Passengers: **8**

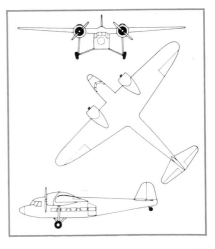

Fokker F.27 Friendship

Rarely in the history of aviation has a commercial aircraft been christened with such a well-omened name as the Fokker Friendship. Conceived in the early 1950s, the Fokker F.27 is today still one of the most popular twin-turbo-prop medium capacity, short-to-medium range transport types available. Its success has been due not only to its excellent general characteristics but also, and above all, to the constant and careful modernization and improvement of the basic design. By July 1, 1977 some 656 examples of all versions (including 205 built under licence in the United States by Fairchild) had been ordered by 145 operators in 56 countries. Apart from being used purely commercially by more than 60 airlines, their use has varied from executive transport to service with civil bodies and organizations, and the military. Even today the history of the Friendship is far from

being a closed book, despite the appearance in the spring of 1967 of its more modern (and no less seasoned) successor, the twin-jet Fokker F.28 Fellowship.

After the success scored by Fokker in the field of commercial transport in the 1920s and 1930s, and dark years of the Second World War, the return to peace made it necessary to completely rebuild and reorganize the works and plant. The end of the war also brought with it a very keen desire by Fokker to regain its former leading-role in the international market for commercial aircraft. With this in mind programmes were launched from 1946 onwards, with the designing of a twin-jet transport model, carrying 17 passengers, powered by two Rolls Royce Nene engines, and capable of flying at 500 mph (800 km/h). Called the F-26 Phantom, this model was, however, never built, mainly because of a lack of funds. Nevertheless, in the early 1950s, Fokker was commissioned by the

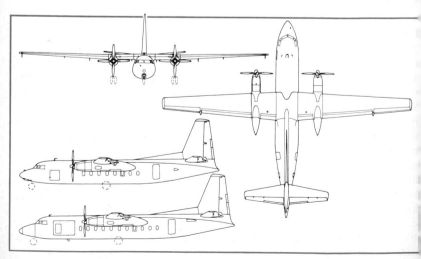

Swedish company SAAB to build six examples of the twin-engined Scandia, for SAS and the Brazilian company VASP. It was more or less at this time that the preliminary studies were started which were to lead to the production of the F.27 Friendship. Here too the point of departure was the need to find a substitute for the American DC-3. In particular, Fokker was well aware of the qualities and drawbacks of the venerable old Dakota. This was because in the immediate postwar period the firm had started to convert numerous C-47s, which had been withdrawn from the Allied air forces, to commercial use. In order to get an authentic idea of the real needs of potential operators, a vast market research survey was carried out; this also made it possible to discard many of the almost 200 design theories that had been piling up the drawing-boards. In this way the final form of the F.27 Friendship took shape. The form of the F.27 was not unlike that of another aircraft, the

Aircraft: **Fokker F.27-100 Friendship**
Manufacturer: **Fokker-VFW N.V.**
Type: **Civil transport**
Year: **1958**
Engines: **Two Rolls-Royce Dart 511-7 turbo-props, 1,710 ehp each**
Wingspan: **95 ft 2 in (29.00 m)**
Length: **77 ft 1 in (23.50 m)**
Height: **27 ft 11 in (8.50 m)**
Weight: **40,500 lb (18,370 kg) (Loaded)**
Cruising speed: **266 mph at 20,000 ft (428 km/h at 6,095 m)**
Ceiling: **29,000 ft (8,840 m)**
Range: **775 miles (1,250 km)**
Crew: **2–3**
Passengers: **40–52**

British Handley Page Herald, which was designed at almost the same time for the same purposes. The Friendship was a high-winged monoplane, with a spacious pressurized fuselage; it adopted a completely retractable tricycle undercarriage. The feature which, to start with at least, distinguished one design from the other was the choice of engines. Handley Page opted for four Alvis Leonides radial engines, while Fokker, from the outset, chose a pair of Rolls-Royce Dart turbo-props. Later on the British aircraft was also fitted with these same

engines, but the delay in doing so was all to the advantage of the Dutch firm.

The F.27 programme went ahead. As from May 1951 a long series of wind-tunnel tests was carried out and in 1952 a mock-up fuselage was built. In the following year the decision was taken to build four prototypes, two for flight tests and two for ground tests. To speed things up it was also decided to put the first prototype in the air without the pressurization system: the maiden flight took place at Schiphol on November 24, 1955. The second prototype made its maiden flight slightly more than a year later on January 31, 1957.

Production started almost simultaneously in Holland and the United States in 1957. The first F.27 in the Dutch series flew on March 23, 1958, while the first model built by Fairchild took to the air twenty days later, on April 13.

The initial version, F.27-100, was followed by the second production model, F.27-200 and F.27A in the USA, with more powerful engines. This

Aircraft: **Fokker F.27-500 Friendship**
Manufacturer: **Fokker-VFW N.V.**
Type: **Civil transport**
Year: **1967**
Engines: **Two Rolls-Royce Dart 532-7** turbo-props, **2,255 ehp each**
Wingspan: **95 ft 2 in (29.00 m)**
Length: **82 ft 2 in (25.04 m)**
Height: **28 ft 7 in (8.71 m)**
Weight: **45,000 lb (20,412 kg) (Loaded)**
Cruising speed: **298 mph at 20,000 ft (48** km/h at **6,095 m)**
Ceiling: **29,500 ft (9,000 m)**
Range: **1,082 miles (1,741 km)**
Crew: **2–4**
Passengers: **36–56**

model was followed by the F.27-300 and the F-27-400 (respectively th F.27B and F.27C from Fairchild) which, apart from having the sam engines as the 100 and 200 series, had large loading door for mixe passenger-cargo use. In Novembe 1967 the first F.27-500 appeared. Thi version had a lengthened fuselage about 5 feet (1.50 m), longer and larger capacity. The F.27-600 wa announced shortly after, to replace th Friendship models in the 200/40 series. Apart from the military version (the main one being the F.27-400 M numerous executive versions were bui by Fairchild.

Noorduyn Norseman

This was one of the most popular utility aircraft of its day, and was specifically designed to operate in the climatic conditions of Canada. The Norseman was robust, sound and versatile, and was capable of being fitted as required with wheels, floats or skis. The prototype made its maiden flight in 1935. The initial production series, called Norseman II with a single 450 hp Wright engine, was followed in 1937 by a more powerful version with a 600 hp Pratt & Whitney radial engine. This version was called the Norseman IV. It had a cruising speed of 148 mph (238 km/h) at 5,000 feet (1,524 m) and a range of some 600 miles (966 km). These aircraft were used satisfactorily by the Royal Canadian Air Force and the U.S. Army Air Forces and more than 900 aircraft were completed. In 1947 there followed a further improved version (Norseman V) which was made by the Canadian Car and Foundry Company, which had taken over Noorduyn Aviation Ltd.

Aircraft: **Noorduyn Norseman IV**
Manufacturer: **Noorduyn Aviation Ltd.**
Type: **Light transport**
Year: **1937**
Engine: **One Pratt & Whitney R-1340-S3H1 Wasp, radial, air-cooled, 600 hp**
Wingspan: **51 ft 8 in (15.75 m)**
Length: **31 ft 9 in (9.68 m)**
Height: **10 ft 1 in (3.07 m)**
Weight: **7,400 lb (3,356 kg) (Loaded)**
Cruising speed: **148 mph (238 km/h)**
Ceiling: **17,000 ft (5,182 m)**
Range: **600 miles (966 km)**
Crew: **1**
Passengers: **8**
Payload: **600 lb (270 kg)**

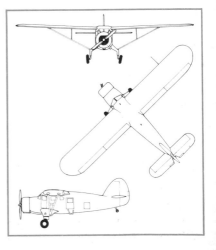

de Havilland DHC-2 Beaver

More than 1,600 aircraft, used in more than 60 countries: such was the exceptional career of this small light utility aeroplane. Robust and versatile, with excellent performances as far as taking off and landing were concerned (STOL), the de Havilland DHC-2 Beaver ended up finding favour with the military and most of the production went to the U.S. Army, the U.S.A.F. and the British Army. In addition this aircraft was sold to the air forces of fifteen or so other countries. It also enjoyed great success in the civil sector, with something approaching 200 aircraft in service all over the world. In 1963, 16 years after the maiden flight by the prototype, a turbo-prop version appeared called the DHC-2 Mk. III Turbo Beaver.

The DHC-2 project was started by de Havilland Canada in the immediate postwar period and represented the first step towards the production of an important family of STOL transport aeroplanes. These aeroplanes were to make their mark on both civil and military markets in the form of the Beavers and their successors the DHC-3 Otter, the DHC-4 Caribou and the DHC-5 Buffalo. The DHC-2 programme was the second completely original one undertaken by the Canadian firm. In fact the de Havilland Aircraft of Canada company, which had been founded way back in 1928 as a subsidiary of the British head office, had operated from the outbreak of the Second World War particularly as a manufacturer of the products designed in Great Britain. Design and construction activities had started during the war and the first original aeroplane had

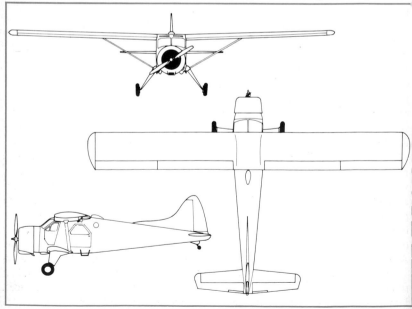

been the DHC 1 Chipmunk. This was a small two-seater training model which, as well as having a production total of 217 in Canada, had been built in Great Britain by the de Havilland Aircraft company. The DHC-2 Beaver prototype made its maiden flight on August 16, 1947. It was a high-winged monoplane, built entirely of metal, powered by a 450 hp Pratt & Whitney Wasp Junior radial engine and capable of carrying seven passengers plus the pilot. The Beaver turned out to be an exceptionally tough and safe aircraft, with excellent flight specifications and a good capacity; it was also extremely versatile. Like the Noorduyn Norseman the DHC-2 could be fitted with wheels, skis or a pair of floats. As a result its success was instant and production went ahead without interruption, particularly thanks to the orders of 968 aircraft from the U.S. Army and U.S.A.F.

In an attempt to improve its all-round performance a 570 hp Alvis Leonides engine was adopted, and a

Aircraft: **de Havilland DHC-2 Beaver 1**
Manufacturer: **de Havilland Aircraft of Canada Ltd.**
Type: **Light transport**
Year: **1947**
Engine: **One Pratt & Whitney R-985-SB3 Wasp Junior, radial with 9 cylinders, air-cooled, 450 hp**
Wingspan: **48 ft 0 in (14.64 m)**
Length: **32 ft 9 in (9.98 m)**
Height: **10 ft 5 in (3.18 m)**
Weight: **5,070 lb (2,300 kg) (Loaded)**
Cruising speed: **143 mph at 5,000 ft (230 km/h at 1,524 m)**
Ceiling: **18,000 ft (5,486 m)**
Range: **740 miles (1,190 km)**
Crew: **1**
Passengers: **7**

small number with this engine were built in Great Britain for the Army. However, a more substantial modification was made in 1963, when de Havilland Canada decided to install in the aircraft a 578 ehp Pratt & Whitney PT6A-6 turbo-prop engine. This modification was made on the 1,562nd production aircraft and the DHC-2 Mk. III Turbo-Beaver made its maiden flight on December 30 of that year.

Canadair C-4

Rarely, in the history of aviation, has so much success been achieved by an aircraft made by radically modifying a type already in production elsewhere, as by the Canadair C-4. This pure hybrid was built, essentially, by replacing the four Pratt & Whitney radial engines by four Rolls-Royce Merlin engines in the Douglas DC-4. In its final form the Canadair C-4 was used both by the military and by Trans Canada Air Lines, Canadian Pacific Airlines and by BOAC. The latter used it on its transcontinental flights from mid-1949 to 1958.

The idea which brought about the four-engined Canadair came way back in 1943 to J. T. Bain, chief engineer at Trans Canada Air Lines. While tackling a study aimed at finding the best types with which to re-equip the company, Bain came to an unusual conclusion: the best-suited aircraft was undoubtedly the Douglas DC-4. However, economically speaking, the large radial engines with which the aircraft was already equipped were certainly not the best engines. Instead Bain suggested using the V-12 Rolls-Royce Merlin engines in the latest version available for commercial use. The idea was put into practice in the immediate postwar period, with encouragement from both Trans Canada Air Lines and the Royal Canadian Air Force, which was also on the lookout for a sound transport aeroplane. The first prototype made its maiden flight on July 20, 1946 and after the trials was delivered to the R.C.A.F. There followed a further six aircraft in the initial series (called

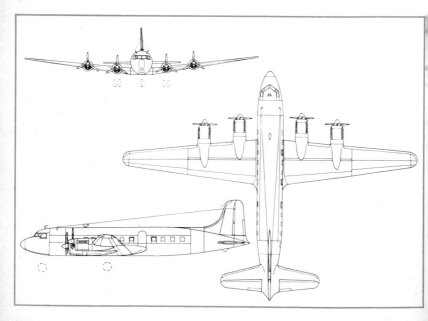

originally DC-4M-1) which were temporarily loaned by the military to Trans Canada. The company put them into service on the North Atlantic route from April 1947 onwards, although these examples had not been equipped with a pressurized cabin. In August of that year, however, the prototype of the final version took to the air (initially called the DC-4M-2) and this did have a pressurization system. Before long an assembly line had been prepared for the construction of 20 aircraft for TCA and 17 aircraft ordered by the R.C.A.F. Trans Canada put the DC-4M-2s, which were then finally called Canadair C-4s, into service from April 1948 onwards and did not start to withdraw them until the mid-1950s.

TCA was followed by two other major airlines: Canadian Pacific, which received four C-4s in the spring of 1949, and BOAC. The latter ended up by becoming the main operator of the four-engined Canadair, putting a fleet of 22 aircraft into operation. The decision to adopt the Canadian aircraft was taken in July 1948, due to the need

Aircraft: **Canadair C-4**
Manufacturer: **Canadair Ltd**
Type: **Civil transport**
Year: **1949**
Engines: **Four Rolls-Royce Merlin 626, V-12, liquid-cooled, 1,760 hp each**
Wingspan: **117 ft 6 in (35.80 m)**
Length: **93 ft 10 in (28.60 m)**
Height: **27 ft 6 in (8.40 m)**
Weight: **82,230 lb (37,300 kg) (Loaded)**
Cruising speed: **230 mph at 16,000 ft (370 km/h at 4,877 m)**
Ceiling: **29,500 ft (9,000 m)**
Range: **3,240 miles (5,214 km)**
Crew: **4**
Passengers: **40–64**

to replenish the BOAC fleet after the failure of the programme which had created the Avro Tudor. The 22 C-4s (called Argonauts by BOAC and each with an individual name) were all delivered by November 1949. At the beginning of the following year BOAC was able to complete the modernization of most of its major routes. During the 1950s the British Argonauts flew more and more intensively, until, in 1958 BOAC started to withdraw them and sell them to smaller companies. In this way their career continued for another ten years.

de Havilland DHC-3 Otter

After the success enjoyed by the DHC-2 Beaver, de Havilland Canada decided to make a larger version of this light aeroplane. The prototype made its maiden flight on December 12, 1951. Although designed mainly for commercial use, the Otter was also popular with the military. Roughly 450 aircraft were produced, almost two-thirds of which were used by the U.S. Air Force (223 aircraft) and the R.C.A.F. (66 aircraft). The remainder went to civil and private operators in 36 countries. Like the Beaver, the DHC-3 Otter had excellent flight characteristics (especially as far as taking-off and landing were concerned) and an almost incredible versatility. It could be fitted as required with wheels, floats, or skis for use in snow-covered regions, and the floor of the cabin was reinforced to enable heavy loads to be carried. The Otter could accommodate 9–14 passengers plus the pilot.

Aircraft: **de Havilland DHC-3 Otter**
Manufacturer: **de Havilland Aircraft of Canada Ltd.**
Type: **Light transport**
Year: **1951**
Engine: **One Pratt & Whitney R-1340-S1H1-G Wasp, radial with 9 cylinders, air-cooled, 600 hp**
Wingspan: **58 ft 0 in (17.69 m)**
Length: **41 ft 10 in (12.75 m)**
Height: **12 ft 7 in (3.83 m)**
Weight: **8,000 lb (3,629 kg) (Loaded)**
Cruising speed: **138 mph at 5,000 ft (222 km/h at 1,524 m)**
Ceiling: **18,800 ft (5,730 m)**
Range: **945 miles (1,520 km)**
Crew: **1**
Passengers: **9–14**

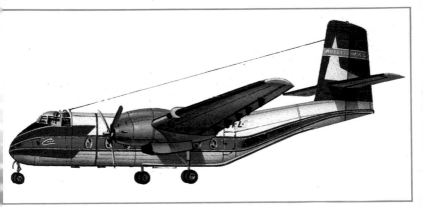

de Havilland DHC-4 Caribou

Although used mainly by the military, especially by the U.S. Army and U.S.A.F. which ordered more than 160 aircraft for tactical transport purposes, the de Havilland DHC-4 Caribou was also fairly successful with civil operators because of its excellent carrying capacity and versatility. This large and heavy twin-engined model in fact echoed almost identically the good take-off and landing features (STOL) of its direct and smaller predecessors, the DHC-2 Beaver and the DHC-3 Otter. The preliminary plans for this project were started in 1956, after discussions between de Havilland and representatives of the U.S. and Canadian armies. The prototype made its maiden flight on July 30, 1958 and was soon followed by the first production aircraft. The total number of de Havilland Caribous manufactured was in excess of 230, and most of these went to the military.

Aircraft: **de Havilland DHC-4 Caribou**
Manufacturer: **de Havilland Aircraft of Canada Ltd.**
Type: **Civil transport**
Year: **1958**
Engines: **Two Pratt & Whitney R-2000-7M2 Twin Wasp, radial with 14 cylinders, air-cooled, 1,450 hp each**
Wingspan: **96 ft 0 in (29.26 m)**
Length: **72 ft 7 in (22.13 m)**
Height: **31 ft 9 in (9.68 m)**
Weight: **26,000 lb (11,793 kg) (Loaded)**
Cruising speed: **182 mph at 7,500 ft (293 km/h at 2,286 m)**
Ceiling: **27,700 ft (8,443 m)**
Range: **1,400 miles (2,253 km)**
Crew: **1–2**
Passengers: **24–30**

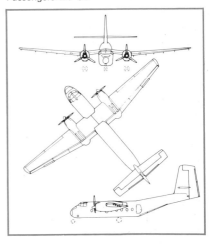

Canadair CL-44

Derived from the CC-106 Yukon military transport which was in turn developed from the British Bristol Britannia commercial four-engined turbo-prop, the Canadair CL-44 became the first all-cargo long-range aeroplane to be equipped with an original goods-loading system. This was provided by having the whole rear section of the fuselage opening: where the tail started it could swing open on hinges, thus making it much easier to stow awkward and bulky cargo. With a total of 27 aircraft built in two major versions, the CL-44 was originally adopted by four operators specializing in large, long-range transportation. These were the Flying Tiger Line, Seaboard World, Slick Airways and Icelandic Airlines (Loftleidir). This latter company also used the four-engined Canadair aircraft for carrying passengers and had the aircraft in its

fleet converted to the CL-44J version which had a lengthened fuselage capable of holding up to a maximum of 214 people.

The idea of making an improved and more powerful version of the already excellent commercial Bristol Britannia came to Canadair in the late 1950s. They were encouraged by the military authorities of the Royal Canadian Air Force who wanted a large capacity strategic transport aircraft. Instead of developing an entirely new project, which would have taken time and a lot of money, it was decided to pursue the same policy that had led to the production of the excellent Canadair C-4: thus they used an air-frame that had already been fully tested and was in production and modified it to specific requirements. The Canadair CL-44 (which took on the military designation CC-106 Yukon) came into being by considerably extending the fuselage of the Britannia and replacing the Bristol

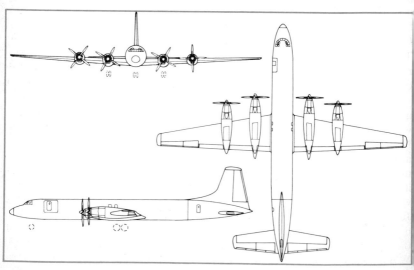

Canadair CL-44D-4 – 1960

Proteus engines with Rolls-Royce Tyne engines which were much more powerful. The prototype of this fine hybrid model made its maiden flight on November 15, 1959 and after a small initial production run for the Royal Canadian Air Force, it was decided to make a version for commercial transport. This was called the CL-44D-4 and although it retained the basic features of the military model, it was fitted with the original loading system. This was achieved by reinforcing the rear fuselage sufficiently and mounting one side of it on large hinges.

The system involved no drawbacks and the prototype of the CL-44D-4 which made its maiden flight on November 16, 1960, obtained its airworthiness certificate after about six months, on June 29, 1961. Before long it was in regular service and proving its well-earned commercial success. In July 1961, the 'Forty-four' (as it was nick-named) was put into operation by the Flying Tiger Line and by Seaboard World Airways, which had ordered,

Aircraft: **Canadair CL-44D-4**
Manufacturer: **Canadair Ltd.**
Type: **Civil transport**
Year: **1960**
Engines: **Four Rolls-Royce Tyne 515-10 turbo-props, 5,730 ehp each**
Wingspan: **142 ft 4 in (43.37 m)**
Length: **136 ft 11 in (41.73 m)**
Height: **38 ft 8 in (11.80 m)**
Weight: **210,000 lb (95,256 kg) (Loaded)**
Cruising speed: **316 mph at 20,350 ft (508 km/h at 6,200 m)**
Ceiling: **30,000 ft (9,144 m)**
Range: **2,875 miles (4,625 km)**
Crew: **3**
Payload: **63,272 lb (28,700 kg)**

respectively, 12 and seven aircraft. Later another two airlines, Slick Airways and Icelandic Airlines each ordered four CL-44D-4s. It was in fact the Icelandic company which first used these large four-engined turbo-props for passenger transport, from 1964 onwards, on the transatlantic route. This cheap, high capacity service turned out to be so popular that Icelandic Airlines requested that the fourth model should be delivered as a CL-44J (with an even longer fuselage, which was available towards the end of 1965) and later it had the other three CL-44D-4s similarly modified.

267

RWD 13

Developed in 1934, the RWD-13 made its maiden flight as a prototype in February of the following year. It was a small, high-winged monoplane, with a mixed structure and covering capable of carrying the pilot and two passengers. The RWD-13 had a cruising speed of 112 mph (180 km/h) and a range of 560 miles (900 km). It was powered by a 130 hp Walter Major engine, but in effect any similar engine on the market could be fitted. To demonstrate this versatility many aircraft were originally equipped with 130 hp de Havilland Gipsy Major engines, while other sorts of engine were used by other operators.

The RWD-13 soon became popular as a touring and executive model and production reached a fairly high pitch, totalling by September 1939 almost 110 examples. Apart from the busy sporting career it enjoyed, the RWD-13 also saw some service as a flying ambulance.

Aircraft: **RWD-13**
Manufacturer: **Doswiadczaine Warsztaty Lotnicze**
Type: **Light transport**
Year: **1935**
Engine: **One Walter Major with 4 straight cylinders, air-cooled, 130 hp**
Wingspan: **37 ft 9 in (11.50 m)**
Length: **25 ft 9 in (7.85 m)**
Height: **6 ft 9 in (2.05 m)**
Weight: **2,050 lb (930 kg) (Loaded)**
Cruising speed: **112 mph (180 km/h)**
Ceiling: **13,800 ft (4,200 m)**
Range: **560 miles (900 km)**
Crew: **1**
Passengers: **2**

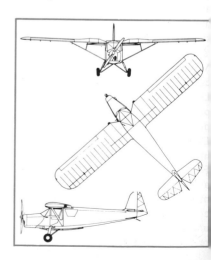

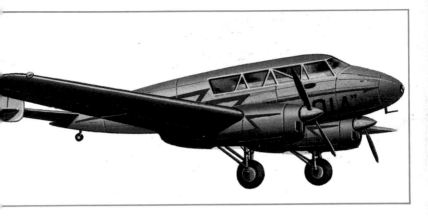

RWD-11

The RWD-11 was expressly ordered by the Polish authorities as a light transport aircraft capable of operating from rough airfields and on difficult routes, but it never actually went into service. In fact the only aircraft ever produced underwent a long and laborious process of development and at the moment of delivery was inexplicably rejected. The project was started in 1933, on the basis of a tender issued the year before by the Polish Ministry of Transport, to which the company PZL had already replied. Despite this initial disadvantage the programme was pursued after a promise of financial backing from the Department of Aeronautical Engineering. The RWD-11 took to the air in February 1936 for the first time. It was an elegant low-winged, twin-engined monoplane with mixed structure and covering, and a retractable undercarriage. The first flight tests revealed a series of minor problems

Aircraft: **RWD-11**
Manufacturer: **Doswiadczaine Warsztaty Lotnicze**
Type: **Civil transport**
Year: **1936**
Engines: **Two Walter Major, 6 straight cylinders, air-cooled, 205 hp each**
Wingspan: **49 ft 10 in (15.20 m)**
Length: **34 ft 11 in (10.65 m)**
Height: **10 ft 10 in (3.30 m)**
Weight: **5,840 lb (2,650 kg) (Loaded)**
Cruising speed: **158 mph (255 km/h)**
Ceiling: **13,500 ft (4,100 m)**
Range: **500 miles (800 km)**
Crew: **2**
Passengers: **6**

including vibration and a degree of instability. It took more than a year to put all these faults right and the aircraft did not re-appear in its final form until late summer in 1937. In particular, the fuselage had been modified and lengthened and the original single rudder had been replaced by two rudders. At that time, however, the RWD-11 had already been refused by the authorities and the last phase in its finishing touches had been carried out independently, with no financial support. Although it passed its various tests and certification trials, the aeroplane remained a prototype.

269

PZL-44 Wicher

Developed with the aim of equipping the Polish airlines with a modern Polish-made commercial aircraft, the PZL-44 was the victim of a long and lively debate between the civil and military authorities. They could not agree on production costs and the aircraft ended up being overshadowed by the Second World War. This elegant twin-engined aeroplane therefore remained at the prototype stage despite its considerable worth. The project was started in the spring of 1936 and the official requests specified that the new aircraft should be of the same class as the Douglas DC-2. It was precisely this request that caused the first delays. The prototype took to the air in March 1938 and tests and trials began. During this phase there were also further delays in development, but the programme halted when the argument over costs started. After the outbreak of the war the abandoned aeroplane was captured by the Russians.

Aircraft: **PZL-44 Wicher**
Manufacturer: **Pantswowe Zaklady Lotnicze**
Type: **Civil transport**
Year: **1938**
Engines: **Two Wright GR-1820-G2 Cyclone, radial with 9 cylinders, air-cooled, 1,000 hp each**
Wingspan: **78 ft 1 in (23.80 m)**
Length: **60 ft 7 in (18.45 m)**
Height: **15 ft 9 in (4.80 m)**
Weight: **21,000 lb (9,500 kg) (Loaded)**
Cruising speed: **174 mph (280 km/h)**
Ceiling: **22,500 ft (6,850 m)**
Range: **1,150 miles (1,840 km)**
Crew: **3–4**
Passengers: **14**

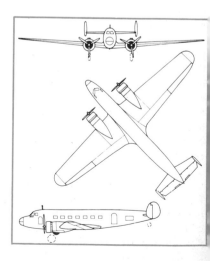

PZL MD-12

The fate of the PZL MD-12 was fairly like that of its prewar predecessor, the PZL-44 Wicher. Once again there had been a request for a Polish-made commercial aeroplane for use by the Polish state airline. This was to replace the ancient Lisunov Li-2 and Ilyushin Il-14 which were currently in use on domestic flights. However, the proposed aircraft was not accepted and remained at the prototype stage. The project was embarked upon by PZL in the late 1950s and the first aircraft flew on July 21, 1959. It was a small four-engined, low-winged type with a tricycle undercarriage, small capacity and suited to operating over short distances. In particular it had been calculated that over distances of up to 250 miles (400 km) its running costs would be 13% lower than those of the Li-2. Clearly these calculations were never verified because after three years of assessment LOT rejected all three prototypes produced.

Aircraft: **PZL MD-12**
Manufacturer: **Pantswowe Zaklady Lotnicze**
Type: **Civil transport**
Year: **1959**
Engines: **Four Narkiewicz WN-3 radial with 7 cylinders, 330 hp each**
Wingspan: **69 ft 11 in (21.31 m)**
Length: **51 ft 10 in (15.80 m)**
Height: **19 ft 1 in (5.82 m)**
Weight: **16,500 lb (7,500 kg) (loaded)**
Cruising speed: **174 mph at 6,560 ft (280 km/h at 2,000 m)**
Ceiling: **17,000 ft (5,200 m)**
Range: **435 miles (700 km)**
Crew: **2**
Passengers: **20**

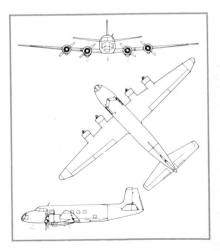

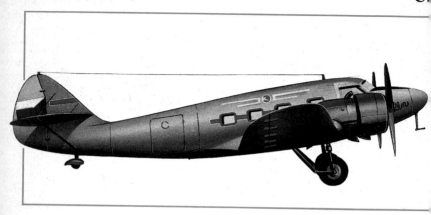

Aero 204

This was one of the few non-military aircraft produced in the late 1930s by the Czech industry. It was a twin-engined, low-winged model with a retractable main undercarriage, a mixed structure and a covering of wood and canvas. It was powered by a pair of Walter Pollux 360 hp radial engines, each of which drove a wooden two-bladed propeller. The Aero 204 had a cruising speed of 178 mph (286 km/h) and a range of 560 miles (900 km). Special care was paid to the furnishing of the main cabin. The eight passengers were accommodated in single seats at the side of the fuselage beside the windows and each one had lighting and ventilation controls, as well having an adjustable backrest. In addition the passenger cabin was heated. Despite its good all-round performance, the Aero 204 was not competitive with the contemporary European and American products and the war halted further development.

Aircraft: **Aero 204**
Manufacturer: **Aero Tovarna Letadel**
Type: **Light transport**
Year: **1937**
Engines: **Two Walter Pollux IIR, radial with 9 cylinders, 360 hp each**
Wingspan: **62 ft 4 in (19.00 m)**
Length: **42 ft 8 in (13.00 m)**
Height: **11 ft 2 in (3.40 m)**
Weight: **9,500 lb (4,300 kg) (Loaded)**
Cruising speed: **178 mph (286 km/h)**
Ceiling: **19,000 ft (5,800 m)**
Range: **560 miles (900 km)**
Crew: **2**
Passengers: **8**

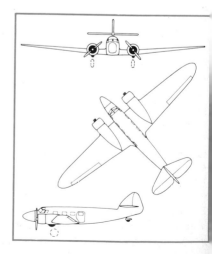

Aero 145

The final version of one of the most successful families of light aircraft produced by the Czech industry in the postwar period was the Aero 145. The 145 derived from the model 45M which had appeared as a prototype in the summer of 1947. In its various versions, this small twin-engined aeroplane was extremely successful commercially and remained in production until 1961. Of the 700 or so aircraft made, almost all were exported. The second production version, called the Super Aero was particularly successful; although it had the same engines as its predecessor, many structural details and much of the equipment had been improved. This aircraft was exported to France, Canada, Switzerland, Brazil, India and Egypt. In particular 130 aircraft went to the U.S.S.R. In Czechoslovakia the Super Aero was used mainly as a flying ambulance. The Aero 145 first appeared in 1958.

Aircraft: **Aero 145**
Manufacturer: **State Industries**
Type: **Light transport**
Year: **1958**
Engines: **Two M.332, with 4 straight cylinders, air-cooled, 140 hp each**
Wingspan: **40 ft 2 in (12.24 m)**
Length: **25 ft 6 in (7.77 m)**
Height: **7 ft 6 in (2.31 m)**
Weight: **3,527 lb (1,600 kg) (Loaded)**
Cruising speed: **155 mph (249 km/h)**
Ceiling: **19,360 ft (5,900 m)**
Range: **1,055 miles (1,697 km)**
Crew: **1**
Passengers: **3–4**

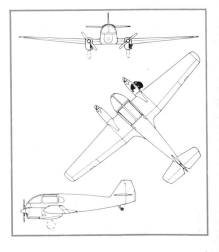

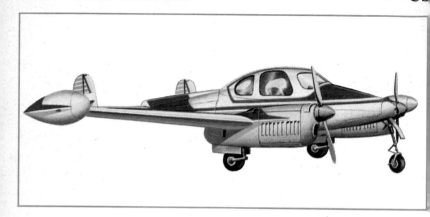

L-200 Morava

The Morava was designed as a successor to the Aero 145. It was more up-to-date, capable of better all-round performance, and endowed with some-what more elegant and aerodynamic lines. The prototype first appeared on April 8, 1957 and was produced in three major versions. The first production model, called the L-200, was powered by two 160 hp Walter Minor engines. The next one, the L-200A, was powered by a pair of 210 hp M.337 engines, but in other respects was identical to the first production model.

The third version, the L-200D which appeared in 1962, had, on the other hand, a series of modifications made to the undercarriage, the hydraulic system, and the three-bladed propellers. Overall the Czech State Industries produced more than 500 examples many of which were exported. The Morava was used above all as an air taxi, especially in the U.S.S.R.

Aircraft: **L-200A Morava**
Manufacturer: **State Industries**
Type: **Light transport**
Year: **1959**
Engines: **Two M.337, with 6 straight cylinders, air-cooled, 210 hp each**
Wingspan: **40 ft 4 in (12.30 m)**
Length: **28 ft 3 in (8.61 m)**
Height: **7 ft 4 in (2.22 m)**
Weight: **4,300 lb (1,950 kg) (Loaded)**
Cruising speed: **182 mph (293 km/h)**
Ceiling: **18,700 ft (5,700 m)**
Range: **1,056 miles (1,700 km)**
Crew: **1**
Passengers: **3–4**

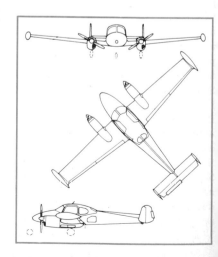

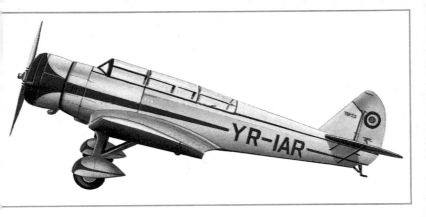

I.A.R. 23

In the 1930s aeronautical engineering in Rumania was a particularly busy industry and even though production was considerably influenced by the Italian and German industries, there was no shortage of original projects, especially where light aeroplanes were concerned. The I.A.R. 23 was one such project. It was a two-seater monoplane, with a mixed structure and covering and a fixed undercarriage. The aeroplane showed itself to be particularly suited to long flights and took part in numerous races. In September 1934, for example, an I.A.R. 23 piloted by Gheorghe Banciulescu took part in three international meetings in the space of five days. On September 15 it flew from Bucharest to Warsaw and back; on September 18, from Pipera to Prague and Bucharest; and on the following day it took part in the long-distance race from Bucharest to Paris, via Vienna.

Aircraft: **I.A.R. 23**
Manufacturer: **Rumanian Aeronautical Industry**
Type: **Competition**
Year: **1934**
Engine: **One Hispano-Suiza 9 Qa, radial with 9 cylinders, air-cooled 340 hp**
Wingspan: **39 ft 4 in (12.00 m)**
Length: **27 ft 5 in (8.35 m)**
Height: **8 ft 10 in (2.70 m)**
Weight: **4,233 lb (1,920 kg) (Loaded)**
Maximum speed: **152 mph (245 km/h)**
Ceiling: **13,500 ft (4,100 m)**
Range: **1,430 miles (2,300 km)**
Crew: **2**

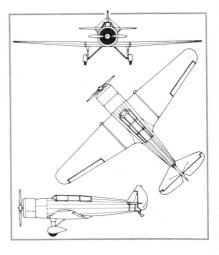

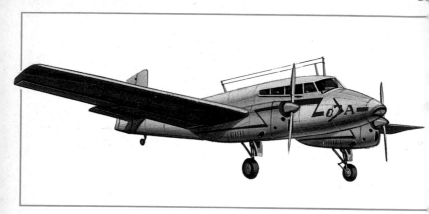

MR-2

Designed in 1953 and initially known as the I.A.R. 814, this small twin-engined model was conceived for light transport and in particular for use as a flying ambulance. Two prototypes were completed and after the various tests and trials the aircraft was put into production as the MR-2. It was built by the Brasov aeronautical works, known as U.R.M.V.-3. The MR-2 was a high-winged monoplane, with a mixed structure and covering and had a retractable main undercarriage. It was powered by a pair of 160 hp Walter Minor engines, each of which drove a variable-pitch two-bladed metal propeller. It had a cruising speed of 171 mph (275 km/h) and a range of 685 miles (1,100 km). The ambulance version of the MR-2 could carry two stretcher patients, plus the crew. There was also an all-cargo version. In this case the seats for the usual complement of five passengers could easily be removed from the cabin.

Aircraft: **MR-2**
Manufacturer: **U.R.M.V.-3**
Type: **Light transport**
Year: **1956**
Engines: **Two Walter Minor 6-III, with 6 straight cylinders, air-cooled, 160 hp each**
Wingspan: **45 ft 11 in (14.00 m)**
Length: **35 ft 9 in (10.90 m)**
Height: **9 ft 1 in (2.76 m)**
Weight: **4,585 lb (2,080 kg) (Loaded)**
Cruising speed: **171 mph (275 km/h)**
Ceiling: **16,000 ft (4,900 m)**
Range: **685 miles (1,100 km)**
Crew: **1**
Passengers: **5**

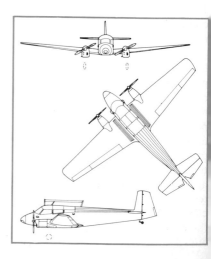

CASA-201 Alcotan

Although destined for military use, the CASA-201 Alcotan occupies an important place in the history of aviation because it was the first twin-engined transport aircraft designed and built entirely by the Spanish aeronautical industry. The prototype made its maiden flight on February 11, 1949 and production totalled 112 aircraft. All these were ordered by the military.

The CASA Alcotan was developed in three major versions: the 201-B, for passenger transport; the 201-F, for radio and navigational training; and the 201-G, for training in bombing and photographic reconnaissance. The transport version had a cruising speed of 193 mph (310 km/h) and a range of 620 miles (1,000 km). As well as being able to accommodate a maximum of ten passengers, it was also possible to convert the 201-B to cargo transport (by removing the seats) and to a flying ambulance.

Aircraft: **CASA-201-B Alcotan**
Manufacturer: **Construcciones Aeronauticas S.A.**
Type: **Civil transport**
Year: **1949**
Engines: **Two Enma Sirio S-VII, radial with 7 cylinders, air-cooled, 500 hp each**
Wingspan: **60 ft 4 in (18.40 m)**
Length: **45 ft 3 in (13.80 m)**
Height: **12 ft 11 in (3.95 m)**
Weight: **12,125 lb (5,500 kg) (Loaded)**
Cruising speed: **193 mph (310 km/h)**
Ceiling: **18,500 ft (5,600 m)**
Range: **620 miles (1,000 km)**
Crew: **2**
Passengers: **8–10**

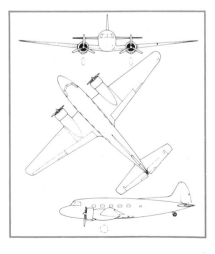

CASA-202 Halcon

After the important experience gained in the field of light transport with the model 201 Alcotan, CASA decided to develop a larger and more modern version. This was called the 202 Halcon and appeared as a prototype in May 1952. However it turned out not to be a successful choice because in effect the new twin-engined model did not differ sufficiently from its predecessor to justify mass-production. In addition, numerous problems emerged during the trials which considerably delayed the final completion of the aeroplane. Production, which totalled twenty aircraft all ordered by the military, did not start for several years and the first series Halcon models did not appear until 1962.

In 1956 CASA had also tried to bring out a version of the Halcon, called the 202-B for executive transport. This aircraft had a longer fuselage, shorter wings and more powerful engines, but it was never built.

Aircraft: **CASA-202 Halcon**
Manufacturer: **Construcciones Aeronauticas S.A.**
Type: **Military transport**
Year: **1952**
Engines: **Two Enma Beta 9C-29-750, radial with 9 cylinders, air-cooled, 750 hp each**
Wingspan: **70 ft 9 in (21.58 m)**
Length: **52 ft 6 in (16.00 m)**
Height: **19 ft 10 in (6.06 m)**
Weight: **18,075 lb (8,200 kg) (Loaded)**
Cruising speed: **205 mph (330 km/h)**
Ceiling: **24,000 ft (7,300 m)**
Range: **1,710 miles (2,750 km)**
Crew: **3**
Passengers: **14**

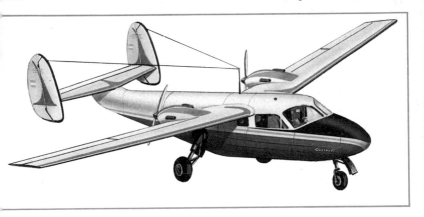

I.A. 45 Querandi

Among the numerous products of the Argentinian industry in the field of light aircraft, the Querandi is one of the most interesting of executive twin-engined designs. Conceived in the mid-1950s by the technicians of the Cordoba nationalized industries, the I.A. 45 made its maiden flight as a prototype on September 23, 1957.

The I.A. 45 Querandi was an elegant high-winged monoplane, built entirely of metal, with a fully retractable tricycle undercarriage, engines mounted in the pusher position and twin fins. The two engines were 150 hp Lycomings, driving variable-pitch twin-bladed metal propellers. The usual capacity was four passengers plus the pilot, but in the version designed for air rescue two stretchers could be carried. It was then decided to make a larger version with more powerful engines. This aircraft, called the I.A. 45B, made its maiden flight as a prototype on December 15, 1960.

Aircraft: **I.A. 45 Querandi**
Manufacturer: **DINFIA**
Type: **Light transport**
Year: **1957**
Engines: **Two Lycoming 0-320, with 4 horizontal cylinders, air-cooled, 150 hp each**
Wingspan: **45 ft 2 in (13.75 m)**
Length: **29 ft 3 in (8.91 m)**
Height: **9 ft 2 in (2.79 m)**
Weight: **4,000 lb (1,800 kg) (Loaded)**
Cruising speed: **152 mph (245 km/h)**
Ceiling: **24,500 ft (7,500 m)**
Range: **700 miles (1,100 km)**
Crew: **1**
Passengers: **4**

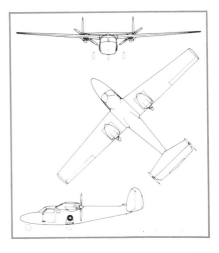

I.A. 35

The I.A. 35 was a forerunner to a large family of twin-engined military transport aircraft, the last of which (the twin-turbo-prop I.A. 50 Guarani II) appeared in the mid-1960s. The Argentinian I.A. 35 made its maiden flight on September 7, 1953.

The I.A. 35 had been conceived for various uses and was produced in five major versions: the I.A. 35-Ia for crew-training; I.A. 35-Ib for training gunners and bomb-aimers; I.A. 35-II for light transport; I.A. 35-III for flying ambulance service; and the I.A. 35-IV for photographic reconnaissance. Amidst all these military versions it was decided to develop one version specifically for civil light transport. This was called the I.A. 35-X-III Pandora and had a modified fuselage. The first prototype of the I.A. 35-X-III flew on May 28, 1960. However there was no follow-up and the only aircraft completed went to the Air Force.

Aircraft: **I.A. 35-X-III**
Manufacturer: **DINFIA**
Type: **Light transport**
Year: **1960**
Engines: **Two I.A.R. 19-C El Indio, radial with 9 cylinders, air-cooled, 840 hp each**
Wingspan: **64 ft 3 in (19.60 m)**
Length: **46 ft 6 in (14.17 m)**
Height: **15 ft 5 in (4.70 m)**
Weight: **13,670 lb (6,200 kg) (Loaded)**
Cruising speed: **191 mph at 9,840 ft (307 km/h at 3,000 m)**
Ceiling: **21,500 ft (6,500 m)**
Range: **950 miles (1,500 km)**
Crew: **3**
Passengers: **10**

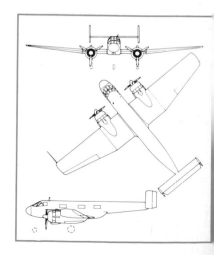

de Havilland DHA-3 Drover

The DHA-3 Drover project was started by the Australian branch of de Havilland immediately after the end of the Second World War. The aim of the project was to meet the urgent local need for a light transport aircraft. The prototype made its maiden flight on January 23, 1948. It was a small low-winged, simple and robust three-engined aircraft, which borrowed many structural components from the D.H. 104 Dove.

Production of the Drover first started in 1949 and ended four years later with the completion of the 20th aircraft. There were two versions: the Mk. 1 which was the basic model; and the Mk. 2 which had modifications to the control surfaces of the wing. This was accompanied in 1960 by the Mk. 3 which had the original Gipsy Major 145 hp engines replaced by 180 hp Lycoming engines, driving constant-pitch propellers.

Aircraft: **de Havilland DHA-3 Drover 3**
Manufacturer: **de Havilland Aircraft Co. (Hawker Siddeley Group)**
Type: **Light transport**
Year: **1960**
Engines: **Three Lycoming 0-360-A1A, with 4 horizontal cylinders, air-cooled, 180 hp each**
Wingspan: **57 ft 0 in (17.37 m)**
Length: **36 ft 6 in (11.12 m)**
Height: **10 ft 9 in (3.27 m)**
Weight: **6,500 lb (2,950 kg) (Loaded)**
Cruising speed: **140 mph (225 km/h)**
Range: **900 miles (1,450 km)**
Crew: **1**
Passengers: **7**

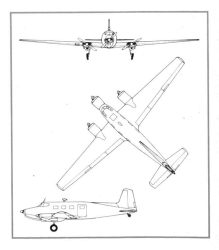

Pilatus PC-6 Porter

The Pilatus PC-6 Porter has shown itself to be one of the most versatile light aircraft produced in Europe in the 1960s, especially since the appearance of the modern successor with a turbo-prop engine, the PC-6 Turbo-Porter.

The project for this robust single-engined model with its STOL characteristics was started in 1957 and the first prototype made its maiden flight on May 4 two years later. Its excellent qualities aroused the immediate interest of the world market and mass production was started not long after. A first batch of twenty aircraft was completed by mid-1961, followed by the same number in the two following years. In 1965, when production was almost wholly taken up with the Turbo-Porter, some fifty aircraft had been delivered to numerous operators in different countries. The Pilatus Porter was built in six major versions, each of which underwent slight modifications.

Aircraft: **Pilatus PC-6 Porter**
Manufacturer: **Pilatus Flugzeugwerke A.G.**
Type: **Light transport**
Year: **1959**
Engine: **One Lycoming GSO-480-B1A6, with 6 horizontal cylinders, air-cooled, 340 hp**
Wingspan: **49 ft 10 in (15.20 m)**
Length: **33 ft 5 in (10.20 m)**
Height: **10 ft 6 in (3.20 m)**
Weight: **4,000 lb (1,800 kg) (Loaded)**
Cruising speed: **135 mph (217 km/h)**
Ceiling: **24,000 ft (7,300 m)**
Range: **750 miles (1,200 km)**
Crew: **1**
Passengers: **5–7**

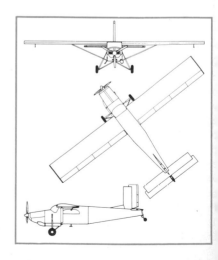

Peking No. 1

Among the first projects developed in the postwar period by the People's Republic of China was the Peking No. 1, which was built in the very short time of slightly more than three months. Its construction was undertaken by the Institute of Aeronautical Engineering of Peking, with the aim of producing a light transport aircraft for use on short domestic flights.

The prototype of the Peking No. 1 made its maiden flight on September 24, 1958 and the first production aircraft were delivered from 1962 onwards. The Peking was a small, low-winged twin-engined aeroplane, built entirely of metal, with a retractable tricycle undercarriage. It was powered by a pair of 260 hp Ivchenko radial engines, built under Soviet licence, which drove variable-pitch two-bladed propellers, also made of metal. The Peking No. 1 had a cruising speed of 162 mph (261 km/h) and a range of 665 miles (1,070 km).

Aircraft: **Peking No. 1**
Manufacturer: **Institute of Aeronautical Engineering of Peking**
Type: **Light transport**
Year: **1958**
Engines: **Two Ivchenko AI-14R, radial with 9 cylinders, air-cooled, 260 hp each**
Wingspan: **57 ft 5 in (17.50 m)**
Length: **42 ft 7 in (12.98 m)**
Height: **–**
Weight: **–**
Cruising speed: **162 mph (261 km/h)**
Ceiling: **15,750 ft (4,800 m)**
Range: **665 miles (1,070 km)**
Crew: **2**
Passengers: **8**

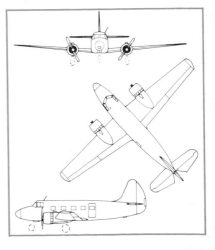

Major Commercial Aircraft

Forty years of air transport represented by the various major aircraft. The purpose of the charts on these pages is to present a concise summary of the development of the commercial aeroplane from its origins up until 1960. In order to make this long trail across forty years as coherent as possible it has been necessary to draw from Volume 2 in this series (World Aircraft 1918–1935) since the aircraft described in this volume are preceded by some of the most important commercial aircraft which went into service before 1935. Thus the aircraft shown here start with the first wood-and-canvas biplanes, such as the Farman F.60 Goliath and end with the commercial jets, many of which are still in service today.

Pre-1935 Aircraft

1919

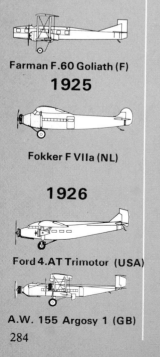

Farman F.60 Goliath (F)

1925

Fokker F VIIa (NL)

1926

Ford 4.AT Trimotor (USA)

A.W. 155 Argosy 1 (GB)

1932

S.M. 71 (I)

1933

Boeing 247 (USA)

1934

Douglas DC-2 (USA)

1935

Bloch 220 (F)

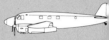

Caudron C-445 Göeland (F)

Macchi M.C.94 (I)

Heinkel He.111 C (D)

Koolhoven F.K.50 (NL

284

Major Commercial Aircraft

1936

Douglas DC-3 (USA)

Short S.23 (GB)

1937

Lockheed 14-F62 Super
Electra (USA)

D.H. 91 Albatross (GB)

S.M. 75 (I)

Fw.200 A Condor (D)

1938

A.W.27 Ensign 1 (GB)

Junkers Ju.90B (D)

Mitsubishi G3M2 (J)

Major Commercial Aircraft

1939

Short S.26 (GB)

Macchi M.C. 100 (I)

1940–1945

1940

Boeing SA-307B
Stratoliner (USA)

Lockheed 18-56
Lodestar (USA)

Curtiss C-46A (USA)

1941

Boeing 314A Yankee
Clipper (USA)

1942

Douglas DC-4 (USA)

Avro 685 York (GB)

Latécoère 631 (F)

1945

Avro 691 Lancastrian
(GB)

Sud-Est SE-161
Languedoc (F)

1946

1947

1948

Martin 2-0-2 (USA)

Boeing 377-10-26
Stratocruiser (USA)

H.P.81 Hermes 4 (GB)

ckers Viking 1 B (GB)

Lockheed L-749
Constellation (USA)

vushin II-12 (USSR)

Convair 240 (USA)

S.M. 95/C (I)

Fiat G.212 CP (I)

Saab 90 A-2
Scandia (S)

Canadair C-4 (CDN)

Major Commercial Aircraft

1949

Sud-Est SE-2010 Armagnac (F)

1950

Vickers Viscount 700 (GB)

1951

Douglas DC-6B (USA

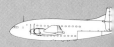

Breguet Br.763 Provence (F)

1952

1953

1954

Lockheed L-1049 Super
Constellation (USA)

Bristol 175 Britannia
102 (GB)

Major Commercial Aircraft

1955

Douglas DC-7C (USA)

1956

1957

Boeing 707-120 (USA)

Tupolev Tu-104A
(USSR)

Ilyushin Il-18V (USSR)

Tupolev Tu-114
Rossiya (USSR)

Major Commercial Aircraft

1958	1959	1960

Douglas DC-8-20 (USA)

Boeing 707-320 (USA)

Avro 748 Series 1 (GB)

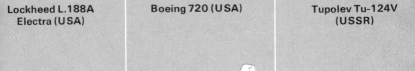

Lockheed L.188A Electra (USA)

Boeing 720 (USA)

Tupolev Tu-124V (USSR)

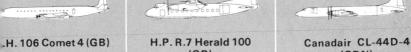

.H. 106 Comet 4 (GB)

H.P. R.7 Herald 100 (GB)

Canadair CL-44D-4 (CDN)

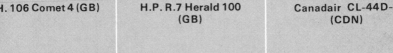

kker F.27 – 100 Friendship (NL)

Antonov An-24V (USSR)

Sud-Aviation SE-210 Caravelle III (F)

1960 – Civil Aviation registration letters

Aden	VR-AAA-VR-AZZ	Ecuador	HC
Afghanistan	YA	Egypt	SU
Albania	ZA	El Salvador	YS
Argentina	LQ, LV	Ethiopia	ET
Australia	VH		
Austria	OE	Falkland Islands	VP-FAA-VP-FZZ
		Fiji Islands	VQ-FAA-VQ-FZZ
Bahamas	VP-BAA-VP-BZZ	Finland	OH
Barbados	VQ-BAA-VQ-BZZ	France	F
Belgium	OO		
Bermuda	VP-BAA-VR-BZZ	Gambia	VP-XAA-VP-XZZ
Bolivia	CP	Germany	D
Botswana	VQ-ZEA-VQ-ZHZ	Ghana	9G
Brazil	PP, PT	Gibraltar	VR-GAA-VR-GZZ
British Honduras	VP-HAA-VP-HZZ	Great Britain	G
British Cameroons	VR-NAA-VR-NZZ	Greece	SX
Brunei	VR-UAA-VR-UZZ	Grenada	VQ-GAA-VQ-GZZ
Bulgaria	LZ	Guatemala	TG
Burma	XY, XZ	Guinea	3X
		Guyana	8R
Cambodia	XU		
Cameroons	TJ	Haiti	HH
Canada	CF	Holland	PH
Central African		Honduras	HR
Federation	VP-YAA-VP-YZZ	Hong Kong	VR-HAA-VR-HZZ
Ceylon	4R	Hungary	HA
Chile	CC		
Colombia	HK	Iceland	TF
Congo	9Q	India	VT
Costa Rica	TI	Indonesia	PK
Cuba	CU	Iran	EP
Cyprus	5B	Iraq	YI
Czechoslovakia	OK	Ireland	EI, EJ
		Israel	4X
Denmark	OY	Italy	I
Dominican		Ivory Coast	TU
Republic	HI		
Dutch Antilles	PJ	Jamaica	VP-JAA-VP-JZZ
Dutch New Guinea	JZ	Japan	JA

Jordan	JY	Republic of China	B
		Romania	YR
Kenya	5Y or VP-KAA-VP-KZZ		
Korea	HL	Sarawak	VR-WAA-VR-WZZ
Kuwait	9K	Saudi Arabia	HZ
		Senegal	6V, 6W
Laos	XW	Seychelles	VQ-SAA-VQ-SZZ
Lebanon	OD	Sierra Leone	VR-LAA-VR-LZZ
Leeward Islands	VP-LAA-VP-LZZ	Singapore	VR-SAA-VR-SZZ
Lethoso	VQ-ZAA-VQ-ZDZ	Somaliland	VP-SAA-VP-SZZ
Liberia	EL	South Africa	ZS, ZT, ZU
Libya	5A	Soviet Union	CCCP
Liechtenstein	HB	Spain	EC
Luxembourg	LX	St. Helena	VQ-HAA-VQ-HZZ
		St. Lucia	VQ-LAA-VQ-LZZ
Malaysia	9M	St. Vincent	VP-VAA-VP-VZZ
Mali	TZ	Sudan	ST
Malta	VP-MAA-VP-MZZ	Surinam	PZ
Mauritius	VQ-MAA-VQ-MZZ	Swaziland	VQ-ZIA-VQ-ZIZ
Mexico	XA, XB, XC	Sweden	SE
Monaco	3A	Switzerland	HB
Morocco	CN	Syria	YK
Nepal	9N	Tanganyika	VR-TAA-VR-TZZ
New Hebrides	YJ	Thailand	HS
New Zealand	ZK, ZL, ZM	Trinidad & Tobago	VP-TAA-VP-TZZ
Nicaragua	AN	Tunisia	TS
Niger	5U	Turkey	TC
Nigeria	5N		
North Borneo	VR-OAA-VR-OZZ	Uganda	VP-UAA-VP-UZZ
Norway	LN	USA	N
		Uruguay	CX
Pakistan	AP		
Panama	HP	Venezuela	YV
Paraguay	ZP	Vietnam	XV
People's Rep of China	XT		
Peru	OB	Yemen	YE
Philippines	PI	Yugoslavia	YU
Poland	SP		
Portugal	CS, CR	Zanzibar	VP-ZAA-VP-ZZZ

Insignia of the major airlines in 1960

From the 1960s onwards the world's airlines both large and small began to use what were often striking and brightly coloured insignia. This can be seen as one of the most significant symptoms of the growing importance and constant expansion of air transport. In the world's seething airports, packed with essentially similar aircraft, it is vital for each airline to stand out and 'fly the flag'. The following pages show the insignia of the world's major airlines as they were in 1960. It is interesting to note that only a few have remained unchanged since then. Most of the insignia have undergone at least one or two modifications, and some have been substantially redesigned.

Aer Lingus (IRL)

Aeroflot (USSR)

Air France (F)

Air India (IND)

Alitalia (I)

AA American Airlines (USA)

Insignia of the major airlines in 1960

BEA British European Airways (GB)

BOAC British Overseas
Airways Corp. (GB)

Capital Airlines (USA)

CSA Ceskoslovenske Aerolinie (CS)

El Al Israel Airlines (IL)

Finnair (SF)

Iberia (E)

Icelandair (IS)

Insignia of the major airlines in 1960

Loftleidir (IS)

Lufthansa (D)

Japan Air Lines (J)

JAT Jugoslovenski Aerotransport (YU)

KLM Koninklijke Luchtvaart Maatschappij NV (NL)

Panair Do Brasil (BR)

Pan American World Airways (USA)

PIA Pakistan International Airlines

Qantas Airways (AUS)

South African Airways (ZA)

Sabena (B)

SAS Scandinavian Airlines
System (S)

Swissair (CH)

TCA Trans Canada Airlines (CDN)

TWA Trans World Airlines (USA)

United Air Lines (USA)

1960 – Principal Airports of the World

Country	City	Airport
Ceylon	Colombo	Katunayake
Colombia	Bogota	El Dorado
Congo	Leopoldville	Ndjili
Czechoslovakia	Prague	Ruzyne
Denmark	Copenhagen	Kastrup
Egypt	Cairo	Cairo International
France	Paris	Orly
France	Paris	Le Bourget
Germany	Berlin	Tempelhof
Germany	Frankfurt	Frankfurt am Main
Ghana	Accra	Accra
Great Britain	London	Gatwick
Great Britain	London	Heathrow
Greece	Athens	Athens
Holland	Amsterdam	Schiphol
Hong Kong	Hong Kong	Hong Kong International
Hungary	Budapest	Ferihegy
Iceland	Keflavik	Keflavik
India	Bombay	Santa Cruz
India	Calcutta	Dum Dum
Iran	Teheran	Mehrabad
Iraq	Baghdad	Baghdad
Ireland	Shannon	Shannon
Israel	Tel Aviv	Lod
Italy	Rome	Ciampino
Italy	Rome	Fiumicino
Japan	Tokyo	Tokyo
Kenya	Nairobi	Nairobi

Height above sea-level		Length of main runway	
(ft)	(m)	(ft)	(m)
28	8.5	6,000	1,828.8
8,355	2,546.6	12,467	3,780
1,014	309.1	15,416	4,698.8
1,246	379.8	7,610	2,319.5
16	4.8	10,826	3,299.8
311	94.8	10,990	3,349.8
292	89	10,893	3,320.2
217	66.1	9,843	3,000
163	49.7	5,280	1,609.3
368	112.2	11,810	3,599.7
221	67.4	7,330	2,234.2
194	59.1	7,000	2,133.6
80	24.4	9,576	2,918.8
90	27.4	8,202	2,500
−13	−3.9	8,366	2,550
15	4.6	8,350	2,545
440	134.1	9,875	3,010
169	51.5	10,015	3,052.6
27	8.2	10,500	3,200.4
13	3.9	7,700	2,347
3,937	1,200	9,840	3,000
112	34.1	7,054	2,150
47	14.3	7,024	2,141
132	40.2	7,741	2,359.5
423	128.9	7,218	2,200
7	2.1	12,795	3,900
7	2.1	8,400	2,560
5,327	1,623.7	10,000	3,048

1960 — Principal Airports of the World

Country	City	Airport
Lebanon	Beirut	Beirut
Mexico	Mexico City	Mexico City
Newfoundland	Gander	Gander
New Zealand	Auckland	Whenupai
Nigeria	Lagos	Lagos
Norway	Oslo	Fornebu
Pakistan	Karachi	Karachi
Peru	Lima	Callao International
Philippines	Manila	Manila International
Poland	Warsaw	Okecie
Portugal	Lisbon	Portela
Romania	Bucharest	Bancasa
Singapore	Singapore	Singapore
South Africa	Capetown	D.F. Malan
South Africa	Johannesburg	Jan Smuts
Soviet Union	Moscow	Sheremetievo
Soviet Union	Moscow	Vnukova
Spain	Madrid	Barajas
Sweden	Stockholm	Arlanda
Switzerland	Geneva	Cointrin
Thailand	Bangkok	Don Muang
Turkey	Ankara	Esenboga
United States	Chicago	O'Hare
United States	Los Angeles	Los Angeles International
United States	New York	New York International
United States	New York	La Guardia
United States	San Francisco	San Francisco
United States	Washington	Dulles International

Height above sea-level		Length of main runway	
(ft)	(m)	(ft)	(m)
85	25.9	10,662	3,249.8
7,340	2,237.2	9,840	2,999.2
496	151.2	8,600	2,621.3
100	30.5	6,590	2,008.6
132	40.2	7,600	2,316.4
56	17.1	5,750	1,752.6
75	22.9	7,500	2,286
105	32	11,482	3,499.7
67	20.4	7,954	2,424.4
345	105.2	6,561	1,999.8
360	109.7	6,824	2,080
297	90.5	7,216	2,199.4
59	18	8,200	2,499.4
151	46	6,900	2,103.1
5,559	1,694.4	14,500	4,419.6
623	189.9	11,480	3,499.1
669	203.9	10,006	3,049.8
1,985	605	10,006	3,049.8
111	33.8	10,826	3,299.8
1,410	429.8	12,800	3,901.4
12	3.7	9,840	2,999.2
3,096	943.7	9,016	2,748.1
667	203.3	11,600	3,525.7
126	38.4	12,000	3,657.6
12	3.7	14,600	4,450
20	6.1	5,914	1,802.6
10	3	9,500	2,895.6
—	—	11,500	3,505.2

Engines

There is no doubt that the jet engine is the leading character in the present-day world of commercial aviation. However it has certainly not been an easy or quick task for the jet engine to oust the piston engine from its ancient and traditional position of number one. In fact in the civil sector the final transition to the revolutionary form of propulsion (apart from the exceptions represented by the operation of the first Comets and the Viscount) only occurred in the latter half of the 1950s, which was some time after the actual origins of the turbo-jet. This phenomenon appears even more anomalous if one considers that, in

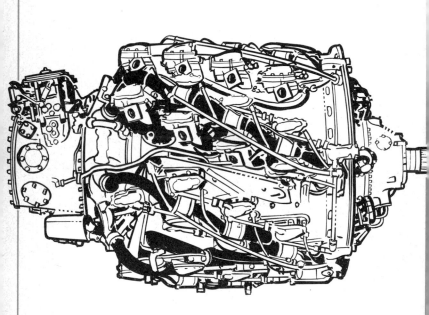

Pratt & Whitney R-4360 Wasp Major – 1943 (USA)

The final development of the radial engines produced by Pratt & Whitney was the series R-4360 Wasp Major, which reached the very limits of performances that could be obtained from a piston engine, and was a leading member of the 3,000–5,000 hp class. It was a large and complicated engine, built around 28 cylinders arranged in four rows: its dry weight was 3,670 lb (1,665 kg). The Wasp Major was designed in the latter years of the Second World War and widely used, especially in the military sector, in the transitional period before the final arrival of the turbine engine. In the civil sector the most important use of the Wasp Major was in the Boeing 377 Stratocruiser.

the years immediately after the Second World War, the development of the jet engine for military uses took on an almost hectic pace. Basically, however, the main cause for the delay in the development of the jet engine was the absolute priority given to the military. As a result air transport was obliged, for some time, to use traditional engines.

This need led to the last stage in the evolution of the piston engine, Once the in-line type of engine had virtually disappeared production focussed on large radial types. For long intercontinental and trans-oceanic flights these were undoubtedly the best-suited engines, even though they were noisy and also caused a lot of vibration.

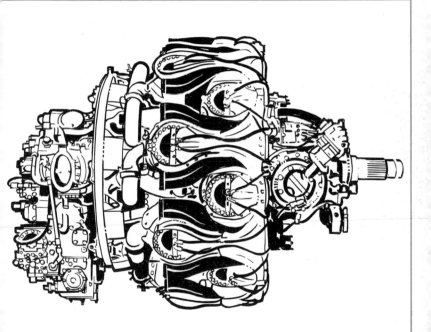

Bristol Centaurus – 1943 (GB)

After the successful Hercules engine, Bristol produced another successful radial engine, the Centaurus. This engine also reached the upper limits for its category, developing in the region of 3,000 hp. The Centaurus derived from the Hercules in its general form (a typical feature was the adoption of valves situated in the cylinders and not in the cylinder-head), but it was considerably bigger and heavier, with eighteen cylinders in two rows instead of fourteen. The Centaurus was used mainly for military purposes, but in the postwar period some of the numerous verions were also put to civil use.

Rolls-Royce Dart – 1945 (GB)

The Rolls-Royce Dart engine was fitted to the first passenger turbo-prop to operate regular services in the world: the Vickers Viscount. The project for this engine was started in 1945, but the basic design was developed via a constant process of updating, which caused the power of the Dart to be increased by more than 150% over the years from the initial 1,000 ehp to the 2,440 ehp, plus a thrust of 670 lb (304 kg) of the series 540. In addition to the Viscount, this engine was also used in other important civil aircraft: in particular it was chosen for the Fokker F.27 Friendship, the Handley Page Herald, the Avro 748 and the Armstrong Whitworth Argosy. The structure of the Rolls-Royce was relatively uncomplicated: a two-stage centrifugal compressor, seven combustion chambers, and a two-stage turbine (series 505 to 514) or three-stage turbine (series 520 onwards). The weight was 1,032 lb (468 kg) in the first version and 1,323 lb (600 kg) in the series 541, and gave a good power weight ratio.

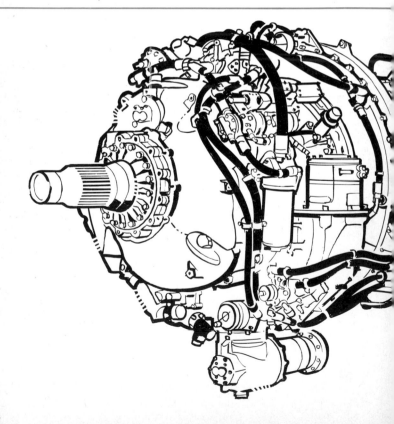

Bristol Proteus – 1947 (GB)

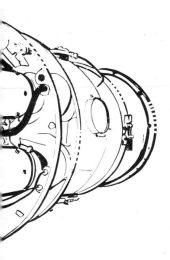

Developed from 1947 onwards, the Bristol Proteus was used in numerous civil and military aeroplanes. In particular, this turbo-prop engine was used in the civil sector in the unsuccessful Saunders-Roe S.R.45 Princess seaplane, and in the Bristol Britannia. During the long process of development which it underwent, the Proteus saw its power constantly increased, until it reached 4,400 ehp in the series 760 which appeared in the early 1960s. Compared with the Rolls-Royce Dart, the Proteus was somewhat more complex: the compressor consisted of twelve axial stages and a centrifugal stage, there were eight combustion chambers, and the turbine consisted of two separate units, each one with two stages: the first driving the compressor, and the second the reduction gear of the propellor shaft. It was also quite heavy: the Proteus 705 installed in the Britannias in the initial series had a dry weight of 2,807 lb (1,273 kg)

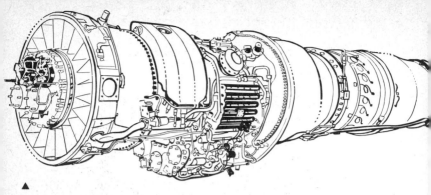

▲

Pratt & Whitney JT-3 – 1949 (USA)

The Pratt & Whitney JT-3 derived directly from the model J-57, which was developed in the late 1940s for military use. In the civil sector, this turbo-jet was used by certain series of the Boeing 707 and the Douglas DC-8, as well as by the Boeing 720. The version mounted in the Boeing 707-120 produced a thrust of 13,500 lb (6,124 kg), but this power was increased by more than 40% in the turbofan version, called the JT3D, which appeared in the early 1960s.

Rolls-Royce Avon – 1950 (GB)

The Rolls-Royce Avon was the turbojet which earned great renown for the British aeronautical industry in the 1950s. It was installed in numerous military aircraft, but it was also developed specifically for civil use as the R.A.29. The initial thrust of 10,500 lb (4,763 kg) on the version installed in the de Havilland Comet increased to 12,500 lb (5,675 kg) in the last versions. The civil Avon engine had a 16-stage axial compressor, 8 combustion chambers and a 3-stage turbine.

▼

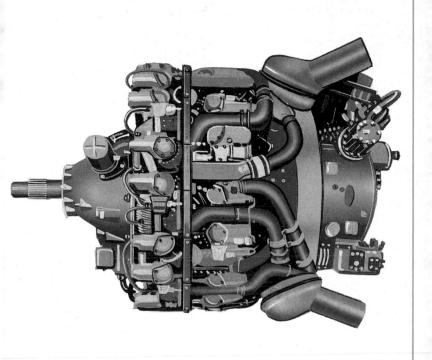

Wright R-3350 Turbo Compound – 1950 (USA)

Like the Pratt & Whitney R-4360 Wasp Major and the British Bristol Centaurus, the Wright R-3350 Turbo Compound was a worthy example of the last generation of piston engines, in which the very limits of power were achieved, and which marked the change-over to the new breed of turbine engines. In particular the Wright Turbo Compound was the leading character in the commercial battle of the mid-1950s between Douglas and Lockheed for the production of a 'better' aeroplane for commercial use. In fact it was adopted by both firms, in what are considered to be the last great civil aircraft with piston

engines: the Douglas DC-7 and the Lockheed Super Constellation. The Wright R-3350 Turbo Compound (also called the TC18) derived directly from the R-3350 Cyclone model, but differed considerably in as much as it incorporated an ingenious system for using the exhaust gases. These were fed into three turbines installed in the rear of the engine, and the turbines, in turn, applied the power thus received directly to the drive shaft, via a set of gears. The increase in power obtained, with the same fuel consumption, was 20%. In some versions the Turbo Compound achieved 3,400 hp at take-off.

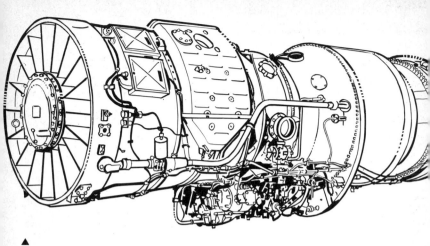

Pratt & Whitney JT-4 – 1951 (USA)

Like the model JT-3, this turbojet was also developed to begin with for military use as the J-75. However, compared with its predecessor it was considerably heavier and more powerful. Some military versions fitted with afterburners could produce a thrust of 26,525 lb (12,030 kg). The first commercial model, called the JT-4A-3 and capable of producing a thrust of 15,800 lb (7,167 kg) was adopted in the initial versions of the Douglas DC-8 and the Boeing 707-320. A turbofan version of the JT-4 was also developed.

Kutznetov NK-12M – 1953 (USSR)

This extremely powerful turbo-prop (in the 12,000–15,000 ehp class) was developed by the Soviet industry particularly for military use. The Kutznetov NK-12M was also used in two very interesting transport aeroplanes, which hallmarked the huge aeronautical growth in the USSR in the 1950s and 1960s: the massive Tupolev Tu-114 and the even larger Antonov An-22. Almost 20 feet (6 m) long and weighing 5,070 lb (2,300 kg) (dry weight), the Kutznetov NK-12M had a 14-stage axial compressor and a 5-stage axial turbine. It transmitted its power to a pair of large counter-rotating propellors.

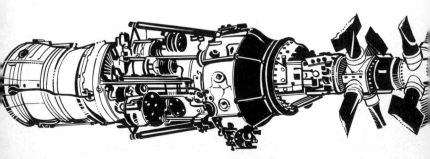

Index

(The numbers in **bold type** refer to an illustration)

311

Bibliography

Books

J. Alexander, *Russian Aircraft since 1940*, Putnam & Co. Ltd., London, 1975.

C. F. Andrews, *Vickers Aircraft since 1908*, Putnam & Co. Ltd., London, 1969.

C. H. Barnes, *Bristol Aircraft since 1910*, Putnam, 1964, 1970 (2 vols).

C. H. Barnes, *Handley Page Aircraft since 1907*, Putnam, 1976.

C. H. Barnes, *Shorts Aircraft since 1900*, Putnam & Co. Ltd., London, 1967.

Peter M. Bowers, *Boeing Aircraft since 1916*, Putnam & Co. Ltd., London, 1966.

Peter W. Brooks, *The Modern Airliner*, Putnam & Co. Ltd., 1961.

Peter W. Brooks, *The World's Airliners*, Putnam, 1962.

D. C. Clayton, *Handley Page, An Aircraft Album*, Ian Allan Ltd., London, 1970.

Maynard Crosby, *Flight Plan for Tomorrow. The Douglas Story: A Condensed History*, Douglas Aircraft Co., Santa Monica, 1962.

R. E. G. Davies, *Airlines of the United States since 1914*, Putnam & Co. Ltd., London.

R. E. G. Davis, *A History of the World's Airlines*, Oxford University Press, London, 1964.

D. M. Desoutter, *All about Aircraft*, Faber & Faber Ltd., London, 1955.

G. R. Duval, *British Flying-Boats and Amphibians 1909-1952*, Putnam & Co. Ltd., London, 1966.

G. R. Duval, *World Flying-Boats – A Pictorial Survey*, D. Bradford Barton, 1975.

H. Emde, *Conquerors of the Air. The Evolution of Aircraft 1903–1945*, Edita Lausanne – Patrick Stephens, 1968.

Paul E. Garber, *The National Aeronautical Collections*, Smithsonian Institution, National Air Museum, 10th edition, Washington, D.C., 1965.

C. V. Glines & W. F. Moseley, *The DC-3 – The Story of a Fabulous Airplane*, J. B. Lippincott, 1966.

H. Hegener, *Fokker – The Man and The Aircraft*, Harleyford, 1961.

Hugo Hooftman, *Russian Aircraft*, Aero Publishers Inc., Fallbrook, California, 1965.

R. J. Hurley, *Martin 2-0-2 and 4-0-4*, Clintor H. Groves, 1976.

D. J. Ingells, *Tin Goose*, Aero Publishers 1968.

A. J. Jackson, *Avro Aircraft since 1908* Putnam & Co. Ltd., London, 1965.

A. J. Jackson, *Blackburn Aircraft Since 1909*, Putnam, 1968.

A. J. Jackson, *British Civil Aircraft 1919–59* (3 vols), Putnam & Co. Ltd., London 1973–74.

A. J. Jackson, *De Havilland Aircraft* Putnam & Co. Ltd., London, 1962.

Derek N. James, *Gloster Aircraft since 1917* Putnam & Co. Ltd., London, 1971.

Jane's 1909–1969: 100 Significant Aircraft Jane's All the World's Aircraft Publishing Co. Ltd., London, 1969.

Joseph P. Juptner, *U.S. Civil Aircraft*, vols 1–6, Aero Publishers Inc., Fallbrook. California, 1962–67.

Reed Kinert, *Racing Planes and Air Races* Aero Publishers Inc., Fallbrook, California 1967–68.

Peter Lewis, *British Racing and Record Breaking Aircraft*, Putnam & Co. Ltd. London, 1971.

Hugh MacDonald, *Aeroflot, Soviet Air Transport since 1923*, Putnam & Co. Ltd. London.

Francis K. Mason, *Hawker Aircraft since 1920*, Putnam & Co. Ltd., London, 1961.

Francis K. Mason-Martin, C. Windrow, *Air Facts and Feats*, Guinness Superlatives Ltd. London, 1970.

Paul R. Matt, *Historical Aviation Album* vols 1–8, Temple City, California, 1965–70.

Kenneth Munson, *Aircraft the World Over* Ian Allan Ltd., London, 1963.

Kenneth Munson, *Airliners Between The Wars 1919–39*, Blandford Press, 1972.

Kenneth Munson, *Airliners Since 1946*, Blandford Press, 1975.

Kenneth Munson, *Civil Aircraft of Yesteryear*, Ian Allan Ltd., London, 1967.

Kenneth Munson, *Civil Airlines since 1946* Blandford Press Ltd., London, 1967.

Kenneth Munson & G. Swanborough *Boeing–An Aircraft Album*, Ian Allan, 1972.

H. J. Nowarra & G. R. Duval, *Russian Civil And Military Aircraft 1884–1969*, Fountain Press, 1971.

Tadashi Nozawa, *Encyclopedia of Japanese Aircraft 1900–1945*, 5 Vols, Shuppan-Kyodo, Tokio, 1958–66.

J. D. Oughton, Bristol – *An Aircraft Album*, Ian Allan, 1973.

Henry R. Palmer Jr., *This was Air Travel*, Superior Publishing Company, 1960.

William Green-Gerald Pollinger, *The Aircraft of the World*, Macdonald & Co. (Publishers) Ltd., 3rd edition, London, 1965.

John B. Rae, *Climb to Greatness. The American Aircraft Industry, 1920–1960*, Massachusetts Institute of Technology Press, Cambridge, USA, 1968.

Ronald Millet-Davis Sawers, *The Technical Development of Modern Aviation*, Routledge & Kegan Paul, London, 1968.

G. R. Simonson, *The History of the American Aircraft Industry (Anthology)*, Massachusetts Institute of Technology Press, Cambridge, USA, 1968.

Page Shamburger, *Classic Monoplanes*, Sports Car Press Ltd., New York, 1966.

Lloyd Morris-Kendall Smith, *Ceiling Unlimited: The Story of American Aviation from Kitty Hawk to Supersonics*, McMillan Co., New York, 1953.

Robert T. Smith, *Classic Biplanes*, Sports Car Press Ltd., New York, 1963.

John Stroud, *Annals of British and Commonwealth Air Transport*, Putnam & Co. Ltd., London, 1962.

John Stroud, *European Transport Aircraft since 1910*, Putnam & Co. Ltd., London, 1966.

John Stroud, *Soviet Transport Aircraft since 1945*, Putnam & Co. Ltd., London, 1962.

John Stroud, *The World's Airliners*, The Bodley Head Ltd., London, 1971.

John Stroud, *The World's Civil Marine Aircraft*, The Bodley Head Ltd, London, 1975.

F. G. Swanborough, *Turbine-Engined Airlines of the World*, Temple Press Book Ltd., London, 1962.

The Lore of Flight, Tre Tryckare Cagner & Co., Gothenburg, 1970.

O. Tapper, *Armstrong Whitworth Aircraft Since 1913*, Putnam, 1973.

H. A. Taylor, *Airspeed Aircraft Since 1931*, Putnam, 1970.

John W. R. Taylor, *Aircraft Sixty Nine*, Ian Allan Ltd., London, 1968.

John W. R. Taylor, *Civil Aircraft of the World*, Ian Allan Ltd., London, 1968.

J. W. R. Taylor & G. Swanborough, *Civil Aircraft Of The World*, Ian Allan, 1974.

Jonathan Thompson, *Italian Civil and Military Aircraft 1930–45*, Aero Publishers Inc., Fallbrook, California, 1963.

P. St. John Turner, *Pictorial History of Pan American World Airways*, Ian Allan, London.

P. St. John Turner, *Heinkel – An Aircraft Album*, Ian Allan, 1970.

P. St. John Turner & H. J. Nowarra, *Junkers – An Aircraft Album*, Ian Allan, 1971.

John W. Underwood, *The World's Famous Racing Aircraft*, Floyd Clymer, Los Angeles, 1955.

Don Vorderman, *The Great Air Races*, Doubleday & Co., Garden City, N.Y., 1969.

Truman C. Weaver, *62 Rare Racing Planes*, Arenar Publications, New York.

Don C. Wigton, *From Jenny to Jet*, Bonanza Books, New York, 1963.

Periodicals

Air Classics, Challenge Publications, Inc., Canoga Park.

Aircraft Illustrated, Ian Allan Ltd., Shepperton.

Aircraft in Profile, Profile Publications Ltd., Windsor.

Air Pictorial, Profile Publications Ltd., Windsor.

Aviation Week & Space Technology, McGraw-Hill, New York.

Esso Air World, Esso International Inc., New York and London.

Flight International, IPC Business Press Ltd., London.

Flying Review International, Haymarket Press Ltd., London.

Annuals

Aerospace Facts and Figures, Aerospace Industries Association of America Inc.

Aviation Week & Space Technology, McGraw-Hill Publications, New York.

Jane's All The World's Aircraft, Sampson Low, Marston & Co. Ltd., London.

J. W. R. Taylor, *Aircraft Annual*, Ian Allan Ltd., London.